In the Classic Mode
The Achievement of Robert Bridges

Roger Fry's portrait of Robert Bridges painted at Chilswell, Boar's Hill, Oxford, February 1923. Fry was a personal friend of Bridges and a well-known painter and art critic. *Courtesy of the Lord Bridges. Photograph by Mrs. Frances Spalding.*

In the Classic Mode
The Achievement of Robert Bridges

Donald E. Stanford

Newark
University of Delaware Press
London: Associated University Presses

© 1978 by Associated University Presses, Inc.

Associated University Presses, Inc.
Cranbury, New Jersey 08512

Associated University Presses
Magdalen House
136–148 Tooley Street
London SE1 2TT, England

Library of Congress Cataloging in Publication Data

Stanford, Donald E., 1913–
    In the classic mode.

    Bibliography: p.
    Includes index.
    1. Bridges, Robert Seymour, 1844–1930—Criticism
and interpretation. I. Title.
PR4161.B6Z864   821'.4   76-27916
ISBN 0-87413-118-9

Other books by DONALD E. STANFORD:
New England Earth
The Traveler
The Poems of Edward Taylor
A Transcript of Edward Taylor's Metrical History of Christianity
Nine Essays in Modern Literature (Editor)
Edward Taylor
Selected Poems of Robert Bridges
Selected Poems of S. Foster Damon

for Maryanna

Contents

Preface

In this book I survey and attempt to evaluate the major achievements of an important poet, scholar, and man of letters whose work in recent years has been neglected. When Robert Bridges's *Testament of Beauty* appeared in 1929 the day after the poet's eighty-fifth birthday, it was enthusiastically received by the critics and achieved a popular success unusual for serious poetry in any age. Several years later, few people were reading Bridges, and fewer still were writing about him. A glance at any standard bibliography from 1935 to 1975 tells the story. The accumulation of articles and books—scholarly, critical, and popular—on Ezra Pound and T. S. Eliot, for example, is enormous and appears to be endless. The entries for Robert Bridges are relatively very few. The Pound-Eliot star was in the ascendancy, and those young intellectuals in the depression years who went for *The Waste Land* and *The Cantos* and for the early poetry of Auden were impatient with the remote and cool classicism of Bridges. It was one of those periodic changes in taste which seem to occur about every half century in the history of literature. *The Waste Land*, published in 1922 (seven years before *The Testament of Beauty*), had, by the mid-thirties, carried all before it. There was a continuing revolution in the arts as well as in society, and the kind of poetry that Bridges wrote—finished, quiet, meditative, beautiful, powerful, and profound—was buried in the libraries in spite of the attempts of a few American critics like Yvor Winters and later Albert Guérard to keep it alive. But tastes change, and almost fifty years after Bridges's death, there are a few signs that there may be a revival of interest in the work of this distinguished poet and in what he stood for.

The terms *classic, classical,* and *classicism* have been frequently used with reference to Bridges's poetry in the text of this book and in the title. Some defense of their use may be needed, particularly in view of the fact that the distinguished scholar Douglas Bush has called Bridges's work romantic, and also in view of the fact that Eliot, who wrote a very different kind of poetry from Bridges, called himself a classicist. Furthermore, Bridges himself praised highly certain romantic poets. He liked some of Keats and he had an embarrassing enthusiasm for Shelley, and he thought that the two most famous neoclassical poets, Dryden and Pope, were very dull dogs indeed. Can the argument that Bridges's verse was predominantly classical be maintained? And what are the virtues, if any, of classicism?

Bridges as a practicing poet (and not merely as a theoretician) rarely departed from the notion that a successful poem should make its appeal *as a whole* and not as a series of disjunctive brilliant parts. The poem should have unity, coherence, and a logically demonstrable structure and be expressed in a language that had beauty without sentimentality and power without sensationalism or vulgarity. Furthermore, he believed that serious poetry should have a rational content that could be discussed intelligently even with those who might disagree with it. For example, he carried on a comprehensible dialogue with George Santayana concerning the philosophical ideas of *The Testament of Beauty* even though the two seemed to be in disagreement about such fundamental terms as *essence* and *influence*. He was, on the other hand, very impatient with William Butler Yeats's irrational occultism, a fact that may have prevented a close friendship between them, for Bridges was fascinated by Yeats as a person and admired his early poetry. But the occultism bored Bridges, if not to tears at least to irritation. As a man of reason, Bridges could discuss his differences with Santayana. He could not do so with the romantic Yeats.

As a technician and as a theoretician Bridges believed that all successful poetry should have a prosody, and he believed that the prosody could be formulated—which he proceeded to do. His various treatises on the subject are not easy reading, but they are an important and necessary part of the total picture. For everything he did in the metrics of his poems—and he experimented with many different rhythms and meters—Bridges had his reasons. His views on the conventional meters of English verse that he himself employed so brilliantly are to be found in his studies on Milton's prosody. The theory behind his early experiments in accentual verse (in collaboration with Hopkins) are set forth in his essay on stress prosody published together in one volume in the final edition of his study of Milton. The extensive experiments in quantitative verse are explained in his 1916 edition of *Ibant Obscuri* and elsewhere. His invention of *neo-Miltonic syllabics*, which led to the "loose Alexandrines" of *The Testament of Beauty,* is analyzed in his "Note on New Verse" reprinted in the *Collected Essays.*

It is this combination of rationally intelligible subject matter and expert craftsmanship that I call *classical.* And there are some further considerations. In his Memoir of Digby Dolben, Bridges said:

> . . . when he [Dolben] began to write poetry he would never have written on any subject that did not deeply move him, nor would he attend to poetry unless it expressed his own emotions. . . . What had led me to poetry was the inexhaustible satisfaction of form, the magic of speech, lying as it seemed to me in the masterly control of the material. . . . Dolben imagined poetic form to be the naive outcome of peculiar personal emotion.[1]

Mastery of form is what we expect in classical verse. Self-expression of one's "peculiar personal emotion" is the hallmark of the romantic school. *The Waste Land,* for instance, is really a romantic poem expressing peculiar personal emotions, in spite of many opinions to the contrary. It is a piece of "rhythmical grumbling" as Eliot himself called it in later years. Now Bridges and his friend Hopkins also had *their* religious problems, and of these three poets, it was Bridges who defined his religious difficulties in verse that comes closest to the classical standards of mastery of form and of clarity, simplicity, and disciplined control of the emotions. In "The Affliction of Richard" he addresses God:

> Though thou, I know not why,
> Didst kill my childish trust,
> That breach with toil did I
> Repair, because I must:
> And spite of frighting schemes,
> With which the fiends of Hell
> Blaspheme thee in my dreams,
> So far I have hoped well.

And it was the Jesuit priest who was indulging in romantic self-expression of his "peculiar personal emotion" when he complained to Christ in "Carrion Comfort":

But ah, but O thou terrible, why wouldst thou rude on me
Thy wring-world right foot rock? lay a lionlimb against me? scan
With darksome devouring eyes my bruise'd bones? and fan,
O in turns of tempest, me heaped there; me frantic to
            avoid thee and flee?[2]

Now the fact that in these two poems Bridges had mastered a conventional metrical form while Hopkins was attempting an unconventional one does not necessarily make Bridges's poem inferior. Hopkins, like most writers of romantic temperament, was excessive in his approach to any subject, and when it came to prosody he was obsessed with the notion of *make it new*. He developed a prosody with a unique system of scansion of unnecessary complexity that no one could follow in its entirety except, perhaps, himself.

Finally, it should be noted that Bridges, more than any other poet of the period, had what one vaguely calls the "Greek spirit." He was, of course, thoroughly familiar with the literature and the philosophy of Greece, and, in his life as well as in his work, he seems to have developed that harmony of mind and heart which one thinks of as the principal attainment of the Greek ideal.

Bridges requested that no biography be written of him, and he destroyed or ordered destroyed many of his letters. Judging from the evidence of the letters that have survived and of the letters and memoirs of those who knew him, he was a man of strong principles and strong opinions who lived through the moral turbulence of the decadence of the 1890s and of the jazz age without revealing any of the weaknesses frequently attributed to the more famous writers of those periods. He did not tolerate fools and flatterers and he never had a large "following." He moved in a small circle of carefully selected friends who had artistic and philosophical interests similar to his own. As far as one can make out at this distance, he had no serious faults. One of his few minor weaknesses, however, was a tendency to think too highly of some of his friends' artistic abilities.

Most of the published pictures of Bridges show him as a striking-looking elderly man with a beard and a leonine head.

There is at least one photograph of him as a young man at Oxford, showing a very handsome, sensitive, yet strong face. He was over six feet tall, athletically built, fond of walking, and, at Oxford, he was considered an excellent oarsman. Contemporary accounts of him frequently refer to his beautiful full-toned voice and his distinguished aristocratic manners.

Robert Seymour Bridges was born October 23, 1844, at Walmer, Kent, in a house near the Channel, the grounds of which are described in his "Elegy: The Summer-House on the Mound." His father, John Thomas Bridges, died in 1853, and his mother, née Harriet Elizabeth Affleck, married the Reverend J. E. N. Molesworth in 1854 and moved with her family to Rochdale. In that same year, Bridges entered Eton where he associated with a group of serious-minded boys who had a strong interest in religion, a group that Digby Dolben joined several years later. He matriculated at Corpus Christi College, Oxford, in 1863. It was during that year that he met Gerard Manley Hopkins. The death in 1866 of his younger brother, Edward, to whom he was very close, seems to have affected him deeply. It was about this time that he was moving away from his earlier high-church views and from the possibility of taking Holy Orders. It was also at this time that his friend Hopkins was moving in the opposite direction, becoming converted to Roman Catholicism in 1867. In that same year Bridges visited Paris, and in December he graduated from Corpus Christi with a second in Greats. The next year he was in Egypt and Syria with his lifelong close friend Lionel Muirhead, and he also visited Germany with William Sanday.

He had by now decided on a medical career, and he entered St. Bartholomew's Hospital as a student in 1869. For the next thirteen years he resided in London, graduating as M. B. Oxon. in 1874 and practicing medicine at St. Bartholomew's and elsewhere until 1881 when he retired after a serious illness. His stepfather had died in 1877. In 1882 Bridges and his mother moved to the attractive village of Yattendon in the Berkshires. There Bridges met Monica, the daughter of the famous architect Alfred Waterhouse. They were married in 1884 and moved into the manor house, an impressive red-brick structure with spacious and lovely grounds. There for over twenty years Bridges wrote his finest lyrics and spent what appears to have been the happiest period of a long and generally happy life, a period beautifully commemorated in his poem "The Sleeping Mansion." In 1907 he built Chilswell House on Boar's Hill overlooking Oxford and lived there until his death on April 21, 1930. He was buried at Yattendon where there is a memorial tablet to him in the church.

In this book I discuss in chapter 1 the short poems in conventional prosody, poems that made Bridges famous and won him the laureateship in 1913, long after he had stopped, or I should say, almost stopped using the conventional and traditional iambic rhythms. In chapter 2 I take up in chronological order Bridges's three experiments in nonconventional meters—the poems in accentual verse that he began to compose early in his career under the encouragement and influence of Hopkins; the experiments in quantitative verse originally inspired by his friend William Johnson Stone's treatise on classical prosody in English; and finally his poems in what he called *neo-Miltonic syllabics.* The next chapter is devoted to a discussion of the two masques and eight plays. Chapter 4 deals with *The Testament of Beauty* and includes a study of the little-known trial texts of that poem. In the final chapter I consider Bridges's literary criticism. Throughout, I have had frequent recourse to Bridges's letters, most of them unpublished.

This book presents the first detailed discussion of Bridges's plays (although Albert Guérard has a brief but brilliant critique of them in his *Robert Bridges,* published over thirty years ago.) The trial texts of *The Testament of Beauty* that are considered in chapter 4 and in its appendix have, to the best of my knowledge, never been analyzed in any detail in print before. There has to date been little study of the poems in classical prosody considered in chapter 2, nor has there, as far as I know, been any extended discussion of Bridges as a critic.

D.E.S.

Acknowledgments

I wish to thank the National Endowment for the Humanities and Dean Max Goodrich and the Louisiana State University Research Council for grants that enabled me to pursue my research on important Robert Bridges manuscripts in Oxford and London. I am indebted to the directors and the courteous staffs of the Louisiana State University Library, the library of the University of South Carolina, the British Library, the library of Worcester College, Oxford, and the Bodleian Library. Mr. Gordon Ray of the Guggenheim Foundation kindly allowed me to examine his holdings of Bridges manuscripts, and Simon Nowell-Smith, who gathered the most impressive collection of Bridges material in private hands, gave me his assistance and encouragement. Mr. Nicolas Barker kindly provided me with a copy of his rare *The Printer and the Poet,* and Professor George Harper sent me transcripts of Bridges's letters to William Butler Yeats.

I am particularly indebted to the late Mrs. Elizabeth Daryush, daughter of Robert Bridges, for her reminiscences of her father and for clarification of a number of matters, to the late Lord Bridges, son of the poet, and to his son the Lord Bridges for their interest and encouragement. I wish to acknowledge also the kindness of Katharine Lady Bridges and of Robert Bridges, grandson of the poet.

The Notes and Bibliography sections of this volume indicate in some measure my debt to previous scholars and critics, but I wish to mention particularly the essays on Bridges, Hopkins, and Elizabeth Daryush by the late Yvor Winters, essays that first aroused my interest in Bridges, and also Albert Guérard's perceptive and intelligent critique, *Robert Bridges: A Study of Traditionalism in Poetry*.

15

Most of all, I wish to acknowledge the ever-devoted help of my wife in preparing and correcting the manuscript of this book.

I wish also to thank the following:

Howard Baker, for permission to quote his poem "Psyche" from his *Ode to the Sea,* published by Alan Swallow (1966).

The Bodleian Library, Oxford, for permission to quote from papers concerning Robert Bridges.

The British Library Board, for permission to quote lines from the Trial Text of *The Testament of Beauty.*

The Macmillan Company, for permission to quote from Thomas Hardy's poem "The Head above the Fog" (in *Collected Poems of Thomas Hardy,* 1968), by permission of the Macmillan Company.

The literary executors of Stanley Morison, for permission to quote from Morison's letter to Bridges, April 19, 1929.

Oxford University Press, for permission to quote from *The Poetical Works of Robert Bridges* and from Gerard Manley Hopkins's poems "Carrion Comfort" and "Duns Scotus's Oxford" (in *The Poems of Gerard Manley Hopkins,* ed. W. H. Gardner and N. H. Mackenzie, 1967), by permission of the Oxford University Press.

In the Classic Mode
The Achievement of Robert Bridges

1

The Traditionalist Poet

The Shorter Poems

Bridges's collection of *Shorter Poems* (1890) [1] established his reputation as one of the great lyric poets in English. Of this book A. E. Housman said that no volume of English verse had ever attained such perfection and anthologists of the future would have immense difficulty in making a selection. [2] In this first collection of the *Shorter Poems* there were a few experiments in accentual meters, and later Bridges wrote poems in classical prosody and in neo-Miltonic syllabics. These experiments and Bridges's explanations of them are important contributions to the theory and history of English prosody, and they resulted in a few beautiful poems that will be discussed in a later chapter. But the bulk of Bridges's lyric poetry is in what Bridges called common or running meter or "old style." It may be more precisely referred to as *accentual syllabic verse.* The accentual syllabic line (usually with an iambic movement), in which the rhythm is measured by a predetermined number of syllables and accents, has been the most common and the most successful meter in English since the sixteenth century. In the hands of a master such as Bridges this meter is capable of the most sensitive and subtle effects, obtained by various means but particularly by the skillful substitution of one kind of foot for another, by the use of light extrametrical syllables, and by the careful handling of quantity in relation to accent. Bridges unfortunately grew tired of it in later years—but not until he had achieved a body of poetry of great

range and delicacy of feeling. Some of these metrical achievements
will be noted in the discussion of individual poems.

Landscape Painting.[3] Although I consider Bridges's poetry to
be primarily classical for reasons given in the Introduction, it
must be admitted that he had a romantic poet's love of rural
England—of the Kentish Downs remembered from childhood, of
the South Downs in the area around his Berkshire home at
Yattendon, of Oxford and its environs, and of the moors and the
sea. He wrote a handful of astonishingly lovely poems depicting
landscapes (often seasonal) , rivers and streams, woods and fields.
His images are precise and his sound effects subtle; usually the
tone is serene and low-pitched. He seldom gives way to the kind
of rhetoric one finds in Shelley's "Ode to the West Wind."
Streams, brooks, rivers inspire some of his loveliest writing.
"There is a hill beside the silver Thames" is one of the best. The
focus of the poem is on a caverned pool beneath the hill described
in the first stanza:

> Swift from the sweltering pasturage he flows:
> His stream, alert to seek the pleasant shade,
> Pictures his gentle purpose, as he goes
> Straight to the caverned pool his toil has made.
> > His winter floods lay bare
> > The stout roots in the air:
> His summer streams are cool, when they have played
> > Among their fibrous hair.

> A rushy island guards the sacred bower,
> And hides it from the meadow, where in peace
> The lazy cows wrench many a scented flower,
> Robbing the golden market of the bees.

To this "purple pool" where nothing grows an occasional angler
comes and sometimes

> > a slow figure 'neath the trees
> In ancient-fashioned smock, with tottering cane.

Otherwise the poet who wishes solitude is safe to bathe in the
stream or arrange his love trysts there. Because he cherishes his

solitude, he wishes to keep the location of his retreat a secret.
This is a perfectly simple poem in praise of retreat to the beauties
and the solitude of nature—without power or depth but successful as a quiet tone poem.

There is a similar theme of retreat in the elegy "Clear and
gentle stream," in which the stream symbolizes the nostalgia for
lost youth,

> Clear and gentle stream!
> Known and loved so long,
> That has heard the song
> And the idle dream
> Of my boyish day;

together with the mature poet's love of rural peace,

> Many an afternoon
> Of the summer day
> Dreaming here I lay;
> And I know how soon,
> Idly at its hour,
> First the deep bell hums
> From the minster tower,
> And then evening comes,
> Creeping up the glade.

These lovely verses open all editions of *Shorter Poems*.

In "Indolence," a river also is the center of interest, and there
is just a hint of allegorical significance. The poet and his companion leave the city by boat late in the afternoon of a hot
summer's day to drift idly downstream

> Past shallow islets floating in the sun,
> Or searching down the banks for rarer flowers
> We lingered out the pleasurable hours.

Toward evening they pass beneath an ancient bridge into a
completely different world of calm and stagnant waters lined
with crumbling walls, deserted wharfs, and vacant sheds—a world
of absolute death:

> Then I who rowed leant on my oar, whose drip
> Fell without sparkling, and I rowed no more.

Sea, clouds, downs, and moors are described in a number of poems,[4] of which "The Downs" (admired by Hopkins) is probably the best. It is discussed in the chapter on accentual verse. "Who has not walked" is one of the loveliest poems of this group. As the poet looks across the Channel from Kent,

> The snow-white clouds he northward chased
> Break into phalanx, line, and band:
> All one way to the south they haste,
> The south, their pleasant fatherland.
>
> From distant hills their shadows creep,
> Arrive in turn and mount the lea,
> And flit across the downs, and leap
> Sheer off the cliff upon the sea;
>
> And sail and sail far out of sight.
> But still I watch their fleecy trains,
> That piling all the south with light,
> Dapple in France the fertile plains.

A few poems are devoted to seasonal landscape.[5] The best of these, "The storm is over," is considered in the chapter on accentual verse. These seasonal poems are usually purely descriptive, without symbolism or even the suggestion of ulterior meaning, and are therefore slight though often charming. From "April 1885":

> Wanton with long delay the gay spring leaping cometh;
> The blackthorn starreth now his bough on the eve of May:
> All day in the sweet box-tree the bee for pleasure hummeth:
> The cuckoo sends afloat his note on the air all day.

Response to Nature. Of the descriptive poems confined to a single scene (rather than a landscape),[6] the best and most famous is the accentual "London Snow" discussed in a later chapter. "The Garden in September"

> Where tomtits, hanging from the drooping heads
> Of giant sunflowers, peck the nutty seeds;
> And in the feathery aster bees on wing
> Seize and set free the honied flowers,
> Till thousand stars leap with their visiting,

with the Keatsian attention to sensuous detail is typical. The inversion of the third foot in the last line quoted is particularly felicitous.

There is an impressive group of poems that may present considerable descriptive detail, but in the depth of feeling aroused in response to beauty in nature they go beyond mere description and often suggest religious, aesthetic, ethical, or metaphysical concepts.[7] A few of these poems (such as "I love all beauteous things") are simple statements of the poet's response to beauty without descriptive detail.

Bridges wrote several eclogues in the classical manner with obvious affinities with Theocritus, Bion, and Virgil. "Eclogue I: The Months" is taken up mainly with the poet's response to beauty in nature as it appears in the change of seasons. The change of seasons implies some consideration of the ravages of time, and Bridges makes the point, repeated in "Elegy: The Summer-House on the Mound" and elsewhere, that the poet can gain a temporary victory over time by evoking the experiences of the past:

> "The passion as I please
> Of that past day I can to-day recall."

The dialogue between the poets Basil and Edward begins on a rocky hill overlooking the vales of Somerset and the sea:

> As there in happy indolence they lay
> And drank the sun, while round the breezy height
> Beneath their feet rabbit and listless ewe
> Nibbled the scented herb and grass at will.

They recall that twelve years ago they had held a friendly competition, each poet composing alternate verses praising the months of the year. Each poet now recites from memory the verses composed by his friend, thus successfully reliving the past in the present and reaffirming that

> Man hath with man on earth no holier bond
> Than that the Muse weaves with her dreamy thread.

They are, in fact, doing more than salvaging the immediate past of the last dozen years. They are evoking the experiences of **centuries ago:**

Like those Sicilian swains, whose doric tongue
After two thousand years is ever young,—
Sweet the pine's murmur, and, shepherd, sweet thy pipe,—
Or that which gentle Virgil, yet unripe,
Of Tityrus sang under the spreading beech
And gave to rustic clowns immortal speech,

and they are reaffirming the immortality of the muse that is
operating in Greek, Roman, and modern times—

But these were men when good Victoria reigned,
Poets themselves, who without shepherd gear
Each of his native fancy sang the year.

This poem has considerably more substance than those previously
discussed. Although the form of the eclogue is derived from the
ancients and the diction occasionally reminds us of Keats, the
poem is more than pastiche. In fact, these echoes of the past in
form and style are appropriate to a major theme of the poem—
the power of poetic inspiration that manifests itself throughout
time, in the Victorian period as well as in the Romantic period
and in the classical era.

Another traditional form, the ode, is effectively employed in
the two odes to spring. The poem is concerned with what one
would call today two life-styles, one based on the country,

And country life I praise,
And lead, because I find
The philosophic mind
Can take no middle ways;
She will not leave her love
To mix with men, her art
Is all to strive above
The crowd, or stand apart,

the other on the city. "Spring Ode I" is an invitation to the
country. "Spring Ode II" is a reply from a city man who accepts
the invitation. Both men are fundamentally hedonistic. The first
finds his joy in the simple unambitious rural life:

For Nature can delight
Fancies unoccupied
With ecstasies so sweet

> As none can even guess,
> Who walk not with the feet
> Of joy in idleness.

The second finds his pleasure in the city in good company, music, literature, and philosophy:

> Or if grave study suit
> The yet unwearied brain,
> Plato can teach again
> And Socrates dispute;
> Till fancy in a dream
> Confront their souls with mine,
> Crowning the mind supreme,
> And her delights divine.

The life-style of Bridges himself was a combination of the best of both worlds.

"The birds that sing on Autumn eves" is worthy of an Elizabethan song writer of the caliber of Campion. The poem is clearly allegorical. The song of the birds in spring represents the enthusiasms and vitality of youthful poets, the songs of autumn the mastery of the mature poet:

> Their notes thro' all the jocund spring
> Were mixed in merry musicking:
> They sang for love the whole day long,
> But now their love is all for song.

> Now each hath perfected his lay
> To praise the year that hastes away:
> They sit on boughs apart, and vie
> In single songs and rich reply.

The unusual inversion of the second and third feet in the line "Now eách háth perfécted his láy," which strongly modulates but does not break the rhythm, is worthy of Campion himself. Bird song is also the direct inspiration of "Larks" and "Asian Birds":

> How the delicious notes
>   come bubbling from their throats!

> Full and sweet how they are shed
> like round pearls from a thread!

Similarly, the pinks in his garden are the subjects of two minor but pleasant poems, "Cheddar Pinks" in neo-Miltonic syllabics and "The pinks along my garden walks."

In "Late Spring Evening" Bridges is attempting a major poem. The first stanza is an address to the "Virgin-mother"— who seems to be a kind of nature goddess, a manifestation of ideal love—and the Muse:

> I saw the Virgin-mother clad in green,
> Walking the sprinkled meadows at sundown;
> While yet the moon's cold flame was hung between
> The day and night, above the dusky town:
> I saw her brighter than the Western gold,
> Whereto she faced in splendour to behold.

As the mystical vision continues, a kind of trancelike state is evoked:

> And o'er the treetops, scattered in mid air,
> The exhausted clouds laden with crimson light
> Floated or seemed to sleep.

This mystical ecstasy rises to a climax in the powerful fifth stanza:

> And when I saw her, then I worshipped her,
> And said.—O bounteous Spring, O beauteous Spring,
> Mother of all my years, thou who dost stir
> My heart to adore thee and my tongue to sing,
>   of my heart's blood the fire,
> Of all my satisfaction the desire!

The Love Poetry. As one would expect of a major lyric poet, many of Bridges's shorter poems are devoted to the subject of love. Some are obviously addressed to a certain lady; others are about love in general.[8] There is an air of conventionality about these love lyrics; they often remind one of Elizabethan songs. Most, while paying due respect to carnal love, seem to be chiefly concerned with spiritual love and beauty. They make an interesting contrast with the love poems of Bridges's contemporary, Thomas Hardy. Hardy's attitude toward women (perhaps influenced by his reading of Schopenhauer, probably influenced by his observation of life) is often one of ironic skepticism. The women in his *Satires of Circumstance* and elsewhere are often deceivers and destroyers of men, and they are treated with a rather shallow cynicism. This treatment of women is never found in Bridges. On the other hand, Hardy wrote a series of powerful love poems addressed to his first wife, Emma Gifford, and several other equally moving poems addressed (probably) to Tryphena Sparks. They have a specificity that Bridges's poetry lacks. For example, in the admirable "The Head above the Fog," which recalls Hardy's trysts with Tryphena on Egdon Heath, the reader has an immediate sense of a particular woman (who wears a plume in her hat) on particular occasions in a particular place, and the effect is one of uncontrived sincerity:

> O the vision keen!—
> Tripping along to me for love
> As in the flesh it used to move,
> Only its hat and plume above
> The evening fog-fleece seen.

In Bridges's love poetry one is always conscious of the craftsman at work, and there is usually a universal quality about it rather than particularity. The poem quite frequently could be about almost any lady almost anywhere. But I do not mean these remarks to be pejorative. The following lines by Bridges are general and "literary" when compared to Hardy; yet they have become a permanent part of the Aubade tradition in English verse. The metrics are beyond praise:

> Awake, my heart, to be loved, awake, awake!
> The darkness silvers away, the morn doth break,
> It leaps in the sky: unrisen lustres slake
> The o'ertaken moon. Awake, O heart, awake!

"Thou didst delight my eyes" records a love that was intense but temporary. The lady who once inspired the poet is now moving other poets to rhyme and is rejoicing other hearts. The first two stanzas state the theme in completely abstract language.

The third stanza illustrates the theme with two metaphors. The poet, although he has lost the lady, is grateful for the redeeming love she gave him, however briefly:

> For what wert thou to me?
> How shall I say? The moon,
> That poured her midnight noon
> Upon his wrecking sea:—
> A sail, that for a day
> Has cheered the castaway.

One of Bridges's best lyrics, "My spirit kisseth thine" defines a love so spiritualized that it almost seems to be a poem about love of God rather than of woman. The final stanzas, which illustrate the mystical ecstasy of the poet's love with a description of sun and a winter landscape, are breathtakingly beautiful:

> Like what the shepherd sees
> On late mid-winter dawns,
> When thro' the branched trees,
> O'er the white-frosted lawns,

> The huge unclouded sun,
> Surprising the world whist,
> Is all uprisen thereon,
> Golden with melting mist.

Bridges wrote several other successful love poems that apparently refer to experiences with an individual lady or ladies. "Wooing" tells of an incident in which the poet had determined to end a love affair. He says his "final" farewell, but then relents:

> And should have lost that day
> My life's delight for ever:
> But when I saw her start
> And turn aside and tremble;—
> Ah! she was true, her heart
> I knew did not dissemble.

"So sweet love seemed that April morn" is a comment on the superiority of mature over youthful love, which seems to refer to Bridges's own personal experience. "I climb the mossy bank of the glade" begins with a specific incident and ends with the comment that the kiss of his mistress combines two fires: that described by the philosopher Heraclitus as the basis of life and that described by the poet Catullus as the essence of desire. "One grief of thine" states that the sorrow of his mistress was a joy to the poet because it drove her into his arms. "Since we loved" is, evidently, a triumphant reference to Bridges's completely happy marriage:

> All my joys my hope excel,
> All my work hath prosper'd well,
> All my songs have happy been,
> O my love, my life, my queen.

"Eros,"[9] one of the most impressive poems in the entire Bridges canon, defines and communicates the power of naked sensuous sexual passion as it is incarnated in the God of Love. Bridges uses the Greek Eros rather than the Roman Cupid in order to avoid the connotations of playfulness and mischievousness sometimes associated with the Roman God. He chooses the same Greek God as his hero of *Eros and Psyche,* and there are overtones of that famous story in "Eros," particularly in the line "And wouldst in darkness come." The meaning of the poem (as I understand it) is this: sexual passion is so dominant a force that even though it subverts reason (indeed, it is completely irrational and hence incompatible with reason) its victims feel that it has a good (a "light") of its own that is superior to reason. At first glance the theme may appear to be identical with Yeats's "Leda and the Swan," but it is not. The implication of Yeats's poem is that sexual experience leads to wisdom. Bridges's poem states that the victim of Eros believes his experience to be superior to the fruits of reason, wisdom, but the word *victim* suggests that Bridges considers this belief to be in error. Yet the poem, although it adopts a critical attitude, is not an attack on Eros. It is a realization of and an evocation of his power. As Robert Beum says, "Part of the poem's charm is that Bridges' critique is put in the most charitable manner compatible with a firm moral attitude. . . . Eros is both king of joy and tyrant; he is essential, and yet he has to be kept in his place."[10] Bridges has been frequently criticized for being too spiritual, formal, and "remote" in his love poetry, and it is true that more poems in *The Growth of Love* sequence are devoted to heavenly or spiritual love than to earthly love. However, "Eros" demonstrates that Bridges was quite capable of appreciating and depicting sensual experience. It should be noted that the poem is universalized: it is about physical love in general and it is in impersonal terms. There is no comparable poem by Bridges dealing with the poet's personal, physical love for an individual woman, a fact that makes his love poetry quite different from the poems Yeats wrote to Maud Gonne and, as previously noted, Hardy wrote to Emma Gifford and Tryphena Sparks.

Many of Bridges's best poems are meditations and are, sometimes, lacking in those qualities which the New Critics have claimed must pertain to any successful poem—immediacy and dramatic appeal. "Eros," however, does have these qualities. The poem is in the form of an apostrophe to the God, or (probably) to a statue or picture of the God. The opening lines set the tone of immediacy, of dramatic urgency:

> Why hast thou nothing in thy face?
> Thou idol of the human race,
> Thou tyrant of the human heart, . . .

Yet, the poet answers, such is the power of "Eros" that his complete lack of intellectuality, of spirituality ("Surely thy body is thy mind"), is disregarded, and in his pure sensuality he becomes "An image of eternal Truth." This sensuality not only takes the place of spirit ("light") but creates a new good, a new "light" of its own as stated in four of the greatest lines in all of Bridges's poetry:

> O king of joy, what is thy thought?
> I dream thou knowest it is nought,
> And wouldst in darkness come, but thou
> Makest the light where'er thou go.

The meter of the poem is perfectly conventional octosyllabic couplets (except for the final tercet), and it is handled with a discipline and a precision that are superior to Milton. There are a very few extrametrical syllables, and those that do occur are there for special effects. As Robert Beum has pointed out[11] the light extrametrical *er* in the line "With thy exuberant flesh so fair," gives a slight yet marked feeling of freedom to the line completely appropriate to the meaning. Similarly, the extrametrical *u* in "In secret sensuous innocence" contributes an appropriately lithe gliding quality to the rhythm. "Eros" is an excellent example of the kind of effects that can be obtained by subtle departures from a fixed and controlled meter. These effects are simply impossible in most free verse or in loosely written metrical verse.

A poem that has grown on me during frequent rereading and after having heard it recited years ago by Robert Hillyer in a lecture is "The evening darkens over." Like "Eros," it is a generalized comment on love, but it is much quieter in tone. It presents a single scene, but the "scenic method" is not made dramatic or immediate as in Hardy. The poem has, rather, the quality of brooding meditation. Rhythm, assonance, sound, a few visual images, and a complicated but unobtrusive rhyme scheme are employed to achieve a minor masterpiece on the theme of the indifference of the physical universe to human needs, in this instance to human love. The significance of the beautifully presented detail is not realized until the final line, which states the theme of the poem:

> The evening darkens over
> After a day so bright
> The windcapt waves discover
> That wild will be the night.
> There's sound of distant thunder.
>
> The latest sea-birds hover
> Along the cliff's sheer height;
> As in the memory wander
> Last flutterings of delight,
> White wings lost on the white.
>
> There's not a ship in sight;
> And as the sun goes under
> Thick clouds conspire to cover
> The moon that should rise yonder.
> Thou art alone, fond lover.

"The Philosopher to His Mistress" and "The Philosopher and His Mistress" are on the same subject—the gulf between the melancholy intellectual and the woman who loves him but

cannot enter into his philosopher's world. The gulf is bridged
by an act of will on the part of the philosopher, who turns his
back (momentarily, it is implied) on his intellectual world to
be made happy in the arms of his mistress. The first is a good
example of the poem of statement in a style that is primarily
though not entirely abstract. The second is a development of a
single simile. The melancholy philosopher who casts a shadow
over the happiness of his mistress is compared to an eclipse of
the moon. The shadow is dispelled and the happiness of the
mistress is restored. As for the philosopher,

> And far my sorrowing shade
>   Will slip to empty space
> Invisible, but made
>   Happier for that embrace.

Two elegies (which are actually love poems) make an inter-
esting contrast. The first, entitled simply "Elegy," which begins
"The wood is bare," recalls the poet's love for a girl now dead.
The poem begins with a description of the woods in winter:

> The wood is bare: a river-mist is steeping
>   The trees that winter's chill of life bereaves:
> Only their stiffened boughs break silence, weeping
>   Over their fallen leaves.

The woods are obviously sharing the grief of the poet. The
pathetic fallacy is operative throughout the poem. The poet
recalls these same woods in a happier mood in spring and summer when he walked in them with his love:

> Yet it was here we walked when ferns were springing,
>   And through the mossy bank shot bud and blade:—
> Here found in summer, when the birds were singing,
>   A green and pleasant shade.

The poet then returns to the present scene where the winter
woods are haunted by the ghost of his dead love:

> So through my heart there winds a track of feeling,
>   A path of memory, that is all her own:
> Whereto her phantom beauty ever stealing
>   Haunts the sad spot alone.

At the end, the poet weeps and despairs of spring. The poem has been criticized for sentimentality and overwriting, with some justification perhaps. Yet the sincerity of his grief somehow survives the rhetoric. In commenting on *The Growth of Love,* Bridges mentioned a lady whom he loved, and who died young. One may surmise that "Elegy" is about her, and one may further surmise that the poet was very close to his material, perhaps too close, and hence the intensity of personal feeling that borders on hysteria and sentimentality.

The other elegy has a more elaborate title—"Elegy: On a Lady Whom Grief for the Death of Her Betrothed Killed." The poet is completely detached from his subject: he was obviously not personally involved with the lady. The style is somewhat cold and formal. Yet the rhetoric is brilliant. The poem is one of the best of the period in the artificial, ornamental style:

> Cloke her in ermine, for the night is cold,
> And wrap her warmly, for the night is long,
> In pious hands the flaming torches hold,
> While her attendants, chosen from among
> Her faithful virgin throng,
> May lay her in her cedar litter,
> Decking her coverlet with sprigs of gold,
> Roses, and lilies white that best befit her.

The preparations for the funeral, the funeral procession, and the union of the ghostly lovers in the afterworld (more pagan than Christian) are described in language worthy of Spenser at his best.

It is difficult to say what will be Bridges's final place in the history of the love lyric. As noted above, he does not dramatize his personal love affairs in the manner of Yeats and Hardy. Yet for that very reason, those love poems of Bridges that are general and universal (such as "Awake my heart") may have a lasting interest as their stylistic virtues are better understood.

Response to Beauty. There are a few poems that are responses to beauty in literature and the arts.[12] "Ye thrilled me" is a criticism of Bridges's enthusiasm for "mournful strains" when he was young. Grown older, he believes that the best of art is gay. In "Eclogue II" Richard and Lawrence, on the occasion of the funeral of the Florentine sculptor Giovanni Duprè[13], discuss his personality and his art. Duprè's works never deserved "The Greek or Tuscan name for beautiful." Instead of becoming a major artist like Michelangelo, he forsook his love of beauty for his love of political action. He made of his life a work of beauty and is now ". . . number'd with the saints, not among them/ Who painted saints." In theme the poem reminds us of several poems by Yeats, such as "Sailing to Byzantium," that deal with the conflict between life and art. But of course the styles of Bridges and of Yeats are entirely different. Yeats usually writes in a highly pitched, figurative, and intense style; Bridges's "Eclogue II" has the tone of quiet meditation. "Emily Brontë" by Bridges, on the other hand, which praises the novelist for her freedom, innocence, wisdom, humility, will power, and courage in the face of death and her capacity for love, is in an ecstatic lyrical style, but it is perhaps not altogether convincing because the terms of praise are so general. They might be used with reference to any person one admires; neither the individual personality of the writer nor any particular characteristic of her work is realized in the poem.

Bridges had a deep and lifelong devotion to music, and there are a number of references to music and musicians throughout his poems. The first edition of *The Growth of Love* was dedicated to Purcell. "To Joseph Joachim," an occasional poem written for the Diamond Jubilee of Joachim, May 16, 1904, and prefixed to the program of the music, is one of Bridges's finest sonnets in the Miltonic manner. Joseph Joachim (1831–1907), a distinguished Hungarian violinist, made his first appearance at the Philharmonic Society in London in 1844 where he played Beethoven's Violin Concerto. He was only thirteen years old at the time and earned the nickname of the Hungarian Boy. At the Diamond Jubilee sixty years later he repeated his performance of the Beethoven Concerto.[14] After 1862 his appearances in London became annual events for which he was credited with raising the standards of musical taste in England. Known as the greatest master of style, repose, and tone of his day, he was famous for his interpretation of his friend Brahms. His quartet ("The Joachim Quartet") gave the premiere performance of Brahms's last chamber work, the great Clarinet Quintet in B Minor. As Bridges's sonnet notes, he also excelled in the interpretation of Bach and Beethoven. "Buch der Lieder" records the poet's enthusiasm when he was young for love songs that now no longer appeal to him. "To Thos. Floyd," another completely successful Miltonic sonnet, is an invitation to his friend to visit Boar's Hill near Oxford where the walls (still roofless) of Bridges's home, Chilswell, are being built. The poem praises the rural scene, country life, and the view of the city of Oxford:

> The lovely city, thronging tower and spire,
> The mind of the wide landscape, dreaming deep,
> Grey-silver in the vale; a shrine where keep
> Memorial hopes their pale celestial fire:
> Like man's immortal conscience of desire,
> The spirit that watcheth in me ev'n in my sleep.

This passage, completely conventional in style, makes an interesting contrast to Hopkins's more ecstatic (and mannered!) description in "Duns Scotus's Oxford":

Towery city and branchy between towers;
Cuckoo-echoing, bell-swarmèd, lark-charmèd, rook-racked, river-rounded;
The dapple-eared lily below thee; that country and town did
Once encounter in, here coped and poisèd powers. . . .

When Bridges wrote his poem in 1906 the arbiters of taste would have considered his lines superior to Hopkins's; today their opinion would probably be in favor of Hopkins. As a result of excessive experimental writing in England and America during the last five decades, there may be another revolution in taste that would favor Bridges.

Philosophical Poems. Bridges wrote a number of poems on various important subjects, more complicated and more profound than those discussed above. For want of a better term I have grouped them together as *philosophical poems*.[15] "The Affliction of Richard," rather widely admired by the critics in Bridges's lifetime but now not frequently anthologized,[16] deals with the religious problem of a typical late-Victorian intellectual. As shown before, Bridges as a young man was seriously considering entering the ministry, but, unlike Hopkins, he seems to have taken the discoveries and attitudes of Victorian scientists seriously, so seriously that his original Christian faith was destroyed. Instead of becoming a minister he decided to become a physician. His loss of faith was followed by a period of skepticism, and this in turn was followed by a new and more mature faith not in dogmatic Christianity but in the existence of a God of Love. This poem defines the nature of that faith based on hope and on the argument that the existence of human love demonstrates the reality of divine love. The poem is in Bridges's plain style at its best—direct, powerful, without ornament or imagery:

> Though thou, I know not why,
> Didst kill my childish trust,
> That breach with toil did I
> Repair, because I must:
>   And spite of frighting schemes,
> With which the fiends of Hell
> Blaspheme thee in my dreams,
> So far I have hoped well.

Victorian skepticism has been overcome by an act of will. "Vision," like "The Affliction of Richard," affirms that faith in Christ is based on love and that the faith of the mature man is even stronger than the ecstasies of youth:

> So 'tis with me; the time hath clear'd
>   Not dull'd my loving: I can see
> Love's passing ecstasies endear'd
>   In aspects of eternity.

The impact of science on Victorian faith is squarely faced in "The sea keeps not the Sabbath day." The poet and his love, as they view the sea whose "noisy toil grindeth the shore," see little evidence of a providential God or a God of love:

> We talk of moons and cooling suns,
> Of geologic time and tide
> The eternal sluggards that abide
> While our fair love so swiftly runs.

They realize that they are "so fugitive a part/ Of what so slowly must expire." Yet their despondency is dispelled momentarily not by a renewal of religious faith but by thoughts of happier days and of pleasures derived from music and poetry, by

> Days that the thought of grief refuse,
> Days that are one with human art,
> Worthy of the Virgilian muse,
> Fit for the gaiety of Mozart.

The attitude here is one often found in Bridges's poetry—a refined intellectual hedonism. "Pater Filio" appears to be addressed to the poet's son Edward, born in 1892. It is darker, more pessimistic than Bridges's other religious poems. As he speaks to the innocent child he foresees the future:

> Why such beauty, to be blighted
>   By the swarm of foul destruction?
> Why such innocence delighted,
>   When sin stalks to thy seduction?
> All the litanies e'er chaunted
> Shall not keep thy faith undaunted.

"Joy sweetest lifeborn joy" is another affirmation of faith in a beneficent Deity, an affirmation that in this instance is not an act of will but is derived instead from intuitive experience, mystical moments of spiritual illumination:

> Then comes the happy moment: not a stir
> In any tree, no portent in the sky:
> The morn doth neither hasten nor defer,
> The morrow hath no name to call it by,
> But life and joy are one,—we know not why,—
> As though our very blood long breathless lain
> Had tasted of the breath of God again.

One of the most powerful of the temptations to skepticism is the notion that although a God of Love may exist, his love is not necessarily directed toward human beings. According to the scientific world view, comparatively new in Bridges's time, we seem to be living in a universe indifferent to human happiness or suffering. This idea (so common in Hardy's poetry) is defined and eventually rejected in this same poem:

> And heaven and all the stable elements
> That guard God's purpose mock us, though the mind
> Be spent in searching: for his old intents
> We see were never for our joy designed:

> They shine as doth the bright sun on the blind,
> Or like his pensioned stars, that hymn above
> His praise, but not toward us, that God is Love.

Even when one is fortunate enough to experience some pleasures, they are merely transitory and therefore they seem to mock us:

> Sense is so tender, O and hope so high,
> That common pleasures mock their hope and sense;
> And swifter than doth lightning from the sky
> The ecstasy they pine for flashes hence.
> . . . .
> Nay even the dear occasion when we know,
> We miss the joy, and on the gliding day
> The special glories float and pass away.

However, all of these occasions of discontent and pessimism are overcome in moments of divine joy that can, by an act of memory, become a permanent source of strength during the rest of our ordinary earthbound existence.

Joy is a frequently expressed emotion throughout Bridges's work. Sometimes it is of divine origin; sometimes it is simply motivated by healthy animal spirits; sometimes it is an aspect of his hedonism and springs from his contented, well-regulated, domestic life in a beautiful area of rural England; sometimes it is primarily aesthetic, a response to beauty in art and nature; and sometimes it is the ecstasy of love. Of these poems "Fortunatus Nimium" is the best known:

> To dream as I may
> And awake when I will
> With the song of the birds
> And the sun on the hill . . .
>
> For a happier lot
> Than God giveth me
> It never hath been
> Nor ever shall be.

The innocent joy of youth, changed yet reaffirmed in maturity, is the theme of "The snow lies sprinkled on the beach." The sea—which is literally the sea but also a symbol of the outer mysterious and potentially hostile world—when confronted by the child, is a motivation of joy that is stronger than fear:

> He from his dim enchanted caves
> With shuddering roar and onrush wild
> Fell down in sacrificial waves
> At feet of his exulting child.

The joy is in part made possible by the innocence of the child. He does not understand the implications of what he is facing. As he grows older and understands more he becomes stoical:

> My heart is now too fixed to bow
> Tho' all his tempests howl at me.

Yet his joy in life (fortified by memories of his youth) continues, although now the joy is more solemn than previously:

> For to the gain life's summer saves,
> My solemn joy's increasing store,
> The tossing of his mournful waves
> Makes sweetest music evermore.

It should be noted in passing that Bridges's optimism is not quite so facile and superficial as that of the earlier Browning. It has been tempered by religious skepticism and by the hardheaded common sense of the practicing physician and by the change in intellectual climate that one associates with the fin de siècle. His joy, as Bridges says in "Fortunatus Nimium," is hard earned; it is all the more convincing to the twentieth-century reader for that reason.

Memories of the joys of youth play an important part in the impressive "Elegy: The Summer-House on the Mound." The poet recalls his childhood at Walmer, Kent. The summer house overlooking the Channel becomes the focus of his nostalgia for the experiences of his youth, the memory of which sustains him during hours of depression:

> There live the memories of my early days,
> There still with childish heart my spirit plays;
> Yea, terror-stricken by the fiend despair
> When she hath fled me, I have found her there;

> And there 'tis ever noon, and glad suns bring
> Alternate days of summer and of spring,
> With childish thought, and childish faces bright,
> And all unknown save but the hour's delight.

It was there that he watched the ships in the harbor below:

> There many an hour I have sat to watch; nay, now
> The brazen disk is cold against my brow,
> And in my sight a circle of the sea
> Enlarged to swiftness, where the salt waves flee,
> And ships in stately motion pass so near
> That what I see is speaking to my ear.

After a detailed description of the ships and of the activities of the sailors, he describes the arrival of Napier's fleet bound for the Baltic. It is one of the most beautiful passages in all of Bridges:

> One noon in March upon that anchoring ground
> Came Napier's fleet unto the Baltic bound:
> Cloudless the sky and calm and blue the sea,
> As round Saint Margaret's cliff mysteriously,
> Those murderous queens walking in Sabbath sleep
> Glided in line upon the windless deep.

The poem concludes with a reference to the death of an old friend of the family, the Duke of Wellington, and to the decline of his family mansion, which has been turned into a convent:

> Within the peach-clad walls that old outlaw,
> The Roman wolf, scratches with privy paw.

It is appropriate that this poem, which expresses respect and even longing for the past as well as the importance of the re-creation of the past in the living present, should be written in heroic couplets. It is one of the few successful poems of the late nineteenth century in this traditional medium, which Bridges handles in a masterful manner, never relinquishing the integrity of the couplet, closing some but running enough over to achieve cumulative effects and to avoid monotony.

    "Eclogue III," an occasional poem written for a Fourth of June Festival at Eton, is, like "The Summer-House on the

Mound," substantially a recollection and re-creation of the pleasures of youth. Richard and Godfrey, old Etonians, meet beside
a stream on the grounds of Eton where

"Nothing is changed, and yet how changed are we!"

Godfrey has returned often to this spot "To live in boyish
memories for an hour," but Richard seldom returns, for he
considers nostalgia dangerous—" 'Twas that I might go on I
looked not back." Two different attitudes are developed toward
the past: (1) That memory of one's boyhood strengthens one
for the difficulties of mature life; (2) That memory is an indulgence in Fancy which cannot live "on real food." It is an
escape from reality. Yet both conclude that perhaps these attitudes
toward the past are not so different after all, for there is no
reality and life itself is a dream. The elegy "Recollections of
Solitude" is also a treatment of past pleasures:

>   therefore it is happy and true
> That memoried joys keep ever their delight
> Like steadfast stars in the blue vault of night.

He described his boyhood as a solitude even though he had
many friends whom he loved and who are not forgotten. Nevertheless, in his youth life held its greatest intensity when he was
alone in the woods and fields or even, later, in his room in
London, for it was then that he was creating and studying poetry:

> O mighty Muse, wooer of virgin thought,
> Beside thy charm all else counteth as nought.
> Building with song a temple of desire.

This elegy is a moving tribute to the Muse, to the importance of
poetry in Bridges's life, to the importance of the poetic imagination to man:

> The only enchantress of the earth that art
> To cheer his day and staunch man's bleeding heart . . .
> Who madest beauty, and from thy boundless store
> Of beauty shalt create for evermore.

There is a particularly fine passage in the second stanza (reminiscent of Keats) that describes the poet's memories of fields, gardens, orchards, woods, rivers, and the sea.

Although, as shown above, joy is a frequently defined experience in Bridges's poetry, its counterpart, melancholy and despair, are also sometimes depicted, and Bridges himself has admitted that as a young poet he was a bit too fond of mournful strains or, as Yvor Winters has remarked, he liked to languish among the tombs. Bridges's beautifully written "Elegy: Sad sombre place" is his best expression of this melancholy attitude. In the eighteenth-century graveyard manner he states in the first stanzas his reasons for seeking out the tombs—he admits that there is pleasure in melancholy, and, furthermore, that this melancholy helps him to control deeper "unquiet sorrows":

> They will not ask why in thy shades I stray,
> Among the tombs finding my rare delight,
> Beneath the sun at indolent noonday,
> Or in the windy moon-enchanted night,
> Who have once reined in their steeds at any shrine,
> And given them water from the well divine.—

The wisdom he learns is the traditional one—that death is the great leveler and the humbler of pride, that death comes to all, and that the private grief that sent him to the graveyard is identical with the grief of other men. He considers the possibility of immortality, but the thought does not bring assurance because he is not certain of our state of being after death:

> And where are all their spirits? Ah! could we tell
> The manner of our being when we die,
> And see beyond the scene we know so well
> The country that so much obscured doth lie!

But the grave at least brings peace, and it is this peace that gives him final control over his feelings:

> Nay, were my last hope quenched I here would sit
> And praise the annihilation of the pit.

The subject matter of the poem is perfectly conventional, but what raises the poem above mediocrity is the absolute control of feeling and the mastery of line rhythm, stanza rhythm, and diction. Particularly felicitous is the line:

> Or in the windy moon-enchanted night.

"Dejection" is another fine example of Bridges's absolute control over his emotions and over his style. (The poem makes an instructive contrast with Coleridge's rhapsodic and sometimes overwritten Ode on the same subject.) The feeling is clearly motivated. The poet's dejection is caused by the betrayal of love and friendship, by the death of loved ones, by obstructionism, and by the usual cares and anxieties of the human condition. The style is impeccable:

> Wherefore to-night so full of care,
> My soul, revolving hopeless strife,
> Pointing at hindrance, and the bare
> Painful escapes of fitful life?
>
> Shaping the doom that may befall
> Be precedent of terror past:
> By love dishonoured, and the call
> Of friendship slighted at the last?

As so often happens in a Bridges poem on this subject, there is a positive and optimistic note at the end. The poet's dejection is almost completely dispelled not by any religious consolation but by the secular pleasures of music and poetry:

> Again shall pleasure overflow
> Thy cup with sweetness, thou shalt taste
> Nothing but sweetness, and shalt grow
> Half sad for sweetness run to waste.

Yet the last two lines must be noted:

> I praise my days for all they bring,
> Yet are they only not enough.

I believe that the last line suggests that the satisfactions derived from the arts are not enough. The poet still needs the kind of consolation one can get only from religious faith.

"Low Barometer," after Yvor Winters called attention to it,[17] has become an anthology piece and justifiably so, for in importance of theme and execution it must be ranked as one of Bridges's masterpieces.

The poem begins with a description of a storm, but it soon becomes apparent that the storm is allegorical. The real subject of the poem is the precarious control by reason and by grace of the irrational forces that afflict man—demonic, archaic, subconscious, and subhuman:

> On such a night, When Air has loosed
> Its guardian grasp on blood and brain,
> Old terrors then of god or ghost
> Creep from their caves to life again;
>
> And Reason kens he herits in
> A haunted house. Tenants unknown
> Assert their squalid lease of sin
> With earlier title than his own.
>
> Unbodied presences, the pack'd
> Pollution and remorse of Time,
> Slipp'd from oblivion reenact
> The horrors of unhouseld crime.

The last stanza quoted is probably Bridges's best expression of supernatural terror. The theme is, of course, common in Hopkins's poetry, particularly in his so-called dark sonnets, but it is unusual to find it so adequately treated by Bridges. There are a few trite phrases (probably echoes of Shakespeare) in the final two stanzas of the poem, but they do not seriously weaken the poem as a whole.

"The Sleeping Mansion" is a backward look at the happiness of his life in the manor house at Yattendon where he had lived after his marriage with Monica Waterhouse. This period (1884–1904), one knows from Bridges's letters and references in several poems, was one of domestic tranquility and great creative accomplishment. The poem begins with a drive along a village lane during which Bridges catches sight for a moment of his former home:

> The place look'd blank and empty,
>   a sleeper's witless face
> which to his mind's enchantment
>   is numb, and gives no trace.

The loneliness of the house is cheered by the presence of its former tenant. The house experiences the same delight that the poet enjoyed while living there:

> I knew what sudden wonder
>   I brought her in my flight;
> what rapturous joy possess'd her,
>   what peace and soft delight.

"The Sleeping Mansion" is a very minor poem, but it is beautifully phrased, and the personification of the house, which might well have been sentimentalized, seems to me completely successful.

"The Great Elm" is of considerably more substance and power than the preceding poem. It begins with an account of a walk in the country during which the poet comes upon a massive and ancient elm that he describes in impressive language. It reminds him of the fabled Elm of Acheron, the last haven of mortal dreams, which grew on the river bank of Hell. This incursion of mythology and the supernatural leads directly to the climax of the poem—the depiction of a transcendental moment in which the poet experiences a union with the eternal mind. The union is described as one in which he discovers and embraces his "other self," his spiritual self:

> He is of such immortal kind,
>   His inwit is so clean,
> So conscient with the eternal Mind—
>   The self of things unseen,
> That when within his world I win,
>   Nor suffer mortal change,
> I am of such immortal kin
>   No dream is half so strange.

As in a similar mystical passage in "Joy sweetest life born joy," mentioned above, the experience is described as being recurrent, ecstatically intense, and relatively brief. The poet attempts to hold the experience in his memory by embodying it in a poem:

> That since he chose that place and time
>   To come again to me,
> I'd hold him fast by magic rhyme
>   Forever to that tree.

Whether one considers this feeling to be one of simple euphoria that most people have experienced from time to time (often in rural surroundings) or whether one considers it to be a genuine mystical rapture depends on one's metaphysical assumptions and on one's subjective response to the quality of the poetry defining the experience. Because of its obvious sincerity, I am more impressed by the poetic expression of supernatural moments in the work of Hopkins and Bridges than I am to the claim of such supernatural communion in *The Four Quartets* of T. S. Eliot.

The philosophical and expository poems "La Gloire de Voltaire" and "To Robert Burns" are Bridges's critique of reason. They introduce themes that are more fully developed in *The Testament of Beauty*. The poem on Voltaire is a dialogue between A (Bridges) and B, a defender of the philosopher, who enumerates his supposed virtues, virtues that are either denied or downgraded by the poet. This poetic indictment of Voltaire charges him with being overly ambitious for worldly fame, lacking in human feeling, a scorner of religion, and a cunning manipulator who feathered his own nest and whose chief interests were comfort, wit, and taste. Those virtues he had, such as industry and gaiety, were "mediocrity pushed to perfection." He used his faculty of reason for superficial witticisms. He was a mere wag with no serious interest in ideas. He was unlike the true philosopher who seeks for wisdom and who realizes that

> . . . the sole fact
> Is the long story of man's growing mind.

True, he fought intolerance, but so did many other people superior to Voltaire including Bayle. He was not a serious reformer and seer like Calvin or Luther. He "degraded art" and "varnished vice." Such a man cannot be praised, for true praise is based on love and to love Voltaire is impossible. The poet has, in fact, just thrown three of his dangerous works behind the fire to keep them out of the hands of his children.

The philosophical thrust of the poem is this—Voltaire (quite aside from his personal deficiencies) misuses the faculty of reason to gain superficial ends. What the proper use of reason should be is demonstrated in "To Robert Burns," which is subtitled "An Epistle on Instinct." In this critique of Burns, Bridges parodies, as it were, Burns's own style:

> Thou art a poet, Robbie Burns,
> Master of words and witty turns,
> Of lilting songs and merry yarns,
>> Drinking and kissing:
> There's much in all thy small concerns,
>> But more that's missing.

Burns is praised for his common sense, his hatred of pretentiousness, and his benevolence. What is missing in Burns is the life of reason. For it is substituted the life of pleasure, the sensual pleasure of the moment. There follows a discussion of the instincts and their relation to reason. There are three instincts: racial, self-preservative, and social. (These become breed, selfhood, and ethic in *The Testament of Beauty*.) Of these, the racial instinct (sex) is the strongest and most tyrannical, and yet reason has tamed sex

> Into a sacramental flame
> Of consecration.

We owe a great deal to the instincts as they functioned in primitive man. By instinct, primitive man founded the bases of art and morals. His lack of analytical reason was, in a way, an advantage, for it saved him from paralysis of the will. Yet his achievements were not completely his own nor did they occur by chance. There was purpose in his development, formulated and guided not by himself but by the Eternal Mind. Burns, like primitive man, did not attain the highest life, the life of the just man as defined by Aristotle. Nevertheless, one should have some sympathy with the primitive instinctive morality of Burns, for by it the poor man was befriended. He had, at least, developed a social conscience.

In these two poems there is some criticism of reason when, as in Voltaire, it is used superficially for shallow wit and for mundane ends. Also, too much analytical reason may paralyze the will. Implicit in these poems is the idea, fully developed in *The Testament of Beauty*, that reason should be used to harmonize and discipline the instincts and in that function it is absolutely necessary to the good life.

Bridges wrote several poems depicting people.[18] With a few exceptions, these are village characters who are not sharply delineated, nor are they analyzed in depth, nor are they personae of a dramatic scene. In this genre Hardy is far superior to Bridges. "The Windmill" is typical. It describes the village miller *in situ*:

> Beside his sacks the miller stands
> On high within the open door:
> A book and pencil in his hands,
> His grist and meal he reckoneth o'er.
>
> . . . .
>
> He gives the creaking sails a spin,
> The circling millstones faster flee,
> The shuddering timbers groan within,
> And down the shoot the meal runs free.

The descriptive detail of the mill and its activity is excellent; the verse rhythms are, as usual, successful, and the comment on the commercialism of the miller at the end gives the poem some thematic point, however slight. But the total result is a very minor local color piece and not a fully developed character sketch. The same comment may be made on "The Winnowers," which is mainly a descriptive poem in praise of country life. "Hodge" praises the strength and courage of a plowman gone to war. He is seen as a type, not as an individual. The poem is a tribute to a way of life rather than a character portrayal. On the other hand, "Simpkin," who is presented in humorous verses reminiscent of Burns, is a fairly vivid description of a village eccentric who may, says Bridges, be a saint:

> And yet since nothing's made in vain,
>   And we must judge our brother
> Unfitted for this world, 'tis plain
>   He's fitted for another.

There is some attempt to dramatize his material in "A Villager." The wife of a laborer tells in dialect (seldom attempted by Bridges) the story of herself and Willie, the handsomest man in town, whom she accepted in marriage although he was beneath her socially. Now old and worn out with poverty and shunned by her shiftless husband, she looks forward to death because her husband, full of remorse, will join her in heaven

> An' come to me there in the land o' bliss
> To give me the love I looked for in this.

In "The Widow," the poet, passing the house of a woman who is rearing the child she bore after her lover was killed in the war, expresses his sympathy and admiration for her courage and says that the child gives her life a sanctifying presence. The poem is a simple statement of a situation without complexity or development. "Millicent" is a charming poem on the affection between the poet, in late middle age, and a young girl. "The Portrait of a Grandfather" (which can be scanned in accentual or in accentual syllabic verse) opens with the striking line

> With mild eyes agaze, and lips ready to speak.

It expresses the poet's admiration for the traditional British family life held together by the bonds of filial love and duty.

Of Bridges's patriotic and war poems,[19] some of which he discarded, the best is probably "Gheluvelt," discussed in the section on classical prosody. "Trafalgar Square" ends with a memorable description of Nelson's statue:

> Who looketh o'er London as if 'twere his own,
> As he standeth in stone, aloft and alone,
> Sailing the sky with one arm and one eye.

"The Chivalry of the Sea" is a stirring tribute to Charles Fisher of Christ Church, Oxford, lost on the ship *Invincible*. The diction is somewhat trite; yet the poem is saved by its rhythms that, no matter how one scans the poem, have the movement of speech-stress verse:

Over the warring waters, beneath the wandering skies
The heart of Britain roameth, the Chivalry of the sea,
Where Spring never bringeth a flower, nor bird singeth in a tree;
Far, afar, O beloved, beyond the sight of our eyes,
Over the warring waters, beneath the stormy skies.

Bridges's occasional poems[20] are not his most memorable achievements. By far the best is the sonnet "To the President of Magdalen College," written in Bridges's impeccable Miltonic style:

> But well-befriended we become good friends,
> Well-honour'd honourable; and all attain
> Somewhat by fathering what fortune sends.

There are a few miscellaneous poems worth considering. "Scream-ing Tarn" is a melodramatic narrative poem, Bridges's only attempt in the genre, and it is surprisingly good. The first stanzas describe the tarn and the cause of its notoriety:

> At mid of night, if one be there,
>   —So say the people of the hill—
> A fearful shriek of death is heard,
>   One sudden scream both loud and shrill.

> And some have seen on stilly nights,
>   And when the moon was clear and round,
> Bubbles which to the surface swam
>   And burst as if they held the sound.—

The rest of the poem tells the story of the scream. In Cavalier days a tavern host with Cromwellian sympathies murders his loyalist guest for the supposed gold in the guest's sack. To his horror he discovers that his victim is a woman disguised as a man and in the sack is not gold but the head of a man, the twin of the murdered woman. The host sinks the body of his victim together with the head of the man in the middle of the tarn and then leaves the area forever. This kind of material is difficult to handle without overwriting, but Bridges's narrative succeeds at every point. It is, in fact, almost as good as several similar poems by Hardy.

"The Isle of Achilles" has as an epigraph three lines from Thetis's final speech in Euripides' *Andromache,* in which the mother of Achilles prophesies to Peleus that the spirit of their son will inhabit an Isle

> whose chalky coasts
> Are laved by the surrounding Euxine deep.

Drawing from other legendary material, Bridges describes the temple of Achilles on the island Leukê where pilgrims of the Greek and Roman world come to consult the oracle and make sacrifices to Achilles and to his friend Patroclus. Here, men have seen in answer to their prayers the figure of Achilles in full armor and the sound of supernatural music, and some in sleep have dreamed that they were entertained by Achilles and Patroclus with wine and music. The poem is in heroic couplets that are composed with the same skill Bridges displayed in his "Summer-House on the Mound." "The Isle of Achilles" has been neglected by critics and anthologists, but in its lucid and calm re-creation of the Greek herioc ideal it seems to me to be a poem worthy of preservation:

> For sure I am that, if man ever was,
> Achilles was a hero, both because
> Of his high birth and beauty, his country's call
> His valour of soul, his early death withal,
> For Homer's praise, the crown of human art;
> And that above all praise he had at heart
> A gentler passion in her sovran sway,
> And when his love died threw his life away.

In these shorter poems one sees the full range of Bridges's accomplishment—his successful treatment of the universal themes of love, death, religious and philosophical questions, and response to beauty in nature and the arts in a variety of poetic forms that are managed with the skill of a scholar of prosody. It is on these poems that Bridges's reputation as a major poet must eventually rest. His chief contemporary competitors, Hardy and Hopkins, are now held in higher esteem than the former poet laureate. When the revolutionary generation (Pound, Eliot, H. D., Marianne Moore, W. C. Williams, and others) caught the imagination of the poetry public in the 1910s and 1920s, it was natural that Hopkins's brilliant experiments in imagery and rhythm should gain the ascendancy. He was a forerunner of the generation that put a high value on intensity of feeling gained by means of striking visual imagery and violent distortion of conventional meter or an abandonment of conventional meter altogether. The ecstasy of H. D.'s poetry is not so very different from that of Hopkins, although the motivations for the ecstasy are fundamentally different. Hardy, much more conventional in his techniques than Hopkins, has become increasingly popular in the last thirty years, partly because of a reaction against the willful obscurity and inordinate complexity of the experimentalists. Hardy can be understood without difficulty and he (like Bridges) wrote movingly on universal themes. His work is frequently marred, in my opinion, by a facile cynicism, but this same cynicism has probably increased his popularity in recent years.

There are already signs of a fundamental change of taste. Readers are beginning to see experimental poetry as a fascinating but minor excursion from the main road of Anglo-American verse, and Hopkins's reputation may be somewhat diminished along with this decline of the experimentalists and by the fact that Hopkins dealt with a limited range of human experience. Hardy's reputation will probably survive, although his range, too, is somewhat narrow, but not as narrow as Hopkins's. One gets tired of Hardy's repetitious determinism and fatalism and his ironies. Furthermore, he deals chiefly with the experience of one kind of people—nonintellectual rural people of the lower class or lower-middle class in England; yet, he understands them perfectly and communicates their feelings with great power. Bridges has much greater intellectual scope than Hardy and far greater artistic mastery of his material; and his learning was greater than that of Hardy. He probably had as much or even more talent than Hardy had, and he had the advantage of a university education. Unlike Hopkins, his best work is in the mainstream of English verse, and the time may come when poems like "Eros" and "The Summer-House on the Mound" will be as highly valued and as frequently anthologized as "Windhover," and "The Convergence of the Twain."

The Growth of Love

In 1876 Edward Bumpus of London brought out an anonymous pamphlet entitled *The Growth of Love/ A Poem/ In Twenty-Four Sonnets.* The first and last sonnets are entitled "Introduction" and "Conclusion" respectively,[21] and these together with the subtitle suggest a unity of subject and a coherence that is in fact not always maintained. According to the "Introduction," which was dropped in subsequent editions and never reprinted by Bridges, the sequence was inspired by a lady "unwon" and now dead:

> Love O'er the noble heart will ne'er abate
>   His empire; he will enter by surprise,
> To conquer till his foes be sworn allies,
> And heart and he become incorporate.

> So the perfected soul, now her own mate,
> Has for her solace neither voice nor eyes,
> Unless the memory of his first disguise
> Quicken the speech of an abolished date.
>
> I pray you, ye that read me, when ye con
> The terms of fancy, question not, nor say
> Who was perchance the lady he looked on?
>
> I tell you she is not of mortal clay:
> Once she was truly, but she died unwon,
> By death transfigured to the light of day.

A definite Platonic note is introduced with this first poem. The author is inspired by the love of a woman "not of mortal clay" and now in heaven. She once was, of course, an earthly woman, but as he remembers their first meeting in "Retrospect" (the second sonnet) he rejects the thought of her special, individual charms, saying that at this, his first love

> . . . all that seemed choice, all that was new,
> Lived in the awakening soul's keen prescience
> At Love's arising. . . .

Although there may be passing references to the body, the emphasis throughout is on spiritual and heavenly beauty. In the next poem, "First Love," he dreams that he, like Adam in Paradise, is encountering Eve for the first time,

> Rending my body where with hurried sound
> I feel my heart beat when I think of thee.

In the succeeding poems the poet recalls various scenes with his lady. But even here the passion is ethereal. As he talks with her,

> She hath the intelligence of heavenly things
> Unsullied by man's mortal overthrow.

There are occasional sonnets on general subjects—such as number 6 entitled "Art," 14, also on art but inspired specifically by the Florentine church of San Miniato, and 20 entitled "Creative Art"—which have only an indirect relationship to his main theme, the worship of heavenly love and beauty once manifested in a certain "unwon" woman. All of the sonnets are in the Italianate form with an obvious influence of Milton, but also with verbal Shakespearean echoes such as "Quicken the speech of an abolished date."

What were Bridges's own feelings about this early volume? McKay in his bibliography[22] quotes from a catalogue (1893) of Edmund Gosse's library: "After a few copies had been distributed the remainder of the edition was burned by the author." Is this true, and if so, why? Bridges may have felt that the poetry was inferior, as he probably did when he destroyed most of his first book, *Poems* (1873).[23] But if he felt that the sonnets were bad, why did he allow the title pages of his anonymous *Poems* (1879) and his anonymous *Poems* (1880) to carry the inscription "By the Author of the *Growth of Love*"? Perhaps he did not destroy the unsold copies of this first edition of *The Growth of Love* until after he had met Monica Waterhouse in 1882 and had decided to address a new, revised, and enlarged sequence to her.

This second edition of *The Growth of Love* (1889) was published by H. Daniel anonymously.[24] It is considerably different in tone and substance from the first. There are seventy-nine sonnets of which fourteen (revised) are taken from the 1876 volume. The rest are new. This sequence is addressed to an earthly woman (Monica Waterhouse, one may conjecture) now won:

> For thou art mine and now I am ashamed
> To have uséd means to win so pure acquist.

The passion is more substantial and considerably more convincing than in the previous sequence; yet the ecstasy of the lover is usually universalized and spiritualized:

> The whole world now is but the minister
> Of thee to me: I see no other scheme
> But universal love, from timeless dream
> Waking to thee his joy's interpreter.

Earthly love occasionally receives its due, but the Platonic note is repeatedly sounded; it is the function of earthly love to lead us to a vision of spiritual beauty, even though few may attain the vision:

All earthly beauty hath one cause and proof,
To lead the pilgrim soul to beauty above:
Yet lieth the greater bliss so far aloof,
That few there be are wean'd from earthly love.

Fifteen of these sonnets are in the Shakespearean form, and the influence of Shakespeare's language as well as of his sonnet form have increased. The rest are Miltonic in form.

Nine years later in volume 1 (1898) of his collected poetical works, Bridges published his third and final revision of *The Growth of Love* and, for the first time, not anonymously. Ten sonnets, none of them of importance, are dropped, the order of the remaining sixty-nine is maintained, and there are no changes in the individual sonnets: the third sequence is similar in purpose, style, and content to the second. The poet's loving response to beauty as it appears in the woman he loves and, finally, his response to the Idea of Beauty in the Platonic sense is the major theme, but also treated is the poet's response to beauty as it is found in nature and in works of art including poetry and music. Hence, there are sonnets that seem to be digressive from the main theme, that refer to various landscapes, towns, and beautiful buildings as seen in Bridges's travels, digressions that give a heterogeneous character to the sequence, at least on first reading, although it may be argued that some of them come under the heading of response to beauty. But there is at least one poem that is completely irrelevant even to this very general theme; yet it is one of the most striking in the entire series. Sonnet 27 expresses the poet's awe (and perhaps revulsion) at the new ironclad steamships that have replaced the sailing vessels:

The fabled sea-snake, old Leviathan,
Or else what grisly beast of scaly chine
That champ'd the ocean-wrack and swash'd the brine,
Before the new and milder days of man,
Had never rib nor bray nor swindging fan
Like his iron swimmer of the Clyde or Tyne,
Late-born of golden seed to breed a line
Of offspring swifter and more huge of plan.

Straight is her going, for upon the sun
When once she hath look'd, her path and place are plain;

With tireless speed she smiteth one by one
The shuddering seas and foams along the main;
And her eased breath, when her wild race is run,
Roars thro' her nostrils like a hurricane.

The poem is out of place in a sequence devoted to loving response to various manifestations of beauty. Yet the writing is of considerable power. It deserves preservation as an individual poem.

An examination of the entire sequence shows that forty-eight sonnets are about love for a woman or about the Platonic idea of love (usually inspired by a woman) or about love in general. Ten sonnets deal with beauty or with loving response to beauty in nature and the arts. Several poems are in groups; for example, 47, 48, 49, and 50 are poems motivated by a sense of loss—the loss may be the loss of a woman, but that is not so stated and they are therefore not included in the poems devoted to love mentioned above. Sonnets 39, 41, and 42 deal with nostalgic memories of childhood of which 41 mentions love. Number 6, a description of the coming of spring with no reference to love, is linked with 7, which states that the loved woman is the spring of the poet's life. Similarly, in sonnet 8 the poet says that beauty is best as it is found in nature, but in the next sonnet he argues that the beauty of his loved one is superior to all other beauty.

A few poems appear to be completely irrelevant, such as 27, quoted above, on the steamship, 15 on the function of reason, and 53 on Hector, although it might be argued that Hector died in a war fought for the love of a beautiful woman. However, the great majority of the poems do deal with love and the various emotions of the lover ranging from despair to ecstasy. There is also the development or "growth of love" from earthly passion to spiritualized vision that has been mentioned. Nevertheless, this final edition of *The Growth of Love* as a whole still has a heterogeneous effect, probably because it was written over a number of years. There is a general theme and a kind of development but no very precise coherence or sequence. In many instances the poems could be rearranged without disturbing any perceptible pattern. Furthermore, as has been frequently noted by the critics, there is a coldness about some of them and the language is sometimes bookish and trite, with too many obvious echoes of Shakespeare and Milton. There are also occasional echoes of Keats, Sidney, and the poetry of Michelangelo and other Italians.

Bridges's lifelong interest in Milton and his study of Milton's prosody are well known; it is therefore not surprising that most of the sonnets (fifty-two of them) are in the Italianate or Miltonic form. Two—numbers 16 and 52—are hybrids but close to the Shakespearean form. Fifteen are Shakespearean with three quatrains and a couplet. It is interesting to note that number 22, "I would be a bird, and straight on wings I arise," which is Miltonic in its rhyme scheme, is, unlike all the other sonnets, in stress prosody and was first published in *Poems* (1879) in small type together with three others to indicate its special prosody.

The Shakespearean influence has been overlooked by most commentators, although not by Guérard.[25] It is evident from unpublished correspondence with Logan Pearsall Smith in the Bodleian library[26] that Bridges as a young man had a high regard for Shakespeare's sonnets but that his admiration diminished in his later years, although as late as 1907 he still liked certain sonnets. Recently published correspondence between Bridges and Samuel Butler concerning Butler's *Shakespeare's Sonnets Reconsidered* (1899) shows that at the turn of the century Bridges concurred with Butler that the poems were the work of a very young poet with the stylistic weaknesses of youth and that Bridges (in sharp disagreement with Butler) considered Shakespeare's sequence to be primarily about idealistic Platonic love as opposed to earthly passion.[27] In *The Growth of Love* Shakespeare is praised in two of the sonnets, and there are at least a dozen easily identifiable verbal echoes of Shakespeare.

Nevertheless, in spite of the obvious weaknesses—occasional imitative and stereotyped language and coldness and aloofness from the subject—*The Growth of Love* may well be the best sonnet sequence since the beginning of the Victorian period. Bridges is thoroughly at home in the form. He has mastered the rhythm and structure of the Italian and the Shakespearean sonnet, and (at its best) his restrained purity of style is superior to the sentimentality of Elizabeth Barrett Browning and Edna St. Vincent Millay. Meredith's *Modern Love* is not, technically, a sonnet sequence, for each poem consists of four quatrains. However, this sequence of short love poems does invite comparison with *The Growth of Love,* to the advantage of Bridges. Meredith's poetry, like his prose, is labored and overwritten. The only nineteenth-century sonnet writer with comparable gifts of style **are the Americans Frederick Goddard Tuckerman and Jones**

Very, and in a few poems they may be superior to Bridges, but their general level is not so high as his.

Eros and Psyche

Today I read through Bridges' mellow tale
Of her whose tact was like a flowery chain,
Psyche, the thwarted one, who could regain
Her naked love within the gods' own pale.

What purity was hers who did not quail
At Pan's full-bellied voice or Death's dank strain?
Though harried, loved the simple sheaves of grain?
Though staunch of purpose, still knew how to fail?

Grace at the earth's black ends!
                                            The tale piles deep
The dull gold leaves from an archaic tree.
But my eclogues must build from cruder thought:
Of shepherds starved, and starved the dusty sheep.

Sadly I linger, loath to part from thee
Who standest gravely fair, and sayest naught.

—Howard Baker, "Psyche"

    O king of joy, what is thy thought?
I dream thou knowest it is nought,
And wouldst in darkness come, but thou
Makest the light where'er thou go.

—Robert Bridges, "Eros"

    I seek no more to see your face; not even the dark of night can be a hindrance to my joy, for I hold you in my arms, light of my life.

—Apuleius, Psyche to Eros, in *The Golden Ass of Apuleius*

Bridges's *Eros and Psyche* is in two versions—the first published in 1885 was reissued in 1894 (reprinted 1895) after some revision. The 1898 reprint in *Collected Poems* is the same as the 1894 version. Bridges considered his poem to be "little more than a translation of Apuleius' tale"[28] and stated that he had read none of the English versions although he had borrowed various rhetorical devices and expressions from many poets including Homer, Spenser, and Shakespeare.[29] The story as it appears in the second-century Latin of Apuleius's *Golden Ass* is called an old wives' tale (*anilibusque fabulis*) by the old hag who tells it to an abducted maiden to cheer her up as she awaits ransom or execution. The story on the surface is pleasant, charming, and touching. Psyche, the most beautiful of three daughters of a king and queen, incurs the jealousy of Venus (Apuleius uses Roman rather than Greek names) because her former devotees are now worshiping Psyche rather than herself. Venus commands her son Cupid to degrade Psyche by compelling her to fall in love with some ignoble and vile man. Meanwhile the father of Psyche, because no mortal had dared offer marriage to his daughter, consults the oracle of Apollo and is instructed to leave his daughter on a mountaintop where she would be married to a creature

> viperous and fierce
> Who flies through aether with fire and sword.

Psyche is taken to a mountaintop to meet her bridegroom. She is transported by the west wind to a valley, finds there a palace, and on entering is ministered to by invisible servants. At night Cupid visits her, makes her his wife, and departs (unseen by Psyche) just before daybreak. Thereafter, Cupid visits his bride unseen, only at night, and warns Psyche against the malevolence of her two jealous sisters who begin to visit her in her palace, transported there by the same west wind that brought Psyche. The sisters eventually extract the information that Psyche (who is now pregnant) has never laid eyes on her husband. They remind her of Apollo's oracle that she would be wed to a serpent, and they convince her that this is the actual case and that her child will be a monster. Psyche is persuaded to cut off her husband's head at night with the aid of a knife and a lighted lamp. The terrified Psyche (forgetting her affection for her husband and his warning) conceals a knife and a lamp near the bed and that night when her husband is asleep, Psyche, with knife in hand, uncovers the lamp and gazes on the love God himself.

Astonished and frightened, she tries to kill herself, but the knife shrinks from the crime and twists itself out of her hand. Psyche, gazing at the beautiful Cupid and accidentally pricking herself on one of his arrows, falls in love with Love and flings herself upon him, but in so doing accidentally spills a drop of burning oil on his shoulder. Cupid awakes and flies off without a word, Psyche clutching his right leg. She falls to the ground, Cupid reproaches her for disregarding his warning, and soars out of sight. Psyche revisits her sisters and tells each of them that Cupid threatened to marry her as punishment for her disobedience. Each sister in turn goes to the mountaintop, entreats the west wind to carry her to Cupid, jumps, and is killed on the rocks below.

Psyche travels from country to country hunting for her husband, while Venus, after learning of Cupid's infatuation for Psyche and his serious illness from the burning oil, offers a reward of seven kisses "and one more sweetly honeyed from the touch of her loving tongue" for her capture. Psyche, after appealing in vain to Juno and Ceres for help, decides to appeal to Venus herself. Dragged into the goddess's presence by her servant Habit, Psyche is whipped and then given four seemingly impossible tasks (or labors, which recall those of Hercules) : the separation of a pile of mixed seeds (accomplished for her by friendly ants) ; the securing of wool from the dangerous golden sheep (done with the friendly advice of a reed) ; the securing of a jar of water from the Styx (accomplished for her by Jupiter's eagle) ; and, finally, the securing of a portion of Proserpine's beauty in a jar (achieved with the advice of a talking tower) .

After the accomplishment of these tasks, Psyche is discovered by Cupid, who has recovered from his burn. Cupid begs Jupiter to allow him to marry Psyche. Jupiter consents, Psyche is made immortal, and after her marriage with Cupid she gives birth to her child, who is named Pleasure.

Bridges includes all the essential elements of the tale in his poem, lengthens the introductory portion, adds some descriptive embellishment of his own and some philosophical interpolation, and hellenizes the story slightly by giving his characters Greek rather than Roman names. He places the story in Crete and refers to Cretan mythology. (Apuleius does not localize the scene.) As he explains in a note,[30] he borrows his description of the sunsets following the eruption of Krakatoa from accounts published at the time.[31] He makes "a gentler characterization of Psyche"[32] and is more careful in his handling of her motivation than is Apuleius. And he adds an anachronic acrostic of PUR-CELL[33] and an equally anachronic reference to Newton's law of gravitation.[34]

Whether or not Apuleius intended his tale (which he put into the mouth of a demented and drunken old woman) to be a parable or an allegory is arguable. Louis C. Purser writes:

> Just a shadow of allegory may have hovered before the mind of Apuleius, owing to Plato and to the Alexandrine poets. It is, however, now generally acknowledged that no consistent allegorical interpretation is to be applied to the story in detail. The story is to be regarded rather as a mere fairy-tale, tricked out with all the airs and graces of Apuleian style.[35]

The characters, in Apuleius, are fairy-tale characters. Venus (again following Purser's commentary) is like one of Grimm's perse-cuting queens, irascible and cruel. In his presentation of her, Apuleius is ironically mocking the gods and goddesses of the old religion. Cupid is primarily an attractive, mischievous boy just grown to manhood. Psyche, far from being a symbol of the Soul, is merely a beautiful fairly-tale princess.

Nevertheless, the tale has frequently been allegorized, or given a symbolic slant, in ancient and modern times, and in the last three decades of this century it has been subjected to Jungian depth analysis. Bridges has told us that he had not read any versions of the story in English. However, he may have been familiar with the brief poems of Meleager (first century B.C.) on Eros and Psyche, which seem to represent the power of passion over the soul. Fulgentius (fifth century) has given us a com-plicated interpretation that sees the story as an allegory of the Soul's (Psyche's) experience with Desire (Cupid). Unseen at night, Desire is controlled and therefore not sinful; but when seen it becomes uncontrolled and evil. In Fulgentius's explana-tion, Venus represents Lust, the King and Queen are God and Matter, the two sisters of Psyche are Flesh and Free Will. G. F. Hildebrand in his edition of Apuleius (1842) gives a list of allegorical interpretations and then his own analysis. He considers the story to have affinities with the doctrine of one of the mystic cults of which Apuleius was a member. Psyche is the pure soul in love with Cupid, Heavenly Love, but opposed by Venus who is Fate. Obstructions are put in Psyche's way by Venus. They are overcome by Psyche's faithfulness to Heavenly Love. Edward Zeller considers the tale to be an allegory of the fallen Soul desiring union with God.[36]

Thus there was, when Bridges came to write his poem in the 1880's, a tradition of allegorical interpretation going back to a date preceding Apuleius's version, and later including Apuleius's version. It was not surprising, then, that Bridges would attempt to give more depth to his poem than that of mere fairy tale. Bridges in fact stated in a letter to Coventry Patmore that both Apuleius's tale and his own poem were allegorical.[37] There are Christian elements in Bridges's *Eros and Psyche* that (like the earlier *Growth of Love*) may be interpreted as a story of the transformation of blind sensual passion (Eros's unseen visits to Psyche at night) to a more spiritualized love (the marriage of Eros and Psyche in Heaven), although this was most certainly not Apuleius's intention. As Albert Guérard has noted, "Cupid is married at the end of Apuleius's story, but merely so that he will be kept out of mischief."[38] Furthermore, Psyche, unlike the fairy princess of Apuleius, is in Bridges's poem the symbol of ideal or spiritual beauty:

> Her vision rather drave from passion's heart
> What earthly soil it had afore possest;
> Since to man's purer unsubstantial part
> The brightness of her presence was addrest.

The Psyche of Bridges is certainly more spiritual than the Psyche of Apuleius. Furthermore, Bridges thought (as he said in his letter to Coventry Patmore) that he had improved on the original Psyche in his analysis of her feminine psychology, that is, in her behavior with respect to the admission of her sisters to her palace (against the wishes of Eros) and in respect to the labors imposed on her by Aphrodite.

When he calls his poem "a faithful translation of Apuleius' story,"[39] Bridges must have meant merely that he was following exactly the chronology of events in the original tale. For Bridges arranges his poem in "twelve measures," one for each month of the year (which Apuleius did not), and he frequently interpolates whole stanzas of description and depiction of character that are not in Apuleius. To list all of them would be tedious, and an example or two must suffice. At the beginning of Apuleius's story Venus calls Cupid to her, expresses her hatred and envy of Psyche, and sends Cupid on his errand of vengeance. Cupid is described by Apuleius as a mischievous and wicked boy as follows:

> Straightway she summoned her winged headstrong boy, that wicked boy, scorner of law and order, who, armed with arrows and torch aflame, speeds through others' homes by night, saps the ties of wedlock, and all unpunished commits hideous crime and uses all his power for ill.[40]

This is considerably changed and expanded by Bridges:

> With that she calls to her her comely boy,
> The limber scion of the God of War,
> The fruit adulterous, which for man's annoy
> To that fierce partner Cytherea bore,
> EROS, the ever young, who only grew
> In mischief, and was Cupid named anew
> In westering aftertime of latin lore.
>
>
> What the first dawn of manhood is, the hour
> When beauty, from its fleshy bud unpent,
> Flaunts like the corol of a summer flower,
> As if all life were for that ornament,
> Such Eros seemed in years, a trifler gay,
> The prodigal of an immortal day
> For ever spending, and yet never spent.
>
>
> His skin is brilliant with the nimble flood
> Of ichor, that comes dancing from his heart,
> Lively as fire, and redder than the blood,
> And maketh in his eyes small flashes dart,
> And curleth his hair golden, and distilleth
> Honey on his tongue, and all his body filleth
> With wanton lightsomeness in every part.
>
>
> Naked he goeth, but with sprightly wings
> Red, iridescent, are his shoulders fledged.

A bow his weapon, which he deftly strings,
And little arrows barb'd and keenly edged;
And these he shooteth true; but else the youth
For all his seeming recketh naught of truth,
But most deceiveth where he most is pledged.

'Tis he that maketh in men's heart a strife
Between remorseful reason and desire,
Till with life lost they lose the love of life,
And by their own hands wretchedly expire;
Or slain in bloody rivalries they miss
Even the short embracement of their bliss,
His smile of fury and his kiss of fire.

He makes the strong man weak, the weak man wild;
Ruins great business and purpose high;
Brings down the wise to folly reconciled,
And martial captains on their knees to sigh:
He changeth dynasties, and on the head
Of duteous heroes, who for honour bled,
Smircheth the laurel that can never die.

(March, stanzas 14–19)

Bridges is not only giving himself an opportunity to write poetic description; he is attempting to restore the very character of the Latin Cupid from that of a mischievous boy-man to Eros, the powerful incarnation of passion.

Undoubtedly, Bridges found delight at this stage of his career in indulging in fanciful invention—some of it quite charming. An example of an exercise in pure rhetoric is found in the launching of Venus on the ocean in stanzas March 24–31, which is expanded from a few lines of the original Latin. The list of names in stanzas 27–28 is not in the original nor is most of the description of the Nereids. The following stanza (number 25) describing the sunset is of special interest, because it was based on observation of a historical event.

Broad and low down, where late the sun had been
A wealth of orange-gold was thickly shed,
Fading above into a field of green,

Like apples ere they ripen into red,
Then to the height a variable hue
Of rose and pink and crimson freak'd with blue,
And olive-border'd clouds o'er lilac led.

On August 26–27, 1883, the volcanic island of Krakatoa in the Dutch East Indies erupted. Most of the island was destroyed and 36,000 people were killed. The explosion caused remarkable sunsets throughout the world in the winter of 1883–84. Bridges saw the sunsets at Yattendon and described one of them in the above passage. They were also described by a number of other writers: the historian G. G. Coulton, Arthur Severn (the friend of John Ruskin), Tennyson, Swinburne, and Hopkins.[41] Hopkins's observations were communicated by a letter dated December 21, 1883, to the editor of *Nature* and were published in that magazine January 3, 1884. Hopkins thought that Bridges had borrowed some of the language of Hopkins's prose account for his poetic description and said so in a letter to Bridges.[42] In commenting on the stanza by Bridges quoted above, R. D. Altick observes: ". . . every color Hopkins uses is present, designated in the same terms, and for the most part arranged in the same order."[43]

But most of the passages in which Bridges "improves" on Apuleius are interpolations of fanciful invention rather than descriptions derived from actual observation. For example, this stanza on Pan is not in the original Latin:

In forehead low, keen eye, and nostril flat
He bore the human grace in mean degree,
But, set beneath his body squat and fat,
Legs like a goat's, and from the hairy knee
The shank fell spare; and, though crosswise he put
His limbs in easeful posture, for the foot
The beast's divided hoof was plain to see.

(August, sta. 13)

One reviewer called this an English Pan![44] The following lovely description of the loquacious and informing gull is not in Apuleius and is pure Bridges. It describes the passage of the gull under water to the bower of Venus:

The eddies from his silver pinions swirl'd
The crimson, green, and yellow floss, that grew
About the caves, and at his passing curl'd
Its graceful silk, and gently waved anew:
Till, oaring here and there, the queen he found
Stray'd from her haunt unto a sandy ground,
Dappl'd with eye-rings in the sunlight blue.

(September, sta. 7)

Hopkins admired this passage: "the seagull under water alone is immortal."[45] The descriptions of Talus (April 13, 14) and of Hermes (November 11, 12) are also inventions.

In thus ornamenting and embellishing his tale Bridges was in a way being true to the spirit of Apuleius if not the letter, for Apuleius himself wrote in the ornamental, or what the rhetoricians called the Asiatic, style. Of this style Professor Purser wrote:

> . . . the easy and commonplace in matter was expressed in the most elaborate and artificial language, and in an elevated tone well suited to recitation. There are an immense profusion and exuberance of words. . . . There is also a frequent use of piquant forms of speech. . . . The rhythms and cadences were carefully studied, and were generally soft and liquid.[46]

The style of Apuleius has been compared to that of Lyly's *Euphues*. Robert Graves considers it so eccentric and extravagant that he thinks Apuleius is parodying the golden style of the professional storytellers of his time (hence the title of Apuleius's book *The Golden Ass*).[47] Bridges's style is, of course, not as eccentric as that of *Euphues* nor does it have the tone of parody, and indeed Bridges probably did not consider it to be the intention of Apuleius to write parody in *Eros and Psyche*. Bridges's style is, however, exuberant, rhetorical, and ornamental and quite different from his own plain style of later years—as it appears in "The Affliction of Richard" for example.

Hopkins and Patmore[48] read a first draft of *Eros and Psyche* in 1884 and commented on the poem in letters and in a review by Patmore. Hopkins thought the poem was full of beauty although it did not attain the elevation of Patmore's *Unknown Eros*. He thought that the poem would deserve and obtain popularity. He admired certain pictorial passages—the description of the Krakatoa sunset (March 24–26) that, as shown, he thought was borrowed from his own account published in *Nature*; the stanza (August 27) describing the fall of Psyche's sister that was brilliant in suggestion although faulty in execution; the depiction of the gull under water (September 5–7). He considered the characterization of Eros to be rather thin—he was merely a "winged Masher." But Psyche was a success, "a sweet little 'body' rather than a 'soul'." Patmore in his review[49] and in a letter to Bridges expressed the opinion that Bridges's *Eros and Psyche* would become the standard transcript of Apuleius's story. Although he Christianizes the pagan story to some extent, he does not overdo it. The style, with many beautiful descriptive touches, is vigorous and perspicuous and as easy to read as a novel. The poem does not attempt the style of highest intensity, but in settling for the lower style he is completely successful and avoids the extravagances of the tense or spasmodic poetry so popular at that time.

The tale of Eros and Psyche has not escaped the attention of the depth psychologists. Erich Neumann, author of *The Great Mother*[50] and *The History of Consciousness*[51] has analyzed the story[52] in great detail in the light of his Jungian theories. Like Bridges, he refers to all the characters by their Greek rather than their Roman names, for he considers the Greek personalities more appropriate for the mythical motifs of the tale.

The central motif, according to Neumann, is the conflict between Aphrodite and Psyche, that is, the conflict between divine beauty and earthly beauty. Aphrodite, who he says is the Jungian archetype, the Great Mother, and her divine son-lover set out to punish human pride as manifested in Psyche, who is being worshipped as a God in place of Aphrodite. She will be punished by the weapon of Eros—Love—and compelled to be consumed with passion for the vilest of men.

Psyche, because no human lover dares wed her, prepares for her marriage as commanded by the Oracle, the "marriage of death" as Neumann calls it. Her wedding procession is more like a funeral procession and is reminiscent of the ancient rites of the lament for Adonis. This marriage of death is a central archetype of the feminine mysteries and central to the Jungian analysis, for, from the viewpoint of feminine psychology, in the matriarchal world every marriage is a rape of Kore (Persephone) by Hades (Pluto), a separation of mother and daughter by the hostile and aggressive male. The marriage of death is followed by the transformation of the maiden into womanhood and a new life. Psyche accepts her fate, whereas the male ego would have struggled against it. She accepts it because she is feminine and because she perceives the underlying meaning of what is happening.

Then comes the reversal. Prepared for death, Psyche experiences the paradise of Eros, an ecstasy of darkness, of not knowing and not seeing. Into this paradise the serpent comes, the envious sisters full of sexual disgust, man-haters, typical of the matriarchate. They plot to destroy her by persuading her to break the taboo against seeing (that is, knowing) her husband. They succeed in evoking the man-hating stratum deep in Psyche's subconscious. "In the same body she hated the beast and loved the husband." They persuade her to symbolically castrate her husband, that is, cut off his head.

By breaking the taboo, Psyche comes into conflict with Eros, is expelled from a blind, dark, purely sensual paradise, and eventually achieves a higher spiritual love and a higher consciousness symbolized by light. In Neumann's words, "It is the awakening of Psyche as the psyche, the fateful moment in the life of the feminine, in which for the first time woman emerges from the darkness of her unconscious and the harshness of her matriarchal captivity and, in individual encounter with the masculine, loves, that is, recognizes, Eros. . . . In the light of her new consciousness she experiences a fateful transformation in which she discovers that the separation between beast and husband is not valid."[53] She has become the fully conscious mature woman whom Eros originally did not want. He preferred the infantile, subservient Psyche. Psyche, however, has found her own identity. Psyche and Eros now confront each other as equals.

Psyche, the representation of human love, is still in conflict with Aphrodite, the Great Mother, because Psyche is rejecting the anonymous force of lust and fertility represented by Aphrodite in favor of personal human love. In her struggle with Aphrodite she becomes a kind of feminine Heracles who wins the love of Eros by performing the four labors delineated above: the sorting of the seeds (a "uroboric mixture of the masculine," according to Neumann) that she accomplishes with the aid of ants (instinctual Chthonic powers of her feminine nature) ; the gathering of a hank of wool from the golden sheep (actually the solar rams of Egyptian legend symbolizing the destructive powers of the masculine), done with the aid of advice from the mantic reed who tells her to confront the solar masculine power with her feminine power at nightfall; the capturing of a vessel of water from the river Styx (symbolic of the stream of eternal male-generative vital energy), achieved with the aid of the eagle (the masculine principle within Psyche herself) ; and, finally, the journey to the underworld to secure some of Persephone's beauty, accomplished with the help of the talking tower (a complex symbol of human culture as well as a phallic symbol). Successful in obtaining a portion of Persephone's beauty ointment, which represents Persephone's eternal youth, the youth of death, she fails to heed the tower's warning (as she had failed to heed Eros's warning), opens the box, seduced by momentary narcissistic love of self, and is overcome by a deathlike sleep; that is, she returns to Persephone. But she is awakened by Eros. Her "failure" in both instances has brought victory. In the words of Neumann again: "In the beginning Psyche sacrificed her Eros-paradise for the sake of her spiritual development; but now she is just as ready to sacrifice her spiritual development for the immortal beauty of Persephone-Aphrodite which will make her pleasing to Eros. . . . It is the beauty of a woman in love, who wishes to be beautiful for the beloved, for Eros."[54] For "no Eros will be able to resist a Psyche anointed with divine beauty."[55] And Aphrodite does not now oppose the new Psyche's deification, for she sees a good deal of herself in "A Psyche who fails, who for the sake of love renounces all principles,"[56] or, in Howard Baker's words, "Though staunch of purpose, yet knew how to fail." Eros too is changed by the human Psyche's sacrifice and love from "a wounded boy to a man and savior."

There is more to Neumann's analysis, but the above summarizes most of the essential details. It is impossible to say how much validity there is in all this and what Bridges would have made of it. But there is some evidence in Bridges's *Eros and Psyche* and in his later "Eros" (1899) that he was aware of the possibility of deeper implications in the story than were immediately discernible in Apuleius's pagan fairy tale or in the later Christian allegorizations of it.

Bridges, like Neumann, is primarily interested in the psychology of the feminine, human Psyche rather than in the male divinity Eros. Bridges's Psyche, like Neumann's, overcomes her terror of being married to a "monster" as the oracle had foretold, for she unconsciously realizes or foresees that good (her fulfillment as a woman) will result. While her parents and friends are expressing their grief during the marriage procession, Bridges's Psyche says,

> Up to the mountain! for I hear the voice
> Of my beloved on the winds, *Rejoice,*
> *Arise, my love, my fair one, and come away!*

She is accepting her fate with considerably more enthusiasm than she does in Apuleius.

In the early part of the story Bridges's Psyche is somewhat "softer" and more feminine than Neumann's or Apuleius's character, particularly in her attitude toward her sisters. She blames herself for their grief caused by her absence and for the grief of her father. She wishes to console them and her father, to share the good news of her happy marriage with them, even against the wishes of Eros. In her relation with her sisters there is no evidence of a stratum of man-hating sexual disgust that Neumann finds in Apuleius's tale, particularly in Apuleius's phrase "in the same body she hated the beast and loved the husband." This expression is not in Bridges's version. Psyche's motivation for agreeing to look on her husband and then kill him in Bridges's tale is a mixture of terror (she believes her sisters' argument, that she is married to a beast) and feminine curiosity:

> But thirsting curiosity to learn
> His secret overcame her simple trust.

Curiosity is not a motive in Apuleius nor in Neumann. Terror and sexual disgust are the motivations. In this respect Neumann appears to be closer to Apuleius than does Bridges. Bridges's Psyche, at this point in the story, is a simple, scared little girl and full of curiosity.

In the performance of her labors in Bridges's version, Psyche shows more initiative and patience than she does in the original story. In the first task, the sorting of the seeds, Apuleius's Psyche is completely helpless. She "never put a hand to that disordered and inextricable mass, but sat in silent stupefaction." But in the poem,

> . . . she intent drew forth with dextrous hand
> The larger seeds, or push'd the smaller back,
> Or light from heavy with her breathing fan'd.

In the second task, the gathering of the golden fleece, the original Psyche goes down to the river to drown herself. Bridges's Psyche hesitates to cross the river to the sheep on the other side, not from fear but because of her desire to

> quit her well
> And in one winning all her woes redeem.

When the third task is set her in Apuleius's story, Psyche's first thought is again suicide. In Bridges's poem, on the contrary,

> Psyche turn'd to tread that desert black
> Since was no fear that could her heart o'erwhelm.

In the final labor Apuleius's Psyche, commanded to descend into Hell to obtain a portion of the beauty of Persephone, immediately climbs a tower to commit suicide. In Bridges's poem she says to Aphrodite "Show me the way."

Bridges's changes of his original material were conscious and deliberate. He wished to make his heroine a courageous and determined woman, now fully awakened to her love and to her loss, and bent on regaining her husband. In this respect, Bridges seems to show more understanding of the development of the feminine Psyche than does Apuleius, and is somewhat closer to Neumann's analysis than is Apuleius. On the other hand, there is little of Neumann's rather farfetched symbolism in Bridges's depiction of the four labors.

In Bridges's *Eros and Psyche,* then, there is the familiar allegory of the growth of love from the purely sensual to the spiritual, the development being manifest chiefly in the character of Psyche, but also in Eros. Bridges Christianized and changed the original story to some extent—particularly in his "feminization" of Psyche—and he added descriptive embellishments, but he did not go to the extremes of the later Jungian depth psychologists and, indeed, he probably would have rejected much of their interpretation.

Portrait of Bridges's mother, née Harriet Elizabeth Affleck, painted by a close friend of Bridges, H. E. Wooldridge of Oxford. *Courtesy of Elizabeth Daryush, daughter of Bridges.*

Monica Waterhouse, daughter of the famous architect Alfred Water-house, and wife of Robert Bridges. This picture was taken in the summer of 1888. *Courtesy of Elizabeth Daryush.*

The poet Elizabeth Daryush, daughter of Robert Bridges. *Courtesy of Elizabeth Daryush.*

The young Robert Bridges, 1862/63. *Courtesy of Robert Bridges (the poet's grandson).*

A close-up of the poet, somewhat later but date unknown. *Courtesy of Robert Bridges.*

Portrait of Bridges by Charles Furse, painted in 1893. *Courtesy of Elizabeth Daryush.*

A photograph of the poet taken in 1913 by Mrs. M. G. Perkins.
Courtesy of Elizabeth Daryush.

Again, the poet in 1913. *Courtesy of Elizabeth Daryush. Photograph by Mrs. M. G. Perkins.*

2

The Experimentalist Poet

> We must get out of the old ruts; the English
> poets have been on the right road, but they have
> worn it into ruts. We must follow the road but
> there is no reason why we should keep to the
> ruts.[1]

> Lawlessness means uncertainty of rhythm, and
> that is the ruin of the verse.[2]

On Rhythm and Meter

As shown above, Bridges composed an impressive body of
poetry in conventional English meters. Nevertheless, almost from
the beginning of his career, he felt dissatisfied, at times, with
English common meter. He wished to experiment with new
meters to achieve new rhythmic effects; yet he never abandoned
his fundamental principle that any poem, to be successful, must
be composed according *to some kind of prosody* that can be
formulated and explained. For Bridges, to abandon prosody
meant to abandon rhythm, or at least effective rhythm, and
without effective rhythm the poem is dead.

In discussing Bridges's various experiments in English prosody
I shall make use of the following terminology:

1. *Accentual syllabic verse*. The meter is determined by
counting syllables and accents. For example, the standard
iambic pentameter line of blank verse has ten syllables with

80

five of them accented. Most of the important poems in English are written in accentual syllabic verse, and most of Bridges's shorter poems as discussed in the previous chapter are written in it. This meter is usually referred to by Bridges and by Hopkins as common or running meter, and by Bridges sometimes as English syllabic meter.

2. *Accentual verse.* The meter is determined by the number of accents per line, with an undetermined number of unaccented syllables. Coleridge's *Christabel* is in accentual verse. Sprung rhythm, which was developed by Hopkins into an elaborate system of prosody, is a special kind of accentual verse. Hopkins refers to a number of Bridges's poems as being written in sprung rhythm, but in Bridges's verse the distortion from normal meter is much less violent than in Hopkins. Bridges wrote a few poems in accentual verse. They are the subject of the following section.

3. *Quantitative verse.* Greek and Latin verse of classical times was written in meters determined by syllable length rather than by accent. Bridges, making use of a quantitative prosody developed for English by William Johnson Stone and modified somewhat by Bridges himself, wrote a number of poems in classical prosody.

4. *Syllabic verse.* The meter is determined by the number of syllables per line, regardless of accent and quantity. Bridges wrote his neo-Miltonic syllabic poems and his *Testament of Beauty* in syllabic verse.

In this chapter, then, Bridges's poems in accentual verse, in quantitative verse, and in neo-Miltonic syllabics will be discussed, and first, the poems in accentual verse. The matter is obscured somewhat by the fact that some of these poems are so close to poems in conventional accentual syllabic prosody that they may be scanned by both systems. For example, "A Passerby," which Bridges considered to be in accentual rhythms, can be scanned in iambic rhythms with considerable substitution of feet with extra metrical syllables and with occasional sprung rhythms. Furthermore, sprung rhythm may be introduced into poems primarily syllabic. I am including in the following section all poems that Bridges himself considered to be in accentual meters (for example, the four poems he put into small print in the 1879 edition of his poems and the three in small print in the 1880 edition) together with those poems which, in my opinion, Bridges considered accentual, although there may be no objective evidence in his letters or elsewhere that he did so. Finally, Hopkins developed an elaborate system for scanning his own poems in sprung rhythm. I have found it of great help in simplifying matters where I consider Bridges's use of sprung rhythm to employ Yvor Winters's definition of sprung rhythm— sprung rhythm occurs whenever two accents are brought together by a means other than normal substitution, such as a trochaic foot for an iambic foot. For example, this line does not employ sprung rhythm although two accents come together:

> I cóme: and ón the eárth stép with glad fóot.

A trochaic foot has been substituted for an iambic in the fourth foot, a situation that occurs frequently in conventional iambic verse. The following line, however, employs true sprung rhythm:

> Wórld's stránd, swáy of the séa.

A distinction should be made between *rhythm* and *meter*. *Meter* is the scansion of the poem, the *arithmetic norm,* as Yvor Winters has called it.[3] *Rhythm* is the actual movement of the verse when read aloud or heard in the mind's ear. Two lines that have exactly the same scansion (iambic pentameter, for example) may have, because of the infinite possibilities for variety in syllable length and degrees of accent, very different rhythms. Bridges was of course aware of this distinction. He sometimes called the meter or arithmetic norm of the line *prosody* and the actual movement of the line when spoken aloud *rhythm.* In analyzing the line

> Of thát Forbídden Treé, whose mórtal tást,

Bridges points out that the accent on *bid* is on a very short syllable, whereas the unaccented syllable that follows (*den*) is relatively long and he says that "this affects the rhythm very deeply, but it does not concern the prosody."[4] This device, of putting the accent on a short syllable and making the unaccented syllable relatively long, is one of the chief means of varying the rhythm in English accentual syllabic verse. It is, incidentally, helpful to remember that the determination of whether a syllable is accented or not (in accentual syllabic verse) is made relative to the other syllable or syllables *within the same foot,* and not relative to other syllables outside the foot. Thus in

Whén to the séssions óf sweet sílent thóught,

of is accented not only according to the prosody or meter but also according to the actual speaking of the line, for it has just slightly more accent than the other syllable in the same foot, *sions,* although considerably less accent than the following unaccented syllable *sweet. Sweet,* when the line is read properly, has less accent than the other syllable in the same foot, *si.* Thus the line is correctly scanned above as iambic pentameter with a trochaic substitution in the first foot; it is *not* scanned thus:

Whén to the séssions of sweét sílent thóught.

This scansion (and reading) gives an insensitive line.

The Poems in Accentual Verse

As far as I can determine, Bridges published approximately twenty poems in accentual verse.[5] The most important of these will be discussed.

Bridges evidently began his experiments in accentual verse around 1877 after his friend Hopkins had composed his first poem in sprung rhythm, "The Wreck of the *Deutschland*" (1875). Undoubtedly he received encouragement from and was influenced by the experiments of his Jesuit friend. Other influences were Milton, Coleridge, Coventry Patmore, Shelley, and Clough.

Coleridge, Hopkins, and Patmore. When Bridges began his experiments in accentual verse, he was familiar with the work of Coleridge in that prosody, and particularly with *Christabel* and with Coleridge's Introduction to *Christabel.* He refers to Coleridge's Introduction at the beginning of his own essay "On the Prosody of Accentual Verse," first published in 1901, revised in 1921,[6] and he quotes from *Christabel* to illustrate the nature of accentual verse. Bridges believed, however, that Coleridge's theory was incomplete and imperfect and his practice sometimes unsatisfactory because of his imperfect theory. Bridges in his essay (which he claims is the first systematic treatment of English stress prosody) formulated seven rules for accentual verse,[7] and he identified seven common stress units or feet.[8] The essay is complex and difficult to follow—more complex than necessary, perhaps. In commenting on Bridges's accentual verse I shall usually follow the simple formula that accentual verse should contain a fixed number of stressed syllables to a line with an indeterminate number of unstressed syllables, and usually I shall not attempt to identify the various kinds of feet according to Bridges's system.

Bridges and Hopkins met as young men at Oxford in 1863.[9] In the long friendship that followed they frequently discussed their metrical experiments in conversations and by letter. We have Hopkins's side of the correspondence but not Bridges's. Nevertheless, one can sometimes determine Bridges's ideas about his own accentual poems from Hopkins's answers to Bridges's letters. Hopkins was also, of course, experimenting with accentual verse in the 1870s, and he wrote his first poem in sprung rhythm, "The Wreck of the *Deutschland*," in 1875. Some of Bridges's poems written after the *"Deutschland"* were considered by both poets to be in sprung rhythm for they use this term in their letters. There was undoubtedly mutual influence, but perhaps the influence of Hopkins on Bridges was the stronger.

Coventry Patmore had also been experimenting with accentual measures. He formulated his views in his "Essay on English Metrical Law," first published in 1857 and subsequently revised and frequently reprinted.[10] Both Bridges and Hopkins were familiar with this essay. Hopkins met Patmore at Stonyhurst in the summer of 1883, and at that time Patmore expressed his admiration for Bridges's poetry. Hopkins had previously expressed his admiration for Patmore's work. Bridges met Patmore in the summer of 1884 on the occasion of Patmore's returning the manuscript of Hopkins's poems to Bridges.[11] Bridges was eager to enlist Patmore's support for the "new prosody" of Hopkins and himself, that is, their experiments in accentual verse. Both Bridges and Hopkins had been impressed by the essay on metrical law, which was a defense of the irregular ode form used by Patmore in his *The Unknown Eros*. A three way correspondence developed.[12] It is evident from the extant letters that Patmore and Bridges discussed Bridges's own poetry. Patmore praises *Prometheus the Firegiver* for instance, a copy of which Hopkins had sent him. Bridges, in turn, sent Hopkins's poetry to Patmore with such comments as it is "affected in style" and he pushes prosody "to its extreme limits" and he has "a wrong notion of rhyme." Yet Bridges praises Hopkins's "subtlety of rhythm" and says that he is unique. Furthermore, Hopkins writes in a system of poetry that Bridges advocates, that is the "new prosody." Patmore replied that Hopkins's poems were like "veins of pure gold imbedded in masses of impracticable quartz." The correspondence demonstrates that by 1883 Bridges and Hopkins thought that they had worked out a new prosody of accentual verse. Bridges's views were eventually published in his essay on accentual prosody. Hopkins's views were not published during his lifetime.[13]

Milton, Shelley and Clough. As early as 1877 Bridges was attempting to use the irregular rhythms of *Samson Agonistes* in his sonnets.[14] A few years later Bridges was at work on a study of Milton's blank verse in *Paradise Lost* and subsequently of the prosody of *Paradise Regained* and *Samson Agonistes,* followed by an essay on English stress prosody. All of this material was revised and brought together in a final edition entitled *Milton's Prosody* (1921).[15]

There were two lines of development in Bridges's own verse that resulted from the study of Milton's prosody: (1) The decision to write several poems in accentual verse, the rhythm being suggested by certain lines in *Samson Agonistes.* (2) The decision (years later) to write poems in what Bridges called *neo-Miltonic syllabics.* This was syllabic verse as distinct from accentual verse. The prosody was derived from modifications of Milton's practice of inverting every foot but the fifth in his blank verse and from certain lines in *Samson Agonistes.* The neo-Miltonic syllabics will be discussed later.

To return to the influence of *Samson Agonistes* on Bridges's accentual verse—Bridges demonstrates in his *Milton's Prosody* that *Samson Agonistes* can be scanned as accentual syllabic verse with many variations and substitutions. But he goes on to say that this scansion is a fiction:

[Milton] wrote in the choruses of *Samson* a rhythmical stressed verse, and scanned it by means of fictions. *He need not have troubled himself about the scansion at all. If the stressed rhythm is the beauty of the verse, it is a sufficient account of it.* But this seems too simple to be understood.[16]

At this stage in his career (the quotation is from an early version of the essay on *Samson*) Bridges felt that Milton (whatever his theory) had, in fact, preceded Coleridge in the writing of speech stress—that is, accentual verse—in some parts of *Samson Agonistes*, and it seems probable that this deduction had some influence on Bridges's own experiments.

Bridges also refers a number of times to the accentual verse of Shelley. He cites about a dozen lines from *The Sensitive Plant* that break several of the rules for stress prosody, and he comes to the conclusion that "Shelley had not, any more than Coleridge, a consistent practice in that system of versification."[17] On the other hand, in spite of Shelley's lack of system, he considers Shelley's "Away, the moor is dark beneath the moon" and his song of the sixth spirit in *Prometheus* to be successful and moving examples of stress verse. Similarly, although he finds some fault with Clough for *his* lack of system, he considers *Bothie* and *Amours* to have a number of satisfactory hexameters. Bridges's analysis of the stress prosody (or rather the lack of it) of these two poets may have had some influence on his own verses.

Hopkins on Bridges's Accentual Poems. The earliest poems in accentual verse to be published by Bridges appeared in his 1879 volume, *Poems.* There were four of them, distinguished from the others by being printed in small type: "A Passer-by," "The Downs," "Sonnet—I would be a bird," and "Early Autumn Sonnet—So hot the noon." Hopkins praised a number of the poems in the 1879 volume in acknowledging his presentation copy, but he was not so enthusiastic about those in accentual verse. "The pieces in sprung rhythm—do not quite satisfy me."[18] He liked "The Downs" the best, thought the "Bird-sonnet" showed "the clearest distortion," disliked "The Passer-by" calling it "that logaoedic dignified-doggrel one Tennyson has employed in 'Maud'," and in a later letter he wrote of the end of the second stanza, " 'Grandest feathery' etc. reminds one of Tennyson's experiments in Alcaics and so on."[19] Of "Early Autumn" Hopkins said it was "very beautiful and tender, but in the octet at all events not perfectly achieved." Abbott considered the sestet to be "finely wrought." Because the poem was never reprinted and is unavailable except in the rare 1879 volume it is here quoted in full.

EARLY AUTUMN
Sonnet.

So hot the noon was, with lilies the bank so gay,
With arrowhead, pink rushes and watermint,
And sapphire flies that darted heavenly glint,
Whether it were Summer still we could not say:

Or if already Autumn had owned the day,
Aglare with smirching gaze on bloom and tint;
And ripening all to death, did parch and stint
The last stooks down at the river, as there we lay.

O poise of my only August! ah! tears and praise
Take now for thy sweet lingering: so few more
Years of delight, swift as delight of days;

Ere fading, falling, dropping, darkening o'er,
The landscape perishes round the miry ways,
And rheumy Winter snows up window and door.

The 1880 *Poems* included three poems in accentual measures all printed in small type: "The Voice of Nature," "On a Dead Child," and "London Snow." In commenting on "The Voice of Nature," which was sent to him in manuscript before publication, Hopkins wrote: "I do not think the rhythm perfect, e.g. 'woodbine with' is a heavy dactyl. Since the syllables in sprung rhythm are not counted, time or equality of strength is of more importance than in common counted rhythm, and your times or strengths do not seem to me equal enough."[20] He recognized a similarity (as did Bridges) of one passage in the poem in which Bridges is describing the ocean,

whose motion
Precipitate all o'errides, and turns, nor abides

with his own lines in the *"Deutschland"*:

throned behind

Death with a sovereignty that heeds but hides, bodes but abides.

However, Hopkins thought the echo unimportant and wrote, "I do not think the line very good; it is besides ambiguous."[21] In spite of the imperfect rhythm, Hopkins, in a later letter, spoke of the poem as being "very fine."[22]

Hopkins's response to "London Snow," the most widely read and most frequently anthologized of all Bridges's poems in "the new prosody," was enthusiastic—"a most beautiful and successful piece . . . charmingly fresh, I do not know what is like it." He noticed (quite correctly) two echoes, "snow mossed wonder," and "O look at the trees," from his own *Deutschland* and his starlight sonnet.[23] He thought the rhythm not quite perfect, and in a subsequent letter he made explicit suggestions for improving the rhythm, but evidently he did not have the text at hand, for he quoted one phrase incorrectly. Hopkins's suggestions would have tightened the rhythm, but fortunately Bridges adopted none of them, for a tighter rhythm to suggest the loosely falling snow would have been inappropriate.

"On a Dead Child" drew immediate negative response. Hopkins said that the rhythm was worse than that of "London Snow": "You are certainly less at your ease in sprung rhythm" and the poem was "Browningese."[24] Evidently Bridges replied that he considered the poem the best he had written, for Hopkins wrote in a later letter:

> The Dead Child is a fine poem, I am aware, but I am not bound to like it best; I do not in fact like it best nor think it the best you have written, as you say it is. I do not think either the rhythm or the thought flowing enough. The diction is not exquisite as yours can be when you are at ease. No, but you say it is severe: perhaps it is bald. But indeed "wise, sad head" and "firm, pale hands" do not strike me as severe at all, nor yet exquisite. Rather they belong to a familiar commonplace about "Reader, have you never hung over the pillow of . . . . pallid cheek, clammy brow . . . . long, long night-watches . . . surely, Sir Josiah Bickerstaff, there is *some* hope! O say not all is over. It cannot be"—You know.[25]

The Feast of Bacchus, which is written in accentual measures, also drew criticism from Hopkins for its meter:

I daresay the metre will serve its purpose which is, I suppose, to give a slight form and pressure to the language and a corresponding degree of idealization, and it may work well on the stage: in itself I do not admire it. The only particular fault I find is that there are many lines in which the pause in the middle, without which, as it seems to me, it is merely prose rhythm and not verse at all, is wanting. I may add that the continual determination to be smooth and lucid in style gives upon the whole a sort of childish effect.[26]

In conclusion, although Hopkins found some good things to say about "London Snow" and a few other poems by Bridges in accentual meters, he felt that Bridges was not at his ease in the "new prosody" and that his best work was done in the common meter, that is, in accentual syllabic verse.

Bridges's Achievements in Stress Prosody. The fundamental principle governing all of Bridges's poems in stress prosody was this—"In this system the natural accentual speech-rhythms come to the front, and are the determining factor of the verse, overruling the syllabic determination."[27] The natural speaking voice can be heard most effectively in the best and most popular of these poems, "London Snow":

> Then boys I heard, as they went to school, calling,
> They gathered up the crystal manna to freeze
> Their tongues with tasting, their hands with snowballing;
>
> Or rioted in a drift, plunging up to the knees;
> Or peering up from under the white-mossed wonder,
> "O look at the trees!" they cried, "O look at the trees!"

The poem achieves its success partly because it is limited in intention—it is primarily descriptive—and it thus avoids the perilously close approach to sentimentality that one finds in a poem like "On a Dead Child." There is, of course, descriptive material in the other accentual poems, but it is incidental to or illustrative of major thematic material.

The description of the London winter scene is a triumph of diction, prosody, and texture that combine to suggest the light mysterious loveliness of the snowfall. Every word and cadence is right, and all of Hopkins's suggested emendations would have been disastrous if accepted, particularly Hopkins's substitution of "London brown" for "the city brown" in line two. Here are the first six lines, which give a fair idea of the quality of the style and of the meter:

When mén were áll asleép the snów came flýing,   (11)
In lárge white flákes fálling on the cíty brówn,   (11)
Steálthily and perpétually séttling and lóosely lýing,   (15)
    Húshing the látest tráffic of the drówsy tówn;   (12)
Deádening, múffling, stífling its múrmurs fáiling;   (12)
Lázily and incéssantly flóating dówn and dówn.   (13)

There are five accents to a line with the metrical accent in every case coinciding with the normal speech accent. There are a variant number of syllables per line as indicated by the figures in parentheses. How should the reader account for the unaccented syllables? It is known from Bridges's correspondence with Hopkins that Bridges considered this poem to be in accentual verse and not in common or (as Bridges sometimes referred to it) in syllabic meter. Bridges has not left his scansion of this poem, but presumably he would apply the seven rules for accentual verse that he later formulated in his essay on stress prosody, and he would make use of any of the seven kinds of feet he identifies in that essay. Perhaps his scansion would look like this:

Whĕn mên | wĕre âll | ăsleêp | thĕ snôw | cāme flÿing,
In lârge | white flâkes | fâllĭng | ŏn thĕ cîtÿ | brôwn,
Steâlthĭlÿ | ănd pĕrpêtŭallÿ | sêttlĭng ănd | lôoselÿ | lÿiňg,
    Hûshĭng | thĕ lâtĕst | trâffĭc | ŏf thĕ drôwsÿ | tôwn;
Deâdĕnĭng, | mûfflĭng, | stîflĭng | ĭts mûrmŭrs | fâilĭng;
Lâzĭlÿ | ănd ĭncêssăntlÿ | flôatĭng | dôwn ănd | dôwn.

The predominant foot in the first line (in Bridges's terminology) is the rising disyllabic U∧ (Accented syllables in Bridges's system are indicated by ∧, unaccented heavy syllables by —, unaccented light syllables by U. A heavy syllable is very long in quantity. A light syllable is relatively short or very short in quantity.)[28] The last foot of this line is britannic or mid-stress trisyllabic —∧U. The predominate foot of the fifth line is falling disyllabic ∧U with a dactyl ∧UU in the first foot and a britannic in the fourth. The second foot of the third line is the five-syllable foot UU∧UU. And so on. The composition of all of the feet follows Bridges's various rules such as grammatical unity (an accent governs its own proclitics and enclitics) and the placing of unstressed heavy syllables (they must be next to an accented syllable). But Bridges's system seems unnecessarily complicated when the actual governing principle is simple—in accentual verse the number of stresses to a line is constant and the stress must coincide with normal speech accent.

Furthermore, it is possible (and simpler!) to scan this passage as accentual syllabic verse with substitutions:

> Whĕn mén | wĕre áll | ăsleép | thĕ snów | căme flýĭng,
> In lárge | whĭte flákes | fállĭng | on the cít|ȳ brówn,
> Steálthĭly | ănd pĕrpét|uălly séttĭ|lĭng ănd lóos|elȳ lýĭng,
> Húshĭng thĕ | látĕst | tráffĭc | ŏf thĕ dŕow|sȳ tówn;
> Deádenĭng, | múfflĭng, | stíflĭng | ĭts múr|mŭrs fáilĭng;
> Lázĭlȳ | ănd ĭncéss|ăntlȳ flóat|ĭng dówn | ănd dówn.

The basic movement is iambic pentameter with feminine endings for lines one, three, and five. There are various trochaic and trisyllabic substitutions as indicated by the scansion. The unaccented syllables of the trisyllabic feet are usually light or very light to give a wavering motion to the lines. This method of scansion seems to me preferable because it is simpler, but regardless of how the poem is scanned, it should be noted again that Bridges's departures from normal accentual syllabic verse in his poems written in the so-called "new prosody," that is, stress prosody, are subtle and cautious, and hence the possibility of applying two systems of scansion. Hopkins's poems in sprung rhythm employ much greater departures from normal accentual syllabic verse. "The Wreck of the *Deutschland*," for example, cannot be scanned in accentual syllabic feet. It can be scanned only by Hopkins's system and only then with difficulty. Fortunately, Hopkins has given us some information on the scansion of this poem, for frequently in dealing with Hopkins's verse it is impossible (without help from Hopkins himself) to determine where the accent is supposed to fall, as in these lines from "The Wreck of the *Deutschland*":

> . . . and dost thou touch me afresh?
> Over again I feel thy finger and find thee.

The daughter of Robert Bridges, Elizabeth Daryush, says of the final line:

I think . . . that on a first reading most people would scan the last line of the first stanza, in spite of the out-setting, as a pentameter, thus:

> Óver agáin I feél thy fínger and fínd thee.

I remember my father quoting this line as an example of how a misunderstanding of Hopkins' mood could lead to a misreading of his meter, for he meant the line to have an accent also on the last syllable, the unexpected sixth foot giving a kind of dramatic devotional emphasis to the final word.[29]

The arbitrary placing of the accent is the chief weakness of Hopkins's system of sprung rhythm, a weakness that seldom occurs in Bridges's verse, although there is one rare example in "London Snow," in the seventh line:

> Silently sifting and veiling road, roof and railing.

How many accents does this line have and where do they fall? The rest of the poem has five accents to a line, but this line appears to have six. Is *roof* accented or not?

But to repeat, the problem is rare in Bridges's accentual verse. Generally speaking, the prosody and the resulting rhythms are under complete control and are completely effective.

"A Passer-by," like "London Snow," is a triumph of rhythmical effectiveness in its description of the movement of the ship and its appearance in the Tahitian port. Particularly fine are these lines:

> Nor is aught from the foaming reef to the snow-capped grandest
> Peak, that is over the feathery palms more fair
> Than thou, so upright, so stately, and still thou standest,

with the run over from *grandest* to *Peak* and the break in rhythm after *Peak*. Also the repetition of the *st* sound in the last line is excellent. The poem has more thematic depth than "London Snow." It is an expression of Bridges's refined hedonism—metaphysical speculation on man's destiny (the ship's destination) is useless. Man should be satisfied with the mere presence of and his ability to respond to beauty. "Beauty enough is thine." There is a serious flaw in the poem, however—the occasional trite, sentimental, and romantic diction, such as "fair rover," "quest," "bosom," and so forth.

"Nightingales" also has an important theme—the greatest art springs from suffering and from desire that transcends circumstances:

> Nay, barren are those mountains and spent the streams:
> Our song is the voice of desire, that haunts our dreams,
> A throe of the heart.

In spite of occasionally trite diction the poem is moving and beautiful, particularly these lines:

> Alone, aloud in the raptured ear of men
> We pour our dark nocturnal secret.

"On a Dead Child," which may derive from Bridges's experience as a physician, was, as shown above, severely criticized by Hopkins, and, indeed, it does approach the sentimental and trite in some of its descriptive detail. However, the last stanza, and especially the final line, seem to me to be an effective expression of a mood one occasionally finds in the early Bridges, a despair motivated by his doubts about the Christian belief in immortality:

> Ah! little at best can all our hopes avail us
> To lift this sorrow, or cheer us, when in the dark,
> Unwilling alone we embark,
> And the the things we have seen and have known and have heard
> of, fail us.

"The hill pines were sighing" is written in a very mild form of accentual verse, with three beats to a line. I say *mild* because the difference between the meter of this poem and one written in conventional accentual syllabic verse is rather slight. The subject is the destruction by man of his natural environment, specifically, in this instance, the cutting down of ancient oak trees. The emotion of the poet is one of outrage and grief, but in the poem the feeling is projected into the nonhuman world of nature, that is, the bird and the pine trees: the human woodsman's heart is, by implication, as hard as the ax he wields:

A ribald cuckoo clamoured,
And out of the copse the stroke
Of the iron axe that hammered
The iron heart of the oak.

Anon a sound appalling,
As a hundred years of pride
Crashed, in the silence falling:
And the shadowy pine-trees sighed.

"Flycatchers" is difficult to analyze metrically. Probably Bridges's intention was an accentual poem with four beats to a line. The rhythm is perhaps not completely successful, but the ironic portrait of the old school master is unforgettable:

> . . . an authoritative old wise-acre
Stood over us and from a desk fed us with flies.

Dead flies—such as litter the library south-window,
That buzzed at the panes until they fell stiff-baked on the sill,
Or are roll'd up asleep i' the blinds at sunrise,
Or wafer'd flat in a shrunken folio.

A dry biped he was, nurtured likewise
On skins and skeletons, stale from top to toe
With all manner of rubbish and all manner of lies.

One is reminded of Sir Walter Alexander Raleigh's description of Bridges as a man who couldn't stand worthless learning and ignorance:

> He is delightfully grumpy. He mentions thing after thing which is commonly believed and says that of course it's not so. He's always right. His intellect has been so completely self-indulged that it now can't understand rubbish. He has never obeyed anyone or adapted himself to anyone, so he's as clear as crystal, and can't do with fogs.[30]

Other poems in which the new prosody seems to be successful and appropriate are "The Voice of Nature," "The Downs," and "The storm is over." Canon Dixon admired the opening lines of the first of these poems:

> I stand on the cliff and watch the veiled sun paling
>   A silver field afar in the mournful sea.

The second poem (admired by Hopkins) was inspired by Bridges's beloved Sussex Downs:[31]

> Where sweeping in phantom silence the cloudland flies;
> With lovely undulation of fall and rise;
>   Entrenched with thickets thorned,
> By delicate miniature dainty flowers adorned!

And, finally, the irregular accentual lines of "The storm is over" are skillfully used to evoke contrasting moods aroused by the havoc of the storm and the calm that follows. The leaves of summer

> In the watery furrows die,
> In grassy pools of the flood they sink and drown,
> Green-golden, orange, vermilion, golden and brown,
> The high year's flaunting crown
> Shattered and trampled down.

> The day is done: the tired land looks for night;
> She prays to the night to keep
> In peace her nerves of delight:
> While silver mist upstealeth silently,
> And the broad cloud-driving moon in the clear sky
> Lifts o'er the firs her shining shield.

The poems in accentual measures are not among Bridges's greatest; yet a few of them are minor poems of great beauty without which our literature would be the poorer.

The Poems in Classical Prosody

Bridges began his experiments in writing poems in English according to Stone's modified rules of classical prosody perhaps as early as 1898,[32] the same year in which his friend William Johnson Stone privately printed his *On the Use of Classical Metres in English*. Bridges was in part motivated by his friendship for Stone, and when Stone died at the early age of twenty-eight he felt bound by a promise to continue his own efforts to write satisfactory English verse in classical meters: "He died in 1901, leaving me bound by a promise that I would give his system a trial. *Ex hypothesi* I worked at first entirely on his lines, and only gradually discovered and eliminated what I considered the faults in his scheme."[33] He was motivated also by his own natural desire to experiment, to achieve certain effects impossible in conventional meters. In a general defense of experimental prosodies, Bridges wrote in 1901: ". . . while almost everybody has a natural liking for the common fundamental rhythms, it is only after a long familiarity with them that the ear grows dissatisfied, and wishes them to be broken; and there are few persons indeed who take such a natural delight in rhythm for its own sake, that they can follow with pleasure a learned rhythm which is very rich in variety, and the beauty of which is perpetual freedom to obey the sense and diction."[34] It was this natural delight in rhythm for its own sake that impelled Bridges to write over thirty-five poems in classical prosody and to undertake his other experiments in accentual verse, in the neo-Miltonic syllabics and in *The Testament of Beauty,* although he knew that he was writing for an extremely small audience. Indeed, in later years, his popularity as poet laureate was considerably diminished as a result of these abstruse experiments.

Bridges has analyzed and defended his adaptation of Stone's rules for his own classical verse in considerable detail in his 1916 edition of *Ibant Obscuri* and elsewhere. His discussions are extremely technical and not more than a handful of scholars and present or potential readers would have the learning or the patience to follow them. The curious may consult the material cited in the appendix to this chapter. However, the novel and unusual rhythmical effects of Bridges's poems in classical prosody may be appreciated by following Stone's advice to those reading his (Stone's) translation into quantitative verse of the *Odyssey,* 6. 85–209: "I ask them to read my verse slowly, with the natural accent unimpaired, and with such stress as they think right on the long syllables by way of ictus."[35]

Bridges's poems in classical prosody fall into two groups—(1) adaptations and translations; (2) original verse. What are the advantages in translating Latin and Greek into English classical hexameters rather than into free verse or into blank verse or the heroic couplet or some other conventional meters? Bridges answers the question: "If an English reader, who is unable to read Greek, is to get a glimpse of what Homer is like, he must read something which does *not* remind him of Milton or Pope or Tennyson or Swinburne, because Homer does not do this."[36] Nevertheless, Bridges realized that one can only approximate the effects of Latin or Greek hexameters in English. Furthermore, the poet should not be bound to follow the classical rules of prosody exactly, but rather he should feel free to alter and adapt them to the peculiar qualities of his native tongue: "there can be no worse folly in an artist than to forgo the advantages of his own medium in the hopeless pursuit of a likeness to the work of some recognized genius. . . ."[37]

Of all his adaptations and paraphrases, perhaps *Ibant Obscuri* is his most impressive. In describing the conditions under which this line by line paraphrase of the *Aeneid*, 6. 268–751, 893–98 was written, Bridges says: "*I had not set myself to translate Virgil* but only to make quantitative hexameters, and had chosen the *Aeneid* merely as heroic material for dactyls and spondees, and as a severe test of my experiment."[38]

The paraphrase was written, then, "to try what Stone's prosody would make of the Aeneid."[39] It was begun at St. Moritz, Switzerland, November 9 and finished December 19, 1905. "And many lines of it," says Bridges, "were composed during delightful skating expeditions to the beautiful lakes before the first smooth transparent ice had been destroyed by the keener frosts of December."[40] In the 1916 edition it is printed with the Latin interlined and with "A Cento of Previous Translations" across the page. This collection was made in the Bodleian library "in the dog-days of 1906, when Oxford was deserted."[41] A number of authors are represented, some evidently for amusement. Bridges does not seem to like most of them (including Dryden and Pope), although he expresses admiration for J. M. King and Charles Symmons.

Book 6 of the *Aeneid*, from which Bridges paraphrases a passage, describes Aeneas's first landing in Italy near Cumae, his interview with the Sibyl at Apollo's shrine and her prophetic oracle, the plucking of the golden bough that will permit him to visit his father Anchises in Hades, the descent into Hades beginning with the words *Ibant Obscuri*, descriptions of various scenes in Hades by his guide the Sibyl, and the interview with

Anchises who instructs him in the mysteries of the soul of the world and of transmigration and shows him the race of heroes who will descend from him and his posterity. The passage that Bridges paraphrases includes descriptions of the place of empty dreams and illusions, the interview with the shade of Palinurus, descriptions of Charon, the drugging of Cerberus, interviews with Dido among the shades of those who died for love and with the shades of Trojan heroes, the realms of Rhadamanthus, the Elysian fields, the meeting with Anchises and Anchises' explanation of the world soul and transmigration and, finally, after a hiatus, a brief description of the gates of horn and ivory.

Those familiar with the translations of Virgil into conventional iambic verse will find Bridges's paraphrase somewhat ponderous and dense at first reading. Probably the best way to respond to Bridges's intentions is to take his translations in small doses, slowly. The following excerpts, which may be compared with the original Latin and with Dryden's translations, are typical. If one reads the Latin, then Bridges's hexameters, and then Dryden's couplets, one may conclude that Bridges's rendition is closer to the rhythm and texture of Virgil's verse than is Dryden's—although Dryden's conventional diction and meter will usually evoke initially the more favorable response. The Latin text and page numbers are from *Ibant Obscuri*.

"Charon" (6. 295–304):

VIRGIL—Hinc via Tartarei quae fert Acherontis ad undas.
    turbidus hic caeno vastaque voragine gurges
    aestuat atque omnem Cocyto eructat harenam.
    portitor has horrendus aquas et flumina servat
    terribili squalore Charon, cui plurima mento
    canities inculta iacet, stant lumina flamma,
    sordidus ex umeris nodo dependet amictus.
    ipse ratem conto subigit velisque ministrat
    et ferruginea subvectat corpora cumba,
    iam senior, sed cruda deo viridisque senectus.

(P. 26)

BRIDGES—Hence is a road that led them a-down to the Tartarean
    streams,

Where Acheron's whirlpool impetuous, into the reeky
Deep of Cokytos disgorgeth, with muddy burden.
These floods one ferryman serveth, most awful of aspect,
Of squalor infernal, Charon: all filthily unkempt
That woolly white cheek-fleece, and fiery the blood-
    shotten eyeballs;
On one shoulder a cloak knotted-up his nudity vaunteth.
He himself plieth oar or pole, manageth tiller and sheet,
And the relics of men in his ash-grey barge ferries over;
Already old, but green to a god and hearty will age be.

DRYDEN—Hence to deep *Acheron* they take their way;
Whose troubled Eddies, thick with Ooze and Clay,
Are whirl'd aloft, and in *Cocytus* lost:
There *Charon* stands, who rules the dreary Coast;
A sordid God; down from his hoary Chin
A length of Beard descends; uncomb'd, unclean:
His Eyes, like hollow Furnaces on Fire:
A Girdle, foul with grease, binds his obscene Attire.
He spreads his Canvas, with his Pole he steers;
The Freights of flitting Ghosts in his thin Bottom bears.
He look'd in Years; yet in his Years were seen
A youthful Vigour, and Autumnal green.

"Aeneas and Dido" (6. 469–76)

VIRGIL—illa solo fixos oculos aversa tenebat
nec magis incepto vultum sermone movetur
quam si dura silex aut stet Marpesia cautes.
tandem corripuit sese atque inimica refugit
in nemus umbriferum, coniunx ubi pristinus illi
respondit curis aequatque Sychaeus amorem
nec minus Aeneas casu concussus iniquo
prosequitur lacrimis longe et miseratur euntem.

(Pp. 46–47)

BRIDGES—She to the ground downcast her eyes in fixity averted;
Nor were her features more by his pleading affected,
Than wer' a face of flint, or of ensculptur'd alabaster.
At length she started disdainful, an' angrily withdrew

Into a shady thicket: where her grief kindly Sychaeus
Sooth'd with other memories, first love and virginal
    embrace.
And ever Aeneas, to remorse by deep pity soften'd,
With brimming eyes pursued her queenly figure
    disappearing.

DRYDEN—Disdainfully she look'd; then turning round,
    But fix'd her Eyes unmov'd upon the Ground.
    And, what he says, and swears, regards no more
    Than the deaf Rocks, when the loud Billows roar.
    But whirl'd away, to shun his hateful sight,
    Hid in the Forest and the Shades of Night.
    Then sought *Sicheus,* thro' the shady Grove,
    Who answer'd all her Cares, and equal'd all her Love.

In these passages it can be seen that Bridges's quantitative
verse is closer to the original in texture and in rational content
than Dryden's couplets. For example, in commenting on the
youthful appearance of the aged Charon, Virgil said

    iam senior, sed cruda deo viridisque senectus,

literally

    already old, but fresh to a God and green [is] old age.

Bridges renders this

    Already old, but green to a God and hearty will age be,

which is very close to the Latin. In Dryden's translation—

    He looked in Years; yet in his Years were seen
    A youthful Vigour, and Autumnal green—

the idea that Charon still possesses youthful vigor because he is
a God is absent, and the pretty locution "Autumnal green" is
not in the original.

Dryden, in short, invents phrases, usually purely decorative
and trite, to fill up his couplets. One more example. The shade
of Dido, unmoved by Aeneas's entreaties, is thus described by
Virgil:

nec magis incepto vultum sermone movetur
quam si dura silex aut stet Marpesia cautes,

literally

no more by [his] begun discourse is she moved in her face
than if she stood hard flint or Marpesian rock.

Bridges renders this

Nor were her features more by his pleading affected
Than wer' a face of flint, or of ensculptured alabaster.

Dryden conjures up a resounding cliché to describe the scene:

And what he says, and swears, regards no more
Than the deaf Rocks, when the loud Billows roar.

Neither the billows nor their roar is in the original Latin.

Bridges's next long classical paraphrase, *Priam and Achilles*, was done "in the fine English summer of 1913, having been mostly pencilled in the hot sunshine on the lawn in front of my house."[42] The poet in his commentary on the poem says that he is attempting to evoke in English the transcendent and remote dream world that Homer created in Greek. In a remarkable passage Bridges tells his readers what Homer has meant to him and what he himself is attempting to achieve not only in this paraphrase from the Greek but also (by implication) in much of his own original verse:

A reader of Homer is like a man in a dream, who enters into a world of strange beauty unlike that which every day besets him: he is far removed from the associations of modern art and civilization, and unless he is enthralled in that dreamlike charm, he has not entered within the magic circle.

This likening of the effect of Homer to the feeling of a dream satisfies me; because, if I set aside the pretentious phantasms of metaphysical significance, and again all merely nonsensical visions, and the nightmare of physical discomfort, then, in the happy dream-land between these, I find a world wherein the emotions are intensified to a supramundane purity and force, such as no human affection however perfect and sanctified can, except in the rarest moments of ecstasy, be found to attain. And I believe that my strongest waking imagination of the higher emotions owes very much to my dream-experiences of their power, just as I know that some of them have been much heightened or strengthened by pictures and statues and music.

Now I have no doubt that this pure efficacy of the emotions in our dreams is mainly due to the absence of all irrelevant impressions, and this is also the main secret of their force in art, and the reason why music is the most emotional of the arts.

It is not strange then if Homer's transcendent and remote art should remind us of a dream-world; and it follows that, if we would reproduce it, we must avoid all irrelevant impressions.[43]

What does Bridges mean by *irrelevant impressions*? He means anything that reminds one of Milton or Pope or Tennyson or Swinburne as he is reading Homer in English. Bridges goes on to discuss the difficulties of achieving his high aims in English verse. He says, ". . . a familiar and perfected modern verse-form must be a bad vehicle for a translation of Homer."[44] He feels that it is more difficult to achieve in English verse the rhythms of Greek than those of Latin poetry. Hence a literal prose translation of the *Iliad* would do less injustice to the original than a conventional poetic translation. He seems to feel that all English poetic translations of Homer are bad. "Can they have thought that Homer wrote in their manner, or did they imagine that they were writing like Homer? Or perhaps they struck a balance, and hoped that Homer's verse was not very good, nor their own very bad."[45]

Bridges's paraphrase from Book 24 (11. 339–660) of the *Iliad* tells the story of Priam's recovery of the body of his son Hector from the Greek camp. After Achilles had killed Hector, he kept the body unburied in revenge of his friend Patroclus's death. Zeus in a vision advised Priam to ransom the body of Hector from Achilles. Priam was promised the assistance of Hermes in entering the Grecian camp. Priam, therefore, sets out on his mission driving his own chariot followed by a mule wagon carrying the ransom and driven by his servant Idaeus. The paraphrase begins with a description of Hermes' flight from Olympus to the meeting with Priam. Hermes

. . . stoop'd quickly to bind his winged shoon on his ankles
Gold-glittering, which bear him aloft whether over the ocean

Journeying, or whether over the broad earth, swift as a wild wind.

Hermes, in the guise of a mortal and supposedly not recognized by Priam and his servant (although Priam suspects who he is), pretends that he is a squire of Achilles and informs Priam that his son's body still lies unburied, though as yet uncorrupted, after twelve days of neglect and dishonor by Achilles, who every morning drags it around the barrow erected to Patroclus:

Nor yet is injury done: thou mightest go thither and see
How dew-fresh he lieth, how free from death's blemish or stain.

Priam, thanking the Gods that they have kept Hector's body free from disfigurement and corruption, attempts to bribe Hermes (as Achilles' supposed squire) to lead him to his patron. Hermes rejects the bribe, but leaping into Priam's chariot, leads Priam and his servant safely to Achilles through the entire Grecian camp "Whom Hermes drow'zd deeply, in senseless slumber immersing." After formally disclosing his identity to Priam, Hermes returns to Olympus, leaving Priam to face Achilles without his help. Achilles is moved by Priam's plea—partly out of pity for Priam's loss of his many sons and because Priam reminds him of his own ancient father. He grants Priam's petition, accepts the ransom, and orders Hector's body to be washed and clothed. He finds it necessary, however, to explain to the spirit of Patroclus that he is getting a good ransom for Hector. In Bridges's version Achilles tells Patroclus that *all* of the ransom will go to him: "Thine is it all, as ever thou sharedst with me in all things." In the original, Achilles offers to share the ransom with Patroclus. (Samuel Butler's translation: "And I will share it equitably with you.") Bridges explains in a note that he couldn't resist the temptation to magnify Achilles' generosity and improve on Homer.

Hector's body is returned to Priam. Achilles and Priam then pass the night in feasting, drinking, and courtly dialogue. The quality of the poetry in this paraphrase is never of the first rank, and yet one may hazard the guess that it comes as close to the original in tone and feeling as any other verse translation.

Bridges's other paraphrases and adaptations in classical prosody are minor in intention and execution. Perhaps the nicest is "Walking Home" from the Chinese:

Thousand threads of rain and fine white wreathing of air-mist
   Hide from us earth's greenness, hide the enarching azure.
Yet will a breath of Spring homeward convoying attend us,
   And the mellow flutings of passionate Philomel.

Of the original poems in classical prosody, the early "Now in Wintry Delights" (written in 1902) is perhaps the best, and, although he spoke with reservations about all of his classical experiments, Bridges himself seems to have been satisfied with it. The poem received a highly favorable review in the *Times Literary Supplement* (April 10, 1903), which Bridges approved. In a letter to Logan Pearsall Smith he wrote, ". . . the Literary Supplement to the Times gave me a full page of approval!! and that the first page. The article was by an expert, and very good. . . ."[46] And again he writes to Smith, "It pleases me very much that you like the *matter* of my Epistles ["Now in Wintry Delights" and "To a Socialist in London"]. There is really no English metre which makes poetry of such subjects, it is like versified prose. Whether Stone's prosody will come to anything, I can't say, but it is worth while trying. I have no convictions."[47] The poem is a letter in verse form to L. M. (Bridges's close friend Lionel Muirhead). There is, in the Bodleian library, a beautifully bound manuscript of this epistle entitled "Lionello. B. C. L. Muirhead/ Robertus Bridges. S. D." written in elaborate script (by Bridges himself) with marginal headings in red indicating topics of the poem. The care Bridges spent on this manuscript indicates the high regard he had for this early experiment in quantitative verse. Bound with the manuscript is a letter to Muirhead explaining the prosody.

The *Times* reviewer of Bridges's poem analyzes the beauty of classical prosody, which is derived from a threefold complexity:

> The beauty of classical versification was, in point of rhythm, determined by three conditions—syllabic, accentual, and quantitative. The line consisted of a number of syllables, which in some metres was absolutely fixed, in others allowed to vary only within narrow limits: on this was superimposed a scheme of quantitative "feet" by the disposition of which the character of the verse was technically determined; on this again an entirely different system of stresses of accents, almost infinitely flexible, and intended in some places to contradict the quantity and in some places to reinforce it.[48]

He goes on to argue that in conventional modern meters, the iambic for example, the mistake is frequently made that quantity and accent are identical, and that quantity is unduly disregarded whereas in classical meters "the whole character of the verse in Greek and Latin depends on the clash of accent and quantity."[49] The modern poet in English, by paying attention to accent only, loses the subtle counterpoint between quantity and accent to be found in classical verse. This argument is, I think, fallacious. Although in modern meters accent is primary, all of our great poets have achieved variety in conventional modern meters by setting up a counterpoint between accent and quantity. Take, for example, Ben Jonson's

> Drink to me only with thine eyes.

The rhythmic beauty of this iambic line is achieved by:

1. Trochaic substitution in the first foot
2. The placing of a word long in quantity (*thine*) in an unaccented position.

In fact, accent and quantity are seldom identical throughout an entire poem in English verse except in doggerel. But to return to Bridges. The anonymous reviewer quite correctly points out that by imitating the classical line that is primarily quantitative and secondarily accentual, Bridges achieves something quite new in English verse—an easy colloquial rhythm rather like a Horatian epistle. He states that "Now in Wintry Delights" is

> a brief survey of man's place in the universe, and the various interests which go to make up the sum of human life; and it reads somewhat as if Horace had been studying the "de Rerum Natura" and had written to tell Maecenas his impressions.[50]

As a good example of a line in which stress conflicts with quantity the reviewer quotes

> He mappeth out the utter wilderness of unlimited space.

"Now in Wintry Delights" begins with a request to L. M. to take this letter as some "account of Will Stone's versification." He reminds his friend that they can remember back fifty years and that they have had the good fortune of a varied and relatively easy life. Yet life is and should be clung to even without those

things that enrich it and that they have enjoyed: the beauties of
nature and of art and love's varied affection. In stressing the
importance of man's response to beauty in nature and in art,
Bridges writes lines that in subject matter and technique are
somewhat similar to passages in *The Testament of Beauty* written
over twenty years later. In fact, the entire poem is a forerunner
of *The Testament of Beauty*:

> Set these out of account, and with them too put away ART,
> Those ravishings of mind, those sensuous intelligences,
> By whose grace the elect enjoy their sacred aloofness
> From Life's meagre affairs, in beauty's regenerate youth
> Reading immortality's sublime revelation, adoring
> Their own heav'nly desire; nor alone in worship assist they,
> But take, call'd of God, part and pleasure in creation
> Of that beauty, the first of His first purposes extoll'd:—

> Yea, set aside with these all NATURE's beauty, the wildwood's
> Flow'ry domain, the flushing, softcrowding loveliness of Spring,
> Lazy Summer's burning dial, the serenely solemn spells
> Of Sibylline Autumn, with gay-wing'd Plenty departing;
> All fair change, whether of seasons or bright recurrent day,
> Morning or eve; the divine night's wonderous empyrean;
> High noon's melting azure, his thin cloud-country, the landscape
> Mountainous or maritime, blue calms of midsummer Ocean,
> Broad corn-grown champaign goldwaving in invisible wind,
> Wide water'd pasture, with shade of whispering aspen;
> All whereby Nature winneth our love, fondly appearing
> As to caress her children, or all that in exaltation
> Lifteth aloft our hearts to an unseen glory beyond her;—

> .   .   .   .

> If from us all these things were taken way, (that is all art
> And all beauty whate'er, and all love's varied affection,)
> Yet would enough subsist in other concerns to suffice us,
> And feed intelligence, and make life's justification.

Putting aside beauty and love, one would still have something
to make life worthwhile—the capacity for metaphysical and
scientific speculation:

> Tis reflective effort of mind that, conscious of itself,
> Is ever exploring nature for principle and cause.

There follow passages on man's accomplishments in astronomy (his mapping of the solar system and the vast regions of space beyond) , on the wonders of light and man's ability to analyze it, followed by a warning that we should not reject the material world that science is mapping out for us in favor of some abstract idealism, for the material world as perceived by the senses is the basis of all our knowledge:

> But since all the knowledge which man was born to attain to
> Hath these only channels, (which must limit and qualify it,)
> We shall con the grammar, the material alphabet of life.
> Yea, ev'n more from error to preserve our inquisitive mind,
> Than to secure well-being against adversity and ill.

Science, then, is to be praised for setting men free from "dreamy scholastic/ Imprisoning." Yet it is odd that so many intellectuals are still interested in studying the superstitions of the past:

> While civilization's advances mutely regarding
> Talk we of old scapegoats, discuss bloodrites, immolations
> Worship of ancestors; explain complexities involved
> Of tribal marriages, derivation of early religions,
> Priestly taboos, totems, archaic mysteries of trees,
> All the devils and dreams abhorr'd of barbarous ages.

This obsession with primitivism and anthropology is perhaps an escape from "the worried congestion of our Victorian era,/ Whose many inventions of world-wide luxury have changed/ Life's very face. . . ." There follows a passage on the decline of medicine during the dark ages when the doctrines of Hippocrates were forgotten. Sunk in superstition, the practice of medicine did not become respectable again until the Victorian discoveries of bacteria and the founding of the science of bacteriology. There is a vivid passage on the deadliness of germs:

> Those swarming parasites, that barely within the detection
> Of manifold search-light, have bred, swimming unsuspected
> Thro' man's brain and limbs, slaying with loathly pollution
> His beauty's children, his sweet scions of affection,
> In fev'rous torment and tears, his home desolating
> Of their fair innocence, breaking his proud passionate heart,
> And his kindly belief in God's good justice arraigning.

Successful in science, we have neglected other human concerns. "Our art/ Self-consciously sickens in qualms of an aesthetic aura/ Noisily in the shallows splashing and disporting uninspired." However, on the positive side, we have got over the superstitions and vain metaphysical speculations of Christian religion and have by the sciences of archaeology and anthropology discovered how these false beliefs arose:

> Science has pierced man's cloudy commonsense,
> Dow'rd his homely vision with more expansive an embrace,
> And the rotten foundation of old superstition exposed.
> That trouble of Pascal, those vain paradoxes of Austin,
> Those Semitic parables of Paul, those tomes of Aquinas,
> All are thrown to the limbo of antediluvian idols,
> Only because we learn mankind's true history, and know
> That not at all from a high perfection sinfully man fell,
> But from baseness arose.

He concludes with an eloquent passage (looking forward once again to *The Testament of Beauty*) on the superiority of Man over Nature in creating the outward forms of beauty. Art is superior to Nature:

> Turn our thought for awhile to the symphonies of Beethoven,
> Or the rever'd preludes of mighty Sebastian: Is there
> One work of Nature's contrivance beautiful as these?
> Judg'd by beauty alone man wins, as sensuous artist.

This poem, then, is a rather loosely organized disquisition in verse on the place of man in the universe. Bridges appears to be a religious and philosophical skeptic, rejecting the older Christian dogma as outworn, accepting with enthusiasm the discoveries of Victorian science, but regretting the failure of progress in the arts, and emphasizing his own personal need for the experience of transcendent beauty that the arts alone can give. The poem looks forward both in technique and in some of its themes to *The Testament of Beauty*. The prosody is not the same as *The Testament of Beauty*, for the *Testament* is not in quantitative verse. Nevertheless, both poems make use of the long cadenced line, and when read in the normal speaking voice without regard to theoretical systems of scansion, the verse of both poems in a number of passages is similar. Furthermore, the structures of

"Wintry Delights" and of the *Testament* are similar. Both poems use a few basic philosophical themes to tie together a series of more or less digressive passages (often descriptive) of great beauty. "Now in Wintry Delights" is an interesting document in the history of Bridges's technical development, of his relationship with the Victorian period that he long outlived, and of his general philosophical position.

In "Epistle to a Socialist in London" Bridges turns from science and metaphysics to politics and social views. These views, which are repeated in *The Testament of Beauty*, exhibit a strong reaction against socialism and an equally strong belief in law and order. He considered socialist doctrines of equality dangerous forerunners of "Red Revolution, a wild Reawakening," and in the event such a revolution occurs—"who shall amend the amenders?" As an aristocrat, he was not sympathetic toward a dictatorship of the proletariat or toward any political movement that seemed to him to be leading in that direction.

In the first few lines of "To a Socialist" he praises Fraser, to whom this verse epistle is addressed, as a man of integrity, even though he, Bridges, disagrees with his humanitarian and socialist views. He criticizes Fraser for being Utopian in believing that most of our ills would be cured if the profits of labor were equally divided. Bridges considers Fraser's views to be "down-leveling." A limit must be fixed to "the folk" or else, as their number is increased, their happiness will diminish. For example, if the famine be relieved in India this season, the next famine will be worse! If man since the time of Adam and Eve had been allowed to propagate freely and live according to the rule "the greatest happiness for the greatest number," the earth would have been overpopulated long ago. Individual effort and heroism give a man ascendancy over his followers and justly so. Struggle and death are the laws of life:

> Who winneth? ah! see!
> Ours have arrived, and he who led their bravery is there.
> None that heard will ever forget that far-echoing cheer:
> Such heard Nelson, above the crashings & thundering of guns:
> At Marathon 'twas heard and all time's story remembers.

The main thrust of the poem is praise of individualism and hope of attainment that would be lost in Socialism's "stingy promise." One can imagine Bridges's opinion of Chairman Mao's China, to which the following verses might apply:

>   . . . the level'd borders, the symmetric allotments,
> Where nothing exceedeth, nothing encroacheth, nor assaileth;
> Where Reason now drudgeth a sad monomaniac, all day
> Watering & weeding, digging & diligently manuring
> Her label'd families, starch-makers, nitrogen-extract-
> Purveyors, classified potherbs & empty pretenders
> Of medical virtues; nay ev'n and *their* little impulse
> T'ward liberal fruiting disallow'd by stern regulation;
> So many beans to a pod, with so many pods to a beanstalk;
> Prun'd, pincht, economiz'd miserly til' all is abortion,
> Save in such specimens as, but for an extravagant care,
> Had miserably perish'd.

Rather than this dreary existence, Bridges prefers "Magnificence, Force, Freedom, Bounty," and he praises the power of wealth:

>   Beautiful is GOLD,
> Clear as a trumpet-call, stirring where'er it appeareth
> All high pow'rs to battle.

And he continues:

>   . . . all eminence is unequal, unequal is unjust,—
> Should that once come about, then alas for this merry England,
> Sunk in a grey monotone of drudgery.

Man, says Bridges, has a right to the pleasures wealth can bring, although the poet's pleasures may be quite different from his wealthy neighbor's. If he had his neighbor's income, he would hire a string quartet while his neighbor enjoyed his motor car "rattling along on a furious engine/ In caoutchouc carapace, with a trail of damnable oilstench." However, "blame not the pleasures; they are not enough; pleasure only/ Makes this life liveable. . . . 'Twas for heavn'ly pleasure that God did first fashion all thing." But pleasure has no place (Bridges claims) in a socialist society, which would destroy "the fair embroideries of life,/ That close-clust'ring man, his comfort pared to the outskirts/ Of his discomfort, may share in meanness unenvied."

Bridges concludes his poem with his parable of the bees. In ancient times the life of the bee was not systematized and regulated as it is today—"Golden abundance/ Was not a State-kept hoard." Whatever happiness the bee seems to have today is an instinctive remembrance of a golden age of freedom, abundance, and long life. But unfortunately for the individual bee, these insects discovered Nature's secret of determining the qualities of their offspring. The race was preferred to the individual. Specialization was developed—the individual bee's life (much shortened) is now spent in a prison of "strictly proportioned" and "loveless labour" for the good of the race. It is the perfect socialist society that Bridges renounces in favor of heroic individualism.

A similar dislike of the systematized life and an honest skepticism that Bridges applied to philosophy, religion, and politics is expressed in "Johannes Milton, Senex." The poet believes in God, yet neither he nor anyone else can know or understand him:

> Therefore will I be bound to no studied system
> Nor argument, nor with delusion enslave me.

Of Bridges's other quantitative verses, the very best appear to me to be the short poems in elegiac distichs. Here are two:

GHOSTS

Mazing around my mind like moths at a shaded candle,
  In my heart like lost bats in a cave fluttering,
Mock ye the charm whereby I thought reverently to lay you,
  When to the wall I nail'd your reticent effigys?

Ἐτώσιον ἄχθος ἀρούρης

Who goes there? God knows. I'm nobody. How should I answer?
  Can't jump over a gate nor run across the meadow.
I'm but an old whitebeard of inane identity. Pass on!
  What's left of me today will very soon be nothing.

The alliteration and smooth cadence of the first line of "Ghosts" are completely successful in suggesting the supernatural, and the broken and "dry" texture of "Who goes there?" makes this a remarkable and powerful poem on death as annihilation. It compares favorably with Wallace Stevens's "The Course of a Particular" but is more compact and direct than Stevens's poem. Yvor Winters considered it one of the finest poems he knew. The title is from the *Iliad* 18.104 and may be translated "a profitless burden upon the earth." It is spoken by Achilles as he laments his failure to save Patroclus and other comrades from death.

The Poems in Neo-Miltonic Syllabics

The Tapestry. Of Bridges's twelve poems in neo-Miltonic syllabics, eleven were first collected in a beautifully printed limited edition, *The Tapestry* (1925). The twelfth poem of the group, "The West Front," was omitted by printer's error, much to the poet's annoyance.[51] Stanley Morison, probably the greatest typographer of the century, was in charge of the printing.[52] Morison first met Bridges when he called on him at Boar's Hill November 8, 1923.[53] He had received the invitation to visit the poet as a result of his letter of October 22, 1923, stating that he was preparing a volume on typography and inquiring if Bridges designed his own volumes. Morison was particularly interested in a flower border that appeared in the *Poems* of 1873 and again in the *Yattendon Hymnal* of 1896—"a more sumptuous presentation of the ancient types than had ever been produced in Fell's day, or since" according to Morison.[54] Morison (born 1889) was more than forty years younger than the poet. Converted to Catholicism in 1908, he was also a staunch Marxist; Bridges, on the other hand, was moderately anti-Romanist and strongly opposed to Socialism. However, in spite of their political and religious differences, the two became good friends, sharing an enthusiasm for fine print. By the time Morison met Bridges he was advancing rapidly in his career as a typographer. He had served on the staff of *The Imprint,* a journal devoted to the study of fine printing. He had helped to set up in Fell type a volume of poems by Alice Meynell. After serving two years in prison as a conscientious objector to World War I, he became manager of the Pelican Press, source of the liveliest typographical design in London. He became typographical advisor to the Cloister Press in Heaton Mersey near Manchester, but then returned to London and became active in the affairs of *The Fleuron,* a journal devoted to fine printing. By 1922, when he became advisor to the Monotype Corporation, he was an acknowledged expert in printing and the history of printing. At the time of his first meeting with Bridges he was collecting material for his *Four Centuries of Fine Printing* published in 1924. He designed the special limited quarto edition of *The Testament of Beauty* in 1929 and became in the same year typographical advisor for *The Times,* in which capacity he was responsible for a complete redesigning of that paper. The first issue in his New Roman type appeared October 3, 1932. He edited and virtually wrote the four volume *History of the Times* (1935–52).

About the time Morison met Bridges, two of his friends— Frederic and Beatrice Ward, both Americans living in London— were developing a new type based on Italian Arrighi that Morison showed to Bridges June 28, 1925, and Bridges agreed to let Morison print a selection of his poems in this type—all in neo-Miltonic syllabics—from the manuscript of his forthcoming volume to be published by the Oxford Press under the title of *New Verse.* The understanding was that this selection (which Morison himself later entitled *The Tapestry*) was to appear before *New Verse.*

Problems occurred immediately. The new type was being founded in Paris, and there were delays for technical reasons. Also, Bridges wished to introduce a new letter *g* that would distinguish between soft and hard *g*'s. The making of the extra letter took time. And by mistake "The West Front" was omitted and this had to be discussed. *The Tapestry* was finally published December 17, 1925, in 150 copies.[55] The special soft *g* was used, but not consistently. Variations on this new type were later used for printing Bridges's *Collected Essays.*

Bridges considered his syllabics to be just as experimental as the free verse of the imagist poets that had gained considerable notoriety following the *Des Imagistes* anthology of 1914. In the printer's note to *The Tapestry* (actually written by Bridges himself) the poet says:

> Mr. Bridges has generously authorized the printing of the following complete collection up to the present date of all his "New Verse" described by him as 'Neo-Miltonic syllabics' and

offered as his considered contribution to the Free Verse controversy.[56]

And in his Preface to *New Verse* (1925) Bridges wrote:

> Part I is in the poet's latest manner and still peculiar to himself: it may be styled *Neo-Miltonic Syllabics* and has been described elsewhere. It pretends to offer their true desideratum to the advocates of Free Verse.[57]

The year before he had written to R. C. Trevelyan, "People are now running after 'free verse.' I say that this stuff is free verse."[58] "This stuff" refers to six of the eleven syllabic poems that were to appear in *The Tapestry*, with particular reference to "Como se Quando," which Trevelyan had praised in an article in *The New Statesman*. In January 1926 he wrote again to Trevelyan, "I agree with the Free versifiers that the old humdrum is worn out: but I am quite orthodox in believing that freedom must be within prosody not without it."[59]

What did Bridges mean by *neo-Miltonic syllabics*? Their meter is explained by Bridges in a brief article written in December 1923,[60] entitled " 'New Verse'/ Explanation of the Prosody of My Late Syllabic 'Free Verse'."[61] The article is written in a condensed style; it is difficult to summarize a summary, but the gist of it appears to be this: Bridges, in his study of Milton's prosody, had discovered that Milton had "freed" every foot in his line except the last foot, in which he allowed extrametrical syllables. Bridges went a step further and "freed" every foot in the line and allowed no extrametrical syllables. Thus, Bridges had a line with a definite number of syllables but an indeterminate number of accents and quantities. Bridges chose to make his line twelve syllables in length. Lines that appear to have more than twelve syllables can be reduced to twelve by elision. By Milton's "freeing the feet" Bridges meant that "there was no place in which any one syllable was necessarily long or short, accented or unaccented, heavy or light." After a great deal of careful technical analysis, Bridges came out with a line that was restricted only by syllable count. As he said, "It was plainly the freest of free verse, there being no speech-rhythm which it would not admit."[62]

Bridges also defends and explains his prosody in a note to the first printing of "Poor Poll." The poem, dated June 3, 1921, is probably the first poem written and printed in the neo-Miltonic twelve-syllable line without a caesural break and is therefore the first poem in what was later to become the "loose Alexandrine" line of *The Testament of Beauty*. Bridges comments on his earlier experiments in the twelve-syllable line printed as two lines of sixes to indicate the caesural break and then discusses his employment in "Poor Poll" of the line without a hemistich or with the hemistich optional. His note, in part, reads:

> To make the hemistich optional, as I have done, is no innovation: Milton would always have had it so; but this liberty when extended to my development of his system gives a result as new and as rich as the earlier experiments gave. The value of it is the consequent freedom of·the diction; no syllable encounters any metrical demand that interferes with its inflexional value as part of the spoken phrase in which it occurs.[63]

As shown above, the poems of *The Tapestry* are in two categories: (1) Those with lines having a strong caesural break in the middle. They were composed as Alexandrines, but are printed in sixes[64] with each line broken in the center:

> A frosty Christmas Eve
>   when the stars were shining.

(2) A twelve-syllable line without a caesural break and printed thus:

> These tapestries have hung fading around my hall.

This line (which became a *Testament of Beauty* line) was suggested by similar verses in Milton's "Nativity Ode" and *Samson Agonistes*:

> Or grovling soild thir crested helmets in the dust.

Of this type of line Bridges wrote: "The characteristic of Milton's twelve-syllable line is his neglect of this [caesural] break, and he makes a verse which has a strong unity in itself, and no tendency to break up."[65]

So much for the prosody of the poems. What of their content?

"Come se quando" has received more favorable comment than any other of the neo-Miltonic poems.[66] The title was sug-

gested by Mrs. Bridges who, on reading the first draft, was struck
by the numerous Dantean similes introduced by "as if . . . when,"
"like as . . . when," and similar phrases. "There are too many
'come se quandos,'" she is reported to have said.[67] "Come se
quando" and the more frequent "come . . . cosi" are introductory
phrases for similes in the *Divinia Commedia*. Bridges committed
the error of substituting *si* for *se*, and the title was not corrected
until recent printings of the *Collected Poems*.[68]

The poem is primarily a meditation on the threat to culture
and civilization when the passions overcome reason—the same
theme (or tenor) as "Low Barometer," which was composed about
the same time. The vehicle is a dream-vision-parable. The narrator, falling asleep at night, sees first "the epiphany of a seraphic
figure" of heroic beauty, with a face like a portrait by Giorgione:

> as if Nature had deign'd to take back from man's hand
> some work of her own as art had refashioned it.

This epiphany of the Greek-Christian ideal of heroic beauty that
"all that looked on loved and many worshipp'd" is blotted out
by passion and fear—the "fear of God." And here there is one
of the many Dantean similes commented on by Mrs. Bridges:

> . . . I saw its smoky shadow of dread;
> and as a vast Plutonian mountain that burieth
> its feet in molten lava and its high peak in heaven,
> whenever it hath decoy'd some dark voyaging storm
> to lave its granite shoulders, dischargeth the flood
> in a thousand torrents o'er its flanks to the plain
> and all the land is vocal with the swirl and gush
> of the hurrying waters, so suddenly in this folk
> a flood of troublous passion arose and mock'd control.

A poet-prophet figure next appears—the familiar alienated
intellectual—who has fled the city to live in wilderness caves.
He makes an impassioned appeal to Themis, the goddess of
Justice, to unveil her eyes and to weigh in her scales on the
one side her "Codes of Justice Duty and Awe," her "penal inter-
dicts" together with the tables of her Law, and on the other side
Mercy, Love, human thought, and suffering, "All tears from
Adam's tears unto the tears of Christ." If mercy, love, and the

experiences of suffering humanity are not enough to outweigh the codes of justice, duty, and law, then the poet tells Justice to bind up her eyes again. He will no more contend, but admit that confusion is the Final Cause. The address to Themis runs for over one hundred thirty lines and there are several fundamental metaphysical questions raised and unanswered, such as the origin and destiny of man and the efficacy of reason in a universe that seems to be largely governed by blind chance. The poet-prophet is, of course, not the spokesman for Robert Bridges who characterizes his plea as "outrageous despair the self pity of mankind." Bridges is obviously more impressed by the figure of heroic beauty that preceded that of the poet.

The poet-prophet figure, having disburdened his heart "to the wilderness and silent sky," is suddenly overwhelmed with "a stream of natural feeling," memories of home and friends. Repenting his abandonment of his people, he returns to the market place of the city and, like an Old Testament prophet, preaches with "strong words of his chasten'd humanity." The people, rising against him, drive him from the city and are about to kill him when the mob is stopped by the sudden appearance of "a white-robed throng that came moving with solemn pace." This "choral convoy" takes the poet into its protection where, after receiving extreme unction, the poet dies. The body is carried in procession "with dirge and shriving prayer" by the priestly host to be buried within a church where it will await the second coming of Christ. The narrator is awakened by the sound of the funeral dirge and by the night wind that returns the reader to the opening lines of the poem, perhaps the best poetry of the entire neo-Miltonic series:

How thickly the far fields of heaven are strewn with stars!
Tho' the open eye of day shendeth them with its glare
yet, if no cloudy wind curtain them nor low mist
of earth blindfold us, soon as Night in grey mantle
wrappeth all else, they appear in their optimacy
from under the ocean or behind the high mountains
climbing in spacious ranks upon the stark-black void:
Ev'n so in our mind's night burn far beacons of thought
and the infinite architecture of our darkness,
the dim essence and being of our mortalities,
is sparkled with fair fire-flecks of eternity
whose measure we know not nor the wealth of their rays.

Of the line "And the infinite architecture of our darkness," Bridges wrote to Trevelyan that it "seems to me one of the most beautiful of the many free rhythms—I have found it one of the lines that first converts the reader."[69]

"Come se Quando," written three years before the first lines of *The Testament of Beauty*, may be considered a preliminary exercise for the longer poem. The prosodic structure—"loose Alexandrines"—is the same as that of the longer poem, and several of the philosophical ideas in "Come se Quando" are given more extensive treatment in the *Testament*. With the exception of the opening lines quoted above, the diction of the earlier poem tends to be stereotyped and the rhythms rather flat. However, Bridges was developing a medium that according to Yvor Winters (referring to a passage in *The Testament of Beauty*, 4, 270–338) is "a new kind of poetry, which, however restricted its possibilities, is nevertheless an enrichment of our experience."[70]

"Poor Poll," as shown above, is the first of the poems in the new twelve-syllable line. In his "Metrical Elucidations" published in the first edition of the poem, Bridges explains that the "poem is privately printed for a few friends who wish to examine the pretensions of the experiment." He goes on to say that he deliberately chose a subject on a low plane and, furthermore, that he introduced quotations from foreign languages "to illustrate how certain well-established and unmistakably alien forms blend comfortably" within the new medium. "Poor Poll," incidentally, was being composed at the same time as *The Waste Land*, and both Bridges and Eliot were looking for a "carry all" medium that would blend excerpts from foreign languages as well as diction from "high" and "low" styles. Bridges found his medium in an adaptation of certain lines from Milton. Eliot found his in an adaptation of the method of Ezra Pound's early *Cantos*.

The vehicle of "Poor Poll" is, as Bridges has stated, on a low plane, but the tenor is not. It is, in fact, the same as that of *The Waste Land*, the destruction of the culture of Western civilization. The poem starts with an incident observed by the poet. A parrot calls loudly for food, but when the pan of "sop" is given him by the cook, the bird surprises the poet by deftly gathering the food in its beak and scattering it on the lawn. Then it "summoned with loud cry the little garden birds/ to take their feast." This incident leads to a meditation involving a number of ideas: the depth of the source of man's benevolence if benevolence can also be found in birds, the possibility that instinct is a better guide to moral behavior than reason, and the ability of the wild bird to adapt to an English domestic life and to mimic languages he cannot understand. In its instinctive desire for the unknown life of the tropics of which it had been robbed by a British sailor, the bird becomes

> —a very figure and image of man's soul on earth
> the almighty cosmic Will fidgeting in a trap—.

In appearance the parrot in "the impeccable spruceness" of his "grey-feather'd poll" might qualify for membership in the House of Lords or the Athenaeum Club, for it has the "simulation of profoundest wisdom." But, the poet continues, in actuality the parrot is not wise but more like an "idle and puzzle-headed" monk in an unfurnished cell who will die in the peace that passes Understanding because he lacks Understanding. The parrot is next asked if he would willingly exchange his present pale, sedentary life with that of the tropical paradise from which he was captured—a monkey's paradise where he would be in constant danger of sudden death. The parrot cannot answer because he cannot understand the question. In fact, there can be no real communication between poet and parrot because the parrot lacks understanding and a sense of values:

> I am writing verses to you & grieve that you sh^d be
> *absolument incapable de les comprendre,*
> *Tu, Polle, nescis ista nec potes scire:—*
> Alas! Iambic, scazon and alexandrine,
> spondee or choriamb, all is alike to you—

The parrot is, by implication, similar to the British public of the 1920s, the parents

> of a new race of beings the unhallow'd offspring
> of them who shall have quite dismember'd & destroy'd
> our temple of Christian faith & fair Hellenic art
> just as that monkey would, poor Polly, have done for you.

Poll is also the victim of the new "monkey's paradise" that would destroy Bridges's ideals, Christian faith and hellenic art. The final lines link the poem thematically with "Come se Quando."

"The Tapestry" is a sequel to "Poor Poll." It begins with a brief account of a young lord who ordered his steward to turn his ancient tapestries to the wall. The mythological scenes, he believed, were out of date for the young, whereas the backs of the tapestries gave "more colour and less solemnity" to the hall for the feast that followed.

The incident is a fable that gives the poet an opportunity to discuss the correct relationship between man and beauty, principally the beauties of nature. There follows an eloquent passage on his awareness from infancy to old age of natural beauty, which includes a fine description of the dawn of the day on which he composed his poem:

> Then looked I forth and lo! The Elysian fields of Dawn!
> and there in naked peace my dumb expectancy
> mirror'd above the hills, a pageant like music
> heard in imagination or the silence of dreams.
> What if I had not seen the cloths of Night take hue
> soft-tinged as of brown bear-skin or green opal spread
> which still persisting through shift imperceptible
> grew to an incandescent copper on a pale light-blue!
> Then one flame-yellow streak pierced thru' the molten bronze
> with lilac freak'd above, where fiëry in red mist
> the orb with slow surprise surged, till his whole blank blaze
> dispell'd from out his path all colour—and Day began.

It was, he goes on to say, the gradual awareness of beauty that helped savage primitive man to become civilized. Then, returning to the tapestries with their faces to the wall:

> I prop so far my slight fable with argument
> to lay malison and ban on the upstart leprous clan
> who wrong Nature's beauty turning her face about.

He has returned to the principal theme of his preceding poem on the parrot. He concludes with the statement that a full appreciation of beauty requires a study of both the back and the front of the tapestry—that is, of the ugly as well as of the beautiful.

In 1917 Bridges resided for a time in Merton College while repairs were being made on Chilswell House. "The College Garden," although written in 1921, refers to the garden at Merton College during that year. The pensive philosopher mentioned in the poem is F. H. Bradley.[71] The theme is in the first line: "The

infinitude of Life is in the Heart of Man," an infinitude that
includes good—the good life being primarily the creation and
contemplation of beauty by means of the imagination. But it
also includes evil as manifested in the blood lust of hunting and
on the battlefields of World War I. Thoughts of the turmoil of
the war sharpen the contrast with the too peaceful garden of
Merton College—deserted of students and empty except for himself, the pensive philosopher, and an aged gardener.

The poem ends with an excellent passage depicting the state
of mind of the seventy-three year old poet:

> I lie, like one who hath wander'd all his summer morn
> among the heathery hills and hath come down at noon
> in a breathless valley upon a mountain-brook
> and for animal recreation of hot fatigue
> hath stripp'd his body naked to lie down and taste
> the play of the cool water on all his limbs and flesh
> and lying in a pebbly shallow beneath the sky
> supine and motionless feeleth each ripple pass
> until his thought is merged in the flow of the stream
> as it cometh upon him and lappeth him there
> stark as a white corpse that stranded upon the stones
> blocketh and for a moment delayeth the current
> ere it can pass to pay its thin tribute of salt
> into the choking storage of the quenchless sea.

Of "The Psalm" Bridges wrote to Trevelyan December 16,
1924, "The shortest of my six poems—attempt at an idyllic effect
—was printed last year in *The Queen* with an ornamental border
etc!! The Editor was (or seemed to be) enthusiastic about it—
tho' he had no chance of scanning it.—Why should it be scanned?
—*No one* ever scanned Milton"[72] The occasion of the poem is
the sound of a Huguenot psalm sung by village folk in an English
church and overheard by Bridges while he was pleasantly talking
with a friend in a meadow. As in "The College Garden," a peaceful scene is interrupted by thoughts of strife and suffering. Bridges
appears to be quite conscious of the fact that his own life in
contrast with that of the world at large has been relatively tran-
quil and idyllic. The substance of the poem is a meditation on the
sufferings of the French protestants during the sixteenth, seventeenth, and eighteenth centuries and an expression of admiration
for their endurance. An earlier poem, "The Summer-House on

the Mound," ends with a reference to the religious quarrels in
England:

> . . . that old outlaw,
> The Roman wolf, scratches with privy paw.

In both poems Bridges is clearly on the side of the protestants.

"Kate's Mother," which Trevelyan described as "a perfect
short story, and a beautiful poem too," is, like "Poor Poll," an
experiment in the new meter as a "carry all" medium suitable
for a wide range of subjects. Bridges wrote to Trevelyan, "I chose
the subject as a simplest childish narrative for test of the metre
—and the general liking for it proves I think that the metre
can carry the highest and lowest business in juxtaposition without embarrassment or bathos: and that is the desideratum in
English versification which I wished to supply. You will have
observed that such a line as e.g. 'For difficulty and roughness
and scorch of the way' which might be out of Dante's Inferno,
does not show."[73]

The poem begins with a description of the house, windmill,
fields, and the sea near the village of Walmer, Kent, with grounds
overlooking the Channel where Bridges spent the first years of
his childhood, the same place as that so beautifully depicted in
"The Summer-House on the Mound." On a July afternoon the
child, his elder sister, and their nurse Kate pay a visit to Kate's
mother—a brief journey that was to the boy an adventure, for
he was going beyond the windmill into new territory. Also, this
was "the first visit of compliment that ever I paid." The visit
is also a journey into a new dimension of childhood experience—
an awareness of human affliction and courage foreshadowed by
these lines:

> For difficulty and roughness and scorch of the way
> then a great Bible-thought came on me: I was going
> like the Israelites of old in the desert of Sin.

They arrive at the straw thatched cottage of Kate's mother
with its typical country garden of sweet william, mint, and jasmin
and its interior that was full of surprises to the boy—a lofty
clock picturing upon its face a full rigged ship and a huge copper
warming pan—but the greatest wonder of all is the old woman
herself:

the wrinkles innumerable of her sallow skin
her thin voice and the trembling of her patient face
as there she swayed incessantly on her rocking-chair
like the ship in the clock: she had sprung into my ken
wholly to enthrall me, a fresh nucleus of life-surprise
such as I knew must hold mystery and could reveal:
for I had observed strange movement of her cotton skirt
and as she sat with one knee across the other, I saw
how her right foot in the air was all a-tremble and jerked
in little restless kicks: so when we sat to feast
about the table spredd with tea and cottage cakes
whenever her eye was off me I watched her furtively
to make myself assured of all the manner and truth
of this new thing, and ere we were sent out to play
(that so Kate might awhile chat with her mother alone)
I knew the SHAKING PALSY.

All of this is quite Wordsworthian and, as an initiation into
evil, a mild performance indeed when one thinks, for example
of the Nick Adams stories of Hemingway. Nevertheless, the poem
has a few charming though very minor passages.

The epitaph on Hubert Hastings Parry, dated 1920 and written for his monument in Gloucester Cathedral, was printed in
The Tapestry but, to the best of my knowledge, not reprinted
elsewhere. I therefore quote it in full:

From boyhood's eager play call'd by the English Muse
Her fine scholar to be than her Master's compeer
A spirit elect whom no unworthy thought might wrong
Nor any fear touch thee joyously o'er life's waves
Navigating thy soul into her holy haven
Long these familiar walls shall re-echo thy song
And this stone remember thy bounteous gaiety
Thy honour and thy grace and the love of thy friends.

The remaining neo-Miltonic poems were written and printed
in lines of six syllables each (with the exception of the 6+5
syllable lines of "Cheddar Pinks"). The first of these, "The
Flowering Tree," is on one of Bridges's favorite subjects—his
response to beauty (and in this poem, beauty's response to him).
The poet falls asleep in the sun and dreams that he is covered
by a flowering tree. He says that, unlike Endymion who slept
by moonlight,

> would I sleep in the sun
> Neath the trees divinely
> with day's azure above
> When my love of Beauty
> is met by beauty's love.

"Noel: Christmas Eve, 1913" was written by the recently appointed poet laureate for King George V who sent it to *The Times* of London where it was published December 24, 1913. During a walk on a frosty Christmas Eve, the poet listens to the church bells:

> And from many a village
> in the water'd valley
> Distant music reach'd me
> peals of bells aringing:
> The constellated sounds
> ran sprinkling on earth's floor
> As the dark vault above
> with stars was spangled o'er.

The use of the words *water'd* and *sprinkling* together with *constellated* and *stars* achieves a very lovely effect of the sound of distant scattered music, reinforced with his reference to the first Christmas in the next stanza when the shepherds

> . . . marveling could not tell
> Whether it were angels
> or the bright stars singing.

In the third stanza the poet blesses the village folk ringing the church bells and in the concluding stanza states what the music meant to him:

> But to me heard afar
> it was starry music
> Angels' song, comforting
> as the comfort of Christ.

Rhythm, imagery, and sound achieve a mood of serenity that makes this poem, Bridges's first as poet laureate, one of his loveliest minor achievements. "In Der Fremde" because of its rhymes could be mistaken for accentual syllabic verse, although Bridges considers it to be in neo-Miltonic syllabics. "The West Front" is of little value and was not reprinted in *The Tapestry*. "Cheddar Pinks," a very slight but charming performance, is on a theme discussed before—the aging poet is reading Homer in his peaceful garden while the world struggles about him. He has a moment of very mild remorse:

> Then felt I like to one
> indulging in sin,

but the remorse is easily dispelled as he busies himself composing his pleasant verses.

How free was Bridges's "free verse"? To what extent did he actually participate in the movement that almost engulfed the poetry of the 1920s? The answer is suggested by Elizabeth Daryush's comment. He was "a keen experimenter" who at the same time wished to preserve "the traditional and characteristic beauties of our language." Robert Beum has said that Bridges's experiments resulted in "free verse which has taken one stride toward regular traditional verse."[74] Sister Mary Berg, in her exhaustive statistical analysis of the neo-Miltonic poems, concluded that Bridges himself thought these poems to be regular traditional verse that has taken one step toward free verse.[75] My own opinion is that by "freeing" all the feet of his twelve-syllable line, Bridges *theoretically* had a medium that could absorb any rhythmical or nonrhythmical matter, but the poet in practice preferred a rising disyllabic meter that Sister Mary describes as "a pervasive, though relaxed, iambic movement."[76] These iambic characteristics became stronger (as Sister Mary has demonstrated) in *The Testament of Beauty*. The rhythms of the neo-Miltonic poems—those which Bridges offered as his contribution to the free verse movement—are considerably less relaxed than those found in the poetry of Sandburg and Amy Lowell, but looser than the rapid cadences of the best free verse poems of Williams, Stevens, Pound, and H. D. As far as subject matter is concerned, Bridges, as shown above, did not follow the suggestions of Pound, Williams, and others that any subject, no matter how trivial (a bathtub, a wheelbarrow), is suitable for "modern verse." In his choice of themes and images Bridges usually maintained the decorum of the traditional classical poet.

3

The Dramatist

The Masques

Bridges began and ended his career as a dramatist with two masques—*Prometheus the Firegiver* composed in 1881 and *Demeter* written in 1904. It is probable that the author did not expect to have *Prometheus* produced, although according to Mrs. Bridges there was, in fact, an amateur production at a boys' school near Newbury. *Demeter* was written by request for performance at Somerville College, Oxford, in 1904, and was repeated fifty years later. The poet's daughter, Mrs. Elizabeth Daryush, who was present at both productions, preferred the first, in which, she told me in an interview, the lady actresses were younger. "The masque was staged out of doors, and to prevent the muslin costumes from blowing in the wind they were dampened, which made them cling more closely than expected to the actresses' youthful figures."

Whether performed or not, a masque has qualities different from the conventional stage play. It is supposed to be poetic, transcendent even, remote from reality, depending for its effect on poetry, music, setting, and costumes rather than on realism and the hurly-burly action of the commercial theater. For these reasons the masque was a genre particularly congenial to a poet of Bridges's temperament, and it therefore may be that his most successful "dramatic" writing is in *Prometheus* and *Demeter*.

126

Prometheus the Firegiver

Readers know from Hopkins's letters to Bridges[1] that a first draft of *Prometheus the Firegiver* had been completed or nearly completed by the spring of 1881, for in a letter dated April 27, 1881,[2] Hopkins asks, "And what is the 1000 line poem about?", which obviously refers to *Prometheus*. There are frequent references to the poem in Hopkins's letters from this date through 1882 and into 1883, and as late as October 31, 1886,[3] Hopkins is still objecting to the phrase "domeless courts," which appeared in the first line of the first draft and was subsequently changed to "aetherial courts." The manuscript of the poem has been lost,[4] but from a reference by Hopkins to "the blotching of the copy with countless corrections,"[5] it is obvious that Bridges heavily revised his original draft. The play may have been begun in Italy where, after a serious attack of pneumonia, Bridges was recuperating during the winter of 1881. Bridges moved to Yattendon in 1882, and it was there that his drama was completed. This "Mask in the Greek Manner" was first published by Daniel in 1883 in a deluxe edition limited to one hundred copies and was issued by Bell in a trade edition in 1884. Mrs. Bridges informed Professor Abbott that the play was acted once only at a boys' grammar school near Newbury in the presence of Bridges.[6]

Bridges, not attempting to restore the lost play of Aeschylus, recreates in his own way the legend of the Titan who, in stealing fire from Zeus and bringing it to man, is, in fact, giving man the opportunity to develop his spiritual and intellectual potentialities by raising him from a brute existence to life in a civilized society. Prometheus appears before the palace of Inachus in Argos. He carries a long reed that holds the stolen fire and, in a prologue, describes the beauties of earth, his love for man, and his desire to win earth's kingdom from the tyranny of Zeus who desires man's destruction or, failing that, wishes to degrade him to the level of the brutes. Prometheus has sent hope to man in visions and dreams to aid him in combating Zeus, and he has chosen Inachus for the gift of fire because he has confidence in his ability to found and civilize a society. He awaits (disguised as a shepherd) the arrival of Inachus before the altar of Zeus where the king is to initiate the ceremony in Zeus's honor. When Inachus enters, Prometheus, commenting on the cold wood on the smokeless altar, announces that there is fire on earth that Inachus may accept for the benefit of mankind if he is willing to dare the wrath of Zeus from whom the fire is stolen. In order to persuade Inachus to accept the gift, Prometheus launches into an attack on the tyranny of Zeus and at the same time praises the dignity and nobility of man. In order to develop the potentialities of man, Inachus must have confidence in his own human power and turn his worship from Zeus to Prometheus. Inachus has more power for good than Zeus has for ill. In describing the nature of the gift he has brought, Prometheus explains the history of fire, which first ruled the world until supplanted by air. Air (as in Bridges's "Low Barometer") is seen as a providential and life-giving force. Air is associated with Reason, which created man at Air's request. Man should forget Zeus, rely on his reason, and trust in Prometheus.

The chorus performs several times in this, the first part of the poem. Immediately after the prologue it sings a hymn to Zeus and describes the birth of Zeus, the dance of the Curetes and Dactyls around the infant Zeus, the marriage of Zeus to Hera, and the gift of the golden apples. At the end of Part 1, the chorus recites an "Ode" on wonder.

Part 2 opens with a conversation between Inachus and his wife, Argeia, concerning the acceptance of the gift of fire. Argeia is terrified at the thought of incurring the wrath of Zeus and recites a long list of punishments meted out by the gods on previous occasions. This is the first example of extended rhetorical augmentation in the masque. Prometheus (under pressure from Inachus) foretells the fate of their daughter Io, who, transformed by Zeus to a heifer, will wander the earth pursued by a gadfly. The long catalogue of places she will visit before finding peace in Egypt is the second example of rhetorical augmentation. Prometheus then foretells his own fate—to be imprisoned on a rock and tortured. Thus, when Inachus accepts the benefits of fire from Prometheus, both giver and receiver are quite aware of the sacrifices being made. Prometheus becomes a sacrificial hero. Before lighting the wood on the altar, Prometheus explains that his motivation is really hatred of Zeus rather than love of man. Prometheus lights the fire, writes his own name on the altar in place of Zeus, and exits unobserved. From now on, man will worship Prometheus rather than Zeus. In this part the chorus sings a hymn on the tragic lot of man after the account of the punishment of Io and Prometheus, a fire-chorus during the lighting of the fire, and a final chorus in praise of Prometheus.

Bridges's treatment of the Prometheus myth naturally invites comparison with the treatment of the myth by Aeschylus and Shelley. The style and structure of his masque has certain affinities with Greek drama and with Milton's *Comus* and *Samson Agonistes*.

There is a widely held theory that Aeschylus's *Prometheus Bound* was the first part of a trilogy, the other two plays (now lost) being *Prometheus Unbound* and *Prometheus the Fire-Bearer*. Neither Shelley in *Prometheus Unbound* nor Bridges in *Prometheus the Firegiver* was attempting a historical restoration of a lost play. Shelley disliked the reconciliation between Prometheus and Jupiter that (according to tradition) ended Aeschylus's version of the story—a reconciliation in which Prometheus was freed in return for revealing his secret: the danger threatened to the empire of Jupiter by the consummation of the marriage between Jupiter and Thetis. Shelley felt this "catastrophe" too feeble. Furthermore, the romantic poet wished to include a great deal of sociological and utopian matter completely foreign to the original Greek. As for the third play of the trilogy, Bridges could not have given us a historical reconstruction even if he had wished to, for very little is known about it. Yet, each poet has, in his own time and way, attempted to repair the loss of the missing drama, and it is not inappropriate to consider the three plays as a trilogy that treats in dramatic form the legend of the Titan Prometheus who, in pity for man, dared the wrath of Zeus to give man the arts of civilization.

In comparing the Shelleyan Prometheus and Bridges's hero, one immediately notices marked differences. Shelley wrote his play to further his sociological and political aims (Bridges did not), and his Prometheus is the hero and herald of a new social order to follow the aftermath of the Napoleonic Wars. The religion of humanity replaces the evil religions of the past. Prometheus becomes not only a hero but the god of this new religion, to be worshipped in place of Jupiter. Shelley's Prometheus is the ideal sacrificial god-hero motivated by love, particularly love for mankind, and forsaking all hatred and revenge. Shelley's play, then, is the romantic poet's prophecy of a new social order.

Shelley's Prometheus is also the focus and symbol of the poet's idealistic metaphysics, Platonic and neo-Platonic—a complete reversal, as Carl Grabo has demonstrated, of his earlier materialism as expressed in *Queen Mab*.[7] As a vehicle for Shelley's idealistic metaphysics, the play becomes a complicated allegory in which the characters are personified abstractions. Asia is passionate creative love, Panthea sympathetic love and hope, Ione the spirit of love in beauty and perhaps memory, Demogorgon necessity, the Furies injustice and violence, and so on. Prometheus himself is not only the regenerator of mankind but, according to Carl Grabo, also the mind or will of man, the oversoul, the personification of mankind as a whole. He has creative will and, in fact, created his enemy Jupiter (Zeus) who attempts to enslave him in the bonds of custom and necessity but falls victim eventually to the assertion of Prometheus's triumphant free will. Both play and protagonist are extremely complex. Carl Grabo says, "The reader of *Prometheus Unbound* comes, with reason, to suspect a double meaning in every line and a symbol in every image."[8]

Bridges' intentions are much less ambitious. His hero is of smaller dimensions than Shelley's; his play is much less complex. It is not systematically allegorical, although there is some symbolism. Bridges's Prometheus suggests the sacrificial Christ and, as Guérard observes, the play "retells the transition of human worship from Zeus to Prometheus, and symbolizes the substitution of the God of Love of the New Testament for the angry God of the Old Testament."[9] But Bridges's hero is not the perfect god-man of Shelley's play. Bridges's Prometheus states at the end of the play, for example, that his principal motive was hatred of Zeus and not love of man, whereas Shelley's hero purges himself of all hatred. Furthermore, Bridges's Prometheus is not the prophet of a new revolutionary social order nor is he a repository for neo-Platonic metaphysics. He, rather, as in the Greek original, is a patron of knowledge who gives the arts of civilization to man.

In tone, style, and dramatic structure as well as in his concept of his hero, Bridges is also closer to the Greek than Shelley. There are passages of considerable grandeur in Shelley's play and a justifiably famous line: "Pinnacled dim in the intense inane." But much of Shelley's play is rhetorical bombast. The Earth says (or sings) :

The joy, the triumph, the delight, the madness!
The boundless, overflowing, bursting gladness,
The vaporous exultation not to be confined!
        Ha! Ha! the animation of delight.

                                (4.321–24)

Bridges's style is sometimes flat, dull, and stereotyped, but it never sinks to this level. As Hopkins has noted, the inspiration for Bridges's choruses is usually Greek; he singles out "O my vague desires" for special praise. The model for the blank verse seems to be Milton's *Comus*, not Shelley (although Bridges admired Shelley), and Milton was closer to the Greek style than Shelley. Guérard has drawn attention to the close parallel (amounting to pastiche) between the opening lines of Bridges's masque and those of *Comus*.

BRIDGES—From high Olympus and the aetherial courts,
        Where mighty Zeus our angry king confirms
        The Fates' decrees and bends the wills of the gods,
        I come: and on the earth step with glad foot.
           This variegated ocean-floor of the air,
        The changeful circle of fair land, that lies
        Heaven's dial, sisterly mirror of night and day:
        The wide o'er-wandered plain, this nether world
        My truant haunt is, when from jealous eyes
        I steal, for hither 'tis I steal, and here
        Unseen repair my joy; yet not unseen
        Methinks, nor seen unguessed of him I seek.

MILTON—Before the starry threshold of *Joves* court
        My mansion is, where those immortal shapes
        Of bright aereal spirits live insphear'd
        In regions mild of calm and serene air,
        Above the smoak and stirr of this dim spot,
        Which men call Earth, and with low-thoughted care
        Confin'd and pester'd in this pinfold heer,
        Strive to keep up a frail and feavourish beeing
        Unmindfull of the crown that vertue gives
        After this mortal change to her true servants
        Amongst the enthron'd gods on sainted seats.

The movement, texture, syntax, and diction of Bridges's lines are obviously in the early Miltonic style of *Comus* and (in my opinion) not inferior to Milton.

It is well known that Milton in his later *Samson Agonistes* was strongly influenced by Aeschylus's *Prometheus Bound*:

> In both plays the action, judged by modern standards, is slight. In both plays all the minor characters are obviously intended to serve as foils for the protagonist. The plot in each consists largely of a series of visits; and in each a greatly suffering hero laments his misery to all who will listen.[10]

Bridges also went back to Greek drama for technical devices such as stichomythia and the chorus, and the form of *Prometheus the Firegiver* is similar to that of *Samson Agonistes* in the same way that Milton's poem has affinities with Aeschylus's *Prometheus Bound*. Yet in tone, as stated above, Bridges's play is much closer to *Comus* than to *Samson Agonistes* or to *Prometheus Bound*, for those plays are tragedies whereas *Prometheus the Firegiver* is a masque. Paulette Hooper notes several characteristics of the masque in Bridges's play—disguise (Prometheus is disguised as a shepherd, which suggests his Christ-like nature), pastoral setting and motifs, a feast or at least preparations for a feast, and dialogue-debate.[11]

In *Prometheus the Firegiver*, Bridges has, in my opinion, achieved a moving closet masque. It would probably not be a success on the stage. It has the unbroken, serene, and slightly remote style that is more effective when read than when acted, and, like Bridges's narrative poem *Eros and Psyche*, the entire drama reminds one of a Greek frieze. As in the much later *Testament of Beauty*, some of the most effective passages are digressive descriptions. In the following dialogue the servant of Inachus is showing Prometheus the faggots he will place on the cold altar of Zeus, hoping for a miraculous fire to light them. The occasion gives Bridges a chance for description not absolutely necessary to the scene yet welcome for its intrinsic beauty:

> SERV.   Thou seest this faggot which I now unbind,
> How it is packed within.
> PR.   I see the cones
> And needles of the fir, which by the wind
> In melancholy places ceaselessly

Sighing are strewn upon the tufted floor.
      SERV.   These took I from a sheltered bank, whereon
The sun looks down at noon; for there is need
The things be dry. these first I spread; and then
Small sticks that snap i' the hand.
      PR.   Such are enough
To burden the slow flight of labouring rooks,
When on the leafless tree-tops in young March
Their glossy herds assembling soothe the air
With cries of solemn joy and cawings loud.
And such the long-necked herons will bear to mend
Their airy platform, when the loving spring
Bids them take thought for their expected young.

                                        (Part 1, ll. 144–59)

There is, then, rather frequent digressive material of this kind, and yet there is a unity of tone throughout, achieved in part by recurrent use of cold-fire imagery.[12] There is also another kind of unity. In this passage from *Prometheus* that, remember, was Bridges's earliest long poem, the spirit of the ancient Greeks as well as the spirit of the elderly poet who many years later completed his career with *The Testament of Beauty* seem to be speaking in unison:

      PR. Nor is there any spirit on Earth astir,
Nor 'neath the airy vault, nor yet beyond
In any dweller in far-reaching space,
Nobler or dearer than the spirit of man:
That spirit which lives in each and will not die,
That wooeth beauty, and for all good things
Urgeth a voice, or in still passion sigheth,
And where he loveth draweth the heart with him.

                                        (Pt. 1, ll. 163–70)

Demeter

Demeter,[13] too, is probably better as a closet drama than it is as a stage play, although it has more of a stage history than *Prometheus*. It was "Written for the Ladies at Somerville College & Acted by Them at the Inauguration of Their New Building in 1904."[14] The original performance of June 11 was repeated by request on June 22. It was acted again at Somerville College June 26, 1954, in celebration of the fiftieth anniversary of the first production.[15] There was also a performance at the Frensham School in New South Wales in 1933.[16] The program of the anniversary production of 1954 carried a poem by Bridges's daughter Elizabeth Daryush, who was also present at the original performance. She draws attention to the relevance of the ancient myth to modern times:

> Fled is that April age; we since have found
> Through two grave wars its winter underground,
> But in an altered world the myth sublime
> Seems even more closely molded to our time.

Music for the first production by Sir Henry Hadow (published by Oxford in 1905) was adapted for the fiftieth anniversary performance with an overture added by Leo Black.[17] A brief account of the first production is in the correspondence between Bridges and Henry Bradley, who attended the Somerville performance. Bradley wrote: "The masque bore the test of representation splendidly . . . I heard only one opinion—that the performance was a thorough success."[18]

Demeter was written over a brief period of time—perhaps as short as four or five weeks.[19] During this period, Bridges's daughter Margaret was seriously ill, and this fact may have deepened and darkened the tone of the masque.[20]

The masque presents the rape of Persephone by Hades, the search for her by her mother, Demeter, and Persephone's return to earth from the underworld for two-thirds of each year. After a prologue by Hades and an opening chorus by the Oceanides on the beauty of spring and of Persephone, Persephone enters accompanied by Artemis, who represents the life of instinct and feeling, and by Athena, who represents the life of wisdom and reason. Persephone, who expresses her joy in the innocent beauties of the flowers that she is gathering for Zeus's festival, is forewarned by Athena that evil and ugliness are as real as beauty and innocence and, in fact, may be the source and cause of beauty on earth. Artemis advises her that in her enjoyment of flowers she is limiting her response to life—animals have more life than flowers and are for that reason more beautiful. At the end of act 1 Persephone, while praising the individual loveliness of each flower she gathers, is carried off by Hades who (with the permission of Zeus) will make her queen of Hell. Throughout this act, the flowerlike Persephone is the epitome and symbol of innocent girlhood.

The reader learns from the chorus that opens the second act that Demeter for ten days has been searching in vain for her daughter. In a dialogue with the chorus, Demeter threatens to annihilate all living things on earth and in heaven by destroying the plants that nourish and sustain life—not an idle threat, for Demeter is goddess of the grain. Hermes enters with a conciliatory message from Zeus requesting Demeter to return to the courts of heaven. Demeter refuses, curses her brother Zeus, and hands Hermes a bag of seeds implying that unless her daughter is returned she will destroy the crops of the earth. At the end of the act the chorus, expressing its grief and terror, decides to seek the help of Poseidon, hoping that if earth and sea are against him, Zeus will order the return of Persephone.

The final act commences a year later with the chorus saluting the dawn and expressing their expectation of Persephone's imminent arrival. Demeter, while hoping for the best, has premonitions of trouble and upon being asked to forego her curse against mankind and the gods if Persephone is not returned, explains that she too learned compassion for man after she had assumed human form and acted as nursemaid for Demophoön, the child of King Keleos who, upon her command, founded the temple and mysteries of Eleusis to teach mankind to live with sorrow. She is overjoyed at the arrival of Persephone led by Hermes at the command of Zeus, but she soon learns that she will have her daughter only two-thirds of the year. During the winter months, as a result of eating the pomegranate seed in Hell, Persephone must return to the underworld. Demeter's grief is assuaged by Persephone, who explains that she also has learned to live with sorrow, that her annual death and rebirth have been decreed by fate, and that she is both a queen and a goddess— queen of the underworld and goddess of flowers. It is obvious that her life with Hades and her vision of pure evil in the Cave of Cacophysia have changed her from an innocent girl to a mature woman, although she does not say so. She promises to join Demeter at the spring festival at Eleusis, and the masque ends with a song by the chorus as they garland Persephone with flowers.

The story of Persephone, like that of Eros and Psyche, has not escaped the attention of the depth psychologists. Erich Neumann writes: "Seen from the standpoint of the matriarchal world, every marriage is a rape of Kore, the virginal bloom, by Hades, the ravishing earthly aspect of the hostile male. . . . The fundamental situation of the feminine . . . is the primordial relation of identity between daughter and mother. For this reason the approach of the male always and in every case means separation. Marriage is always a mystery, but also a mystery of death. . . . [It] is for the feminine destiny, transformation, and the profoundest mystery of life. . . . It is no accident that the central symbol of maiden-hood is a flower. . . . and it is extremely significant that the consummation of marriage, the destruction of virginity, should be known as deflowering."[21] In telling the story of Demeter grieving at her separation from her daughter and of Persephone's mysterious transformation from girlhood to womanhood as a result of her experience with Hades, Bridges is dealing with archetypal material before it was subjected to the analysis of Jung, Kerényi, and Neumann. However, his poetic rendition of this material is not only true to its sources, including the Homeric Hymn to Demeter, but it also has affinities with and foreshadows later psychological analyses.

The blank verse of *Demeter* is, perhaps, not quite so impres-sive as that of the earlier *Prometheus,* nor is it as close to Milton's *Comus.* It is somewhat looser in its rhythms and textures, perhaps because of Bridges's experiments in classical prosody that he undertook during the period between the writing of the two masques. There is one speech by Hermes, for instance, near the end of the second act, in which Bridges tells us in his notes to the first edition[22] that he deliberately introduces a sapphic line and several hexameters to express in halting meter the embarrass-ment of Hermes in delivering his awkward message from Zeus. On the whole, however, the verse maintains a quality of grave beauty quite appropriate to the masque form and its classical subject. Flower imagery is dominant and recurrent. There are several extraordinarily lovely passages that anticipate similar descriptions in *The Testament of Beauty.* In these lines from act 2 Demeter is threatening to destroy the crops and in their place plant the wild flowers loved by Persephone:

> There shall be dearth, and yet so gay the dearth
> That all the land shall look in holiday

With mockery of foison; every field
With splendour aflame. For wheat the useless poppy
In sheeted scarlet; and for barley and oats
The blue and yellow weeds that mock men's toil,
Centaury and marigold in chequer'd plots:
Where seed is sown, or none, shall dandelions
And wretched ragwort vie, orchis and iris
And garish daisy, and for every flower
That in this vale she pluckt, shall spring a thousand.
Where'er she stept anemones shall crowd,
And the sweet violet.

(2.547–59)

Bridges had been experimenting with poems in Stone's classical prosody for several years before he started composing *Demeter*. Three of the choruses of *Demeter* are in this prosody. The three-part chorus that opens act 1 is in choriambics with what Bridges called "freak" rhymes in the second part;[23] the song that opens act 3 is in alcaics followed by an ode in iambics. These opening lines of the chorus from the first act are a fair sample of Bridges's skill in handling the stately yet dancelike rhythms of the classical choriambic metre:

Gay and lovely is earth, man's decorate dwelling;
With fresh beauty ever varying hour to hour.
As now bathed in azure joy she awakeneth
With bright morn to the sun's life-giving effluence,
Or sunk into solemn darkness aneath the stars
In mysterious awe slumbereth out the night,
Then from darkness again plunging again to day.

(1.56–62)

The Plays

In addition to his two masques, Bridges wrote eight plays between the years 1882 and 1894. He stated that all except *Nero 1* were intended for the stage, but only one, his least serious drama, *The Humours of the Court,* received a production of professional caliber when the Oxford University Dramatic Society staged it in London in 1930. *Achilles in Scyros* was given an amateur performance by the ladies of Cheltenham College in 1912, which Bridges called a failure. During the course of writing the plays and shortly thereafter, he expressed in his letters the hope and indeed the expectation that some of them would be produced. But by 1907, when he wrote the letter to A. H. Bullen quoted below, he was probably resigned to their being relegated to the status of closet drama. Bridges (as far as I can determine) did not frequently attend the theater, and he probably had little or no knowledge of the practical side of play production. Furthermore, he refused to be unduly influenced by the tastes of a large public audience, and he was quite conscious of the fact that his plays, whether read or staged, would have only a limited, elite following. He felt, quite correctly, that the drama of his day had been debased by appealing to popular taste. In writing to Bullen on October 15, 1907, concerning a review of his essay on the influence of the audience on Shakespeare, he said, ". . . there are always plenty of brutes, and the London audiences do more harm to the drama today than they did in Shakespeare's time— but in a different manner. They are a chief cause of the badness of the art."[24]

Bridges's plays, then, must be considered as closet drama, to be read as literature with the action occurring in the mind's eye only. And this is not a bad fate. Most Elizabethan plays except for a dozen or so by Shakespeare and several by Marlowe and Jonson are seldom acted today with any great success. Yet many Elizabethan plays, including, of course, those by Shakespeare, have great interest when read. Most readers were moved by *Hamlet, Othello,* and *Macbeth* before seeing those plays staged. And indeed many were somewhat disappointed when they first saw them in a dramatic production. They did not come up to the performances viewed in the imagination. And as for *Lear,* I never have seen an adequate production of it. Yet the play can be read and reread as a work of literature. Poetic closet drama, then, as Yvor Winters, Albert Guérard, and others have argued, is a legitimate literary genre. And as representatives of this genre, Bridges's best plays—*Nero 1* and *2, The Christian Captives,* and *Achilles in Scyros*—hold a distinguished place in the history of poetic drama, comparable, certainly, to the plays of Yeats and Eliot.

The Nero Plays

. . . since the drama of Nero's court is above all one of character, we must admit our inability to penetrate the innermost workings of the heart of the chief actors: no one can pretend to understand Nero, Agrippina, or even Seneca fully.[25]

When the mother of Nero, the formidable Agrippina, took as her third husband her uncle, the Emperor Claudius, she immediately put into execution her plan to bring her own son to the throne instead of the legitimate heir, Britannicus, the son of Claudius. She had Seneca recalled from exile and made tutor to her son; she assigned her man Afranius Burrus as praetorian prefect in charge of the guard. Nero was thus placed under the care and protection of a renowned philosopher and a highly esteemed soldier. Claudius was persuaded to adopt Nero as a guardian to the younger Britannicus and to marry him to his own daughter Octavia, sister of Britannicus. By the time he was fifteen he was making public appearances and speaking before the Senate. Agrippina believed that once her "pumpkin" husband[26] was dead and her son on the throne, her ascendancy over the young and grateful son would be assured and her own political power absolute. To hasten the demise of her elderly husband, she had her specialist Locusta prepare a dish of poisoned mushrooms for him (mushrooms being one of his favorite dishes), and when the poison was too slow in working and Claudius seemed in danger of recovery, she hastened his demise by inducing her physician to tickle his throat with a poisoned feather. This had the desired effect, and Seneca was instructed to prepare the inaugural address for the new emperor as Agrippina destroyed the will of Claudius, which named his own son Britannicus as heir to the throne.

Nero had not reached his seventeenth birthday when he ascended the throne in A.D. 54. He was still under the domination of Seneca, and for a short time his reign prospered. He was hailed as the new Augustus. Seneca dedicated his essay *Clementia* to him, and upon Seneca's advice he stressed clemency in his first speeches. He seems to have been at this time not unattractive physically and fond of games, music, poetry, and feasting—all

of which made him popular. However, domestic difficulties with
Octavia, the jealousy of his mother who felt herself neglected,
the necessity (as he felt it) of getting rid of his rival Britannicus,
his egomaniacal and grandiose schemes for glorifying himself
and his reign by enlarging his palaces and rebuilding Rome,
and his extravagant licentiousness soon brought him into disrepute. By the time he had cut his throat at the age of thirty, he
had murdered his stepbrother Britannicus by poisoning his wine
at one of his feasts, had killed his own mother for conspiring
with Britannicus against him, had ordered the suicide of Seneca,
had divorced his wife Octavia on trumped up charges of adultery
and then had ordered her murder, had sent countless men he
considered his enemies to death, and had persecuted the Christians
on the false charge of burning Rome.

The story of Nero is dramatic to the point of melodrama, and
several of the characters, particularly Agrippina and Seneca and
perhaps Nero himself, appear to be of sufficient complexity to
interest a playwright with any pretension to psychological and
philosophical insights. Yet before Bridges's dramas, only one
important play on the subject (Racine's *Britannicus*) had been
written in any language.[27]

Bridges, in his letters to Samuel Butler, has left us a brief
account of his composition of the two Nero plays:

> I always wished to write drama. I began at school. When I
> seriously set to the work I approached the difficulties thro' a
> masque "Prometheus the Firegiver."
>
> Next I took a historical subject which gave me characters
> and plot, and used the Shakespearian form as the best known
> to me: and I wrote "Nero pt I." I never meant it for more
> than an exercise, else I shd not have taken the cumbrous
> Shakespearian form, with its innumerable drampers [*dramatis
> personae*] and frequent changes of scene. This play was a good
> deal read and praised by historians—so I did print it.
>
> After that I went on my own way and the other plays are
> such as I shd like to see on the stage. Except that "Nero II"
> which I was much urged to write in continuation of "Nero I"
> has some of the difficulties of the first part, and tho' it is made
> for acting, yet it wd need trouble and expense and a very strong
> cast to put it on the stage. I think perhaps it is the best thing
> I have done.[28]

Nero 1 was first published in 1885 and *Nero 2* was first published
in 1894. The evidence in Bridges's letters to Hopkins suggests

that *Nero 1* was begun as early as 1882 and perhaps finished or almost finished by the spring of 1883.[29] There is no evidence as to the exact date of composition of *Nero 2,* but in all probability at least nine years intervened between the writing of the two parts—years that were largely taken up with the composition of at least five other plays. One would expect, therefore, that as the result of experience, *Nero 2* would be superior to the first part, and indeed Bridges felt that it was the best play he had written. *Nero 1,* however, has been more favorably received by those few critics who have read Bridges's plays. It is possible that *Nero 2* would act better than *Nero 1;* however, as closet drama, *Nero 1* appears to have more unity and coherence and dramatic appeal. Guérard was quite correct in noting the fragmentary structure of *Nero 2.*[30]

Nero 1, subtitled "An historical Tragedy of the first part of the reign of the emperor Nero," covers the years A.D. 54–59. As the play opens one finds that the brash young Nero, recently proclaimed emperor, has already by his youthful follies upset honest and conservative senators like Thrasea and Priscus, alienated his mother Agrippina by neglecting her, and has mistreated and alienated his wife Octavia. The central dramatic conflict of the play has started—the struggle between Nero and his mother for control of the empire. Nero's suspicion of Britannicus, dislike of his wife, and (soon to begin) infatuation with Poppaea, wife of his friend Otho, are complicating and contributory factors of this dominating central conflict. As Thrasea and Priscus discuss the political situation, they express the conviction that the best hope for the Empire lies in the fact that Seneca may still have some influence over his former pupil. In his first appearance on the stage, Nero is laying grandiose plans for the enlargement of his palace and he quite callously orders his friend Rufus's house destroyed to make room for it, and then just as grandiloquently promises to give Rufus twice what his house is worth. He is already showing symptoms of a pride that will develop into paranoia. He believes that the civilized world has its epitome in him and what is good for him is good for the world:

> Be all human hopes summed up in mine
> And reach their goal.

By satisfying his own desires and aspirations he will bring in an age of universal joy and peace. At the end of the first scene he

asks Otho to bring Poppaea to supper, which Otho declines to
do. During the remainder of the first act Octavia is seen com-
plaining to her brother, Britannicus, of Nero's neglect and of
his suspicion that she is plotting to remove Nero and elevate
her brother; Agrippina is seen turning against her son and
attempting to persuade Brittanicus to conspire to have Nero
removed and he, the righful heir, made emperor. Britannicus,
at first suspicious, finally agrees to have Burrus, praetorian
prefect, sounded out. If he can be won over, he will bring the
guards with him, and Nero can be removed without civil war.
In the next act Burrus and Seneca (who both owe their positions
at court to Agrippina) refuse to enter into her plot to supplant
Nero with Britannicus, and in a typical tirade she threatens
vengeance on them both. A counterplot against Agrippina is
launched by her sister-in-law Domitia (whose husband Agrippina
had murdered). She plans to further Poppaea's suit of Nero so
that Poppaea's influence will supplant Agrippina's; then (because through her astrologer she has learned of Agrippina's
intrigue against Nero) she hastens to inform Nero of his mother's
intrigues against him. Nero is convinced (or pretends to be
convinced) and confronts his mother with the charges; she makes
counter charges against Seneca and Burrus. Nero appears to
change his mind and believe his mother. This is the first of a
series of apparent vacillations by Nero who seems too easily
swayed first by one person and then by another. On the other
hand, there are suggestions in Bridges's portrayal of his character
that he believes most of the people surrounding him are secret
enemies and that he decides early in his career to get rid of them.
The climactic scene in act 3 is the poisoning of Britannicus at
Nero's supper party. The destruction of the legitimate heir was
probably inevitable, but it was hastened by Nero's growing
awareness of the intrigues swirling around him. Before the death
of Britannicus, Seneca had informed Nero of Agrippina's attempt to seduce him into a plot to elevate Britannicus, and
he advised the exile of Nero's mother, for without her presence
Britannicus would be no longer dangerous. Nero explains in
a soliloquy that he will destroy Britannicus first and, if necessary,
take care of his mother later. In the fourth act Poppaea is succeeding in her plans to implicate Nero, and Domitia is plotting
to use Poppaea's growing influence to destroy Agrippina. She
arranges to have her friend Paris tell Nero when he is drunk

the false story that Agrippina is planning to marry the nobleman Plautus and put him on the throne. The story will be supported by Poppaea, who also wants to get rid of Agrippina. The charge is made and Nero appears to believe it, but is cautioned by Burrus to give Agrippina a chance to defend herself, which she easily does, and Nero seems to change his mind again, but when Agrippina asks him to dismiss Poppaea, Nero (inflamed by his passion for Otho's wife) decides that Agrippina must be removed. He calls in his admiral and arranges to have her drowned at sea in what will appear to be an accident. In the final act Nero (who has some ability as an amateur actor) convinces both Seneca and his mother that he and Agrippina are reconciled. While Seneca is congratulating himself on his success in persuading Nero to adopt a moderate course, Agrippina is cajoled aboard a ship of the Roman navy. The canopy above her, weighted with lead, collapses, but she escapes by swimming ashore, much to Nero's astonishment and wrath. She pretends to be unaware of the plot against her, but in vain. Nero orders his guard to murder her, and Seneca, who is present, does not interfere. She dies bravely, asking a soldier to kill her by piercing the womb that bore her monstrous son.

Nero 2, subtitled "From the Death of Burrus to the Death of Seneca Comprising the Conspiracy of Piso," covers the years A.D. 64–65 and, as its subtitle states, is concerned mainly with the conspiracy of Piso and its failure. During the first act it is learned that Nero is now married to Poppaea, that Burrus is dead and has been succeeded by the villainous Tigellinus, that Caesar, under his influence and with Seneca out of favor, has lost all restraint, and that a plot, later known as Piso's conspiracy, is being formed against him. The conspirators call on Seneca at his house, acquaint him with the conspiracy, and offer to make him Caesar. He declines and refuses to take an active part in the plot. (The degree of the historical Seneca's involvement has not been established. In Bridges's play Seneca has knowledge of the conspiracy and thus is technically guilty of treason for not revealing it to Nero.) Seneca realizes the danger he is in because of his knowledge; yet he cannot save himself by betraying his friends. He resolves on retirement, renunciation of his wealth, and withdrawal from Rome. When his wife Paullina enters with the news that Rome is burning he, in an unheroic moment, **exclaims**

                                                a general calamity
      Might turn attention from me.

The flames of burning Rome that can be seen in the background
rage throughout the second act and rise to a climax in the final
scene. Nero is in good spirits throughout the act; his palace
has been saved from the flames; he (under the influence of
Tigellinus) thinks the people are for him because of his lavish
entertainments; he looks forward to an extravagant feast at
Agrippa's pool when the flames subside; he plans to build a new
Rome in which the good life will be achieved by everyone
following his own natural desires. He casually orders the deaths
of Sylla and Plautus upon the advice of Tigellinus. He refuses
Seneca's request for retirement and, after a preliminary show
of cordiality, berates him for his pompous and pious rhetoric.
The act ends with a quarrel between Nero and his new wife,
who has insisted that he get rid of his former mistress Acte.
The crescendo of the flames of burning Rome in the background
is symbolic of her jealousy. In act 3 Nero has blamed the burning
of Rome on the Christians. Clitus, a Christian convert and brother
to the beautiful Epicharis, a non-Christian girl who has been
briefly seen earlier serving drinks to naval officers in a tavern, is
being dragged off by the pagan mob to be burnt, with Epicharis
following, begging for mercy. She soon becomes involved in the
plot against Nero, motivated by the desire to avenge her brother's
death, and, in her endurance under torture, she is, finally, the
bravest and indeed the most admirable character in the play.
The nobleman Piso has been informed of the conspiracy and
agrees to accept the crown after Nero is dead, but he will take
no active part in the proposed assassination of Caesar. In the
following act, Epicharis, who has taken on the assignment of
winning over Proculus, admiral of the navy, to the side of the
conspirators, fails in her mission and is haled before Nero. But
she half convinces him (with the aid of a friend of Seneca) that
it was all a jest. Caesar has her kept under custody. When the
failure of Epicharis's mission is apparent, the conspirators in
desperation arrange to kill Nero the following day. In the meantime Nero learns from another conspirator, Scevinus, who had
imprudently boasted of his plans to stab Caesar, that the plot
in which Epicharis was involved was real, and, furious at being
tricked by a beautiful but common woman, he orders her tor-

tured. The act ends with Nero blaming all his troubles on the Christians and with his statement *"I am their Anti-Christ."* The final act is taken up mainly with the trial of the conspirators with (ironically) one of them as yet uncharged—Rufus, acting as judge. Under threat of torture, the names of all involved in the plot are divulged; even Rufus is denounced and arrested as the trial ends. One of the guilty party, in order to escape torture, falsely denounces Seneca as having an active part in the plot. Epicharis, broken on the wheel, is carried in a litter to give substantiating evidence for the prosecution by naming the conspirators—but instead in her dying speech she denounces Nero and states that all the world hates him. Nero is reluctant to order the execution of his old teacher Seneca; but Tigellinus convinces him it is the politic thing to do. Even if Seneca is innocent, he no longer admires his former pupil and will in fact turn many against him. In the final scene Seneca, in imitation of Socrates, discourses with his friends on immortality before he allows his veins to be opened. Paullina, his wife, insists on dying with him as the curtain falls. It should be added that the historical Paullina allowed her arms to be bound up again and survived her husband, but this is not in the play.

The dominating characters in these two plays are Nero, Agrippina, and Seneca, and of these Seneca is the most complex and the most interesting. Bridges's depiction of this sometimes paradoxical and morally inconsistent character appears to be in accord with the prevailing scholarly opinion; perhaps Bridges's philosopher is a shade more admirable than his original. There is some evidence to justify the charge that the historical Seneca in his activities at Nero's court was at times self-serving and almost cowardly, particularly in his apparent connivance at Britannicus's death. A. Momigliano says: "Seneca and Burrus cannot well have been unaware of the plot against Britannicus; in any event here as on other occasions they showed themselves prepared to accept a *fait accompli*."[31] Seneca of course owed a debt to Agrippina for recalling him from the exile imposed by Claudius and appointing him as tutor to Nero. He began repaying his debt by writing a stinging satire against Claudius, *Apocolocyntosis,* shortly after the murdered emperor had been deified by Nero and Agrippina. The deification of Claudius was a fraud as far as Agrippina was concerned; she knew that eventually the murder would be widely known, and she probably welcomed the tarnishing of her victim's image. Eventually Agrippina became a threat to Nero (or so he supposed), and it is probable that the historical Seneca was aware of the murder plot against her and did nothing to check it. As public feeling against Nero grew it is also likely that Seneca joined Piso's conspiracy against him. Tacitus is not sure whether he was an active participant or not, but the modern scholar Momigliano states: "There can be no doubt that Seneca shared in the conspiracy."[32] A. P. Ball summarizes Seneca's character: ". . . he preached stoical detachment and rolled in material opulence, he taught virtue and yet remained at Nero's court, he praised Claudius in *Consolatio ad Polybium* while Claudius was alive and heaped mockery on Claudius as soon as he was dead."[33] Yet all accounts agree that after being convicted of treason he met his end with dignity and courage.

Bridges's Seneca is the astute politician, quite aware of his responsibilities as tutor and advisor to the young Nero and proud of his ability to manage these dangerous court personalities (setting one off against the other) for the advantage of the state. He says early in *Nero 1*:

> I place them all as chess men, and I find
> Delight in difficulty.

> (2.1.471–72)

He is at this point guilty of intellectual pride. He thinks he can move men like pieces in a game; he soon finds that he cannot do so, and he loses control of both Nero and Agrippina. In Seneca there is pride caused by awareness of superior intellect; in Nero, pride motivated by superior political power. Both men are destroyed by their hubris, although it should be added that in Nero's case he is eventually a pathological personality, which is not true of Seneca. Seneca refuses to blame himself for the way his pupil is turning out. On learning of Nero's plot against his mother, he says: "I take unto myself no self reproach." Up to this point Seneca has been loyal to his emperor and, in fact, had advised him for the good of the state to get rid of Agrippina —but by exile, not murder. The murder of Agrippina turns out to be too much for Seneca, although he did nothing to stop it. In *Nero 2* he walks the fine line between loyalty to his friends,

the Pisan conspirators whom he does not betray, and fidelity to
his oath to Nero. He compromises by begging Nero for the
opportunity to get rid of his wealth and return to the country, a
request that is refused. From then on his role is passive, and
when he is falsely accused by Natalis of taking an active part
in the conspiracy, he submits to Nero's will and commits suicide.

The character of Seneca as Bridges conceived it is summed
up in speeches by two relatively honest men, Burrus and Thrasea.
Burrus says to his face in *Nero 1*:

> I know you, Seneca,
> For a man of many parts, a scholar, poet,
> Lawyer, and politician, what you will;
> A courtier too besides, a man of business,
> A money-maker; in short, a man of the world,
> That like a ship lifting to every wave,
> Heeling to every blast, makes good her way
> And leaves no track. Now what I ask is this:
> How ride so lightly with the times, and yet
> Be the unbending stoic, the philosopher,
> The rock, I say, that planted in the deep
> Moves not a hair, but sees the buffeting breakers
> Boil and withdraw? Which is the matter, Seneca?
> Nay, 'tis a pertinent and friendly question—
> I'll take your answer as we go along.

(5.1.2757–72)

But they exit before Seneca can reply. Thrasea, as honest as
Burrus and probably more astute, when Priscus tells him in
Nero 2 that he has joined a plot to kill Nero and elevate Seneca,
gives the following devastating portrait of the philosopher:

> Think you that he,
> Who laughed at Claudius' death; who let be slain
> His old friend and protectress Agrippina;
> Who glozed the murder of Britannicus;
> Who hid his protest when Octavia fell;
> That he will turn about and say, "Such things
> I did for Nero, and the good of Rome:
> Now, since he sings at Naples on the stage,
> I do repent me, and will kill my pupil;
> Will take myself the power I made for him,

And shew how I intended he should rule!"
This were a Roman but not Seneca.

(1.1.102–13)

It is obvious that Bridges is quite aware of the paradoxical
nature of the historical character he is attempting to re-create.

All accounts agree on the calmness with which the Stoic
philosopher met his death, and the final scene in *Nero 2* in
which he says farewell to his friends is perhaps the most moving
in the two plays:

These be the last hours of my life: I'd say
To you, my friends, what I have most at heart.
And first rejoice with me that I depart
With all my senses perfect, not as some,
Tortured by pain and praying for release;
Nor like a man, who walking in the dark,
Comes to a brink upright, and steppeth over
Unhesitatingly, because he knows not.
Nor is my term much shortened, I shall die
Like aged Socrates, and with his hope
That the spirit doth not perish;—I mean not
A senseless immortality of fame:
That I shall have, but more I'll have; I dream
Of life in which I may be Seneca again,
Seneca still.
    Thr. Now if thou couldst convince us,
Seneca, of that 'twere worthy thy last hour.
Teach me to picture what thou thinkst to see,
That land betwixt oblivion and regret;
Where is't? how is it?
    Sen.   It lies not in the scope
Of demonstration, Thrasea; but my heart
Bears witness to it: the best that I could say
Is in my books. What all mankind desires,
The mind requires; what it requires believes:
And calls it truth. I hold that one God made us,
And at our death receives our spirits kindly:
We shall meet elsewhere those whom we leave here.

(5.5.2604–28)

The character of Agrippina presents fewer problems to the

dramatist. She is all of a piece—a completely ruthless and ambitious woman, a Lady Macbeth many times over (compare her murder record with that of Shakespeare's character!), with a lust for power that she gains with the aid of sexual appeal, profound guile, a resolute will, and unflinching courage and physical stamina. She is, of course, completely without conscience or remorse. One cannot imagine her (to compare her with Lady Macbeth again) in a sleepwalking scene. She is the evil woman incarnate, yet with qualities that compel admiration—her complete discipline over her emotions and her courage. After having been deceived (a rare event in her life) by Nero's show of reconciliation, she escapes from his murder plot by swimming ashore and then is composed enough to pretend to her son that she has no suspicion of him. Bridges, I believe, has been successful in re-creating this formidable person. The ferocity of her nature is clearly evident in her tirade against Seneca when (in *Nero 1*) the philosopher refused to join the plot against Nero:

> Philosopher! come, teach me thy philosophy.
> Tell me how I may be a dauntless Stoic
> And a most pitiful ass. Show me thy method
> Of magnanimity and self-denial,
> Which makes of slaves the richest men in Rome.
> Philosopher! Ay, thou that teachest youth
> Dishonesty, and coinest honied speeches
> To gloss iniquity, sand without lime,
> Out, out upon thee!
> Thou miserable, painful, hackney-themed
> Botcher of tragedies, that deem'st thyself
> A new Euripides, a second Cato:
> A pedant rather, pander and murderer.
> I'll let Rome know how pumpkin Claudius died;
> I'll not be ashamed to say, 'twas I that spiced
> His fatal mushroom. Honest Seneca
> Stood by and smiled.

(2.1.633–49)

Her courage and self-control are most clearly manifested in the final moments of her life. Paris describes her murder in Part 1:

> None answered, and awhile
> Was such delay as makes the indivisible

And smallest point of time various and broad;
For Agrippina, when she saw her lie
Fail of its aim, ventured no more, as knowing
There was no wiser plea; but let her eyes
Indifferently wander round her foes,
Counting their strength. Then looked I to have seen
Her spring, for her cheeks swelled, and 'neath her robe
Her foot moved; ay, and had she been but armed,
One would have fallen. But if she had the thought
She set it by, choosing to take her death
With dignity. Then Anicetus raised
His sword, and I fled out beyond the door
To see no more. First Tigellinus' voice,
"To death, thou wretch!" then blows, but not a groan;
Only she showed her spirit to the last,
And made some choice of death, offering her body,
"That bare the monster," crying with that curse,
"Strike here, strike here!"

(5.2.3199–217)

According to the literary tradition that has come down to us, Nero was as ferocious as his mother. But, partly no doubt because of his youth, his emotions were less controlled, and, in fact, he seems in Bridges's plays to be fairly easily controlled by others. Like Agrippina he is completely immoral and insensitive. His willpower, unlike Agrippina's, is softened by debauchery. Bridges's Nero makes a number of speeches characterizing himself and his philosophy, such as the following from Part 2:

Well, and is't not sense
To seek for happiness the natural way?
Not by the notions of philosophers,
Who fashion theoretic right and wrong
From books; or if they judge mankind at all,
Judge by themselves, who are unlike the rest,
Scarce human. 'Tis the soundest principle
To follow nature; and what nature is
I well perceive. I judge all by myself.
The appetites are universal gifts:
Caesar will never stoop to flatter Caesar
By such pretence of difference, nor withhold
From others what himself loves. I believe

That no man in the world worth calling man
Is what philosophers term pure and good;—
Nor woman either. All would gratify
The strong desires of nature, and all shall,
While I am emperor.

(2.767–85)

Men, he says in the above passage, should follow their natural desires, and he will, by his example, encourage them to do so. However, when Seneca and Poppaea follow *their* natural desires Nero takes a different attitude:

See how
'Tis private pleasure that she seeks, nought else:
And Seneca the same. That's the true fire,
That burns unquenchable in all human hearts.
Let it rage, and consume the rotten timbers
Of old convention, the dry mouldering houses
Of sad philosophy, that in their stead
I may build up the free and ample structure
Of modern wisdom.

(*Nero 2*, 2.1020–28)

Here the private appetites are seen as a destructive force that Nero may employ for final universal good. The passions will destroy the old Rome, and on its ashes he will build a new Rome. The speech has a modern ring, and like modern revolutionists he never defines clearly and consistently the nature of the new society he will build.

Petronius, the probable author of the famous *Satyricon,* was, according to legend, the complete hedonist, the refined and elegant voluptuary, the arbiter of taste (such as it was) at Nero's court. He spent his days in sleep and his nights in various pleasures including the reading and writing of poetry. He defends his life style:

You little think
What charm the witching night hath for her lovers:
How her solemnity doth deepen thought,
And bring again the lost hellenic Muse
To sing from heaven: Or on moonlit swards

Of fancy shadows in transfigured scene
The history of man.—Thus, like a god,
I dwell; and take the early morning cries
For calls to sleep; and from divinity
Fall to forgetfulness, while bustling day
Ravages life; and know no more of it,—
Your riot and din, the plots and crimes of Rome,—
Than doth a diver in Arabian seas,
Plunging for pearls beneath the lonely blue:
But o'er my slumbering head soft airs of dreamland
Rock their wild honey-blooms, till the sly stars
Once more are venturing forth, and I awake.

(*Nero 2*, 3.2.1393–410)

For him, poetry was of some importance as one of the arts, but the greatest of all the arts, he argues at Nero's banquet, is cookery. A nice bit of irony occurs when, at the height of his peroration on the benefits of healthful cookery, Britannicus falls dead from Nero's poisoned wine. In *Nero 2*, Petronius plays host to the Pisan conspirators but takes no active part in the plot. Nevertheless, Nero condemns him. According to legend, he was a long time dying—opening his veins, then binding them up again so that he could finish his account of Nero's secret debaucheries. It was sent to Nero under seal; the seal was then broken to prevent its misuse. His last act before he died was to break a statue that he knew Nero coveted.

Epicharis gets a brief mention in Tacitus as a member of the Pisan conspiracy who refused to talk under torture and who committed suicide by strangling herself on her litter while she was being questioned. In Bridges's play she died under similar circumstances, but not by suicide. The motivation for her fortitude is not given in Tacitus, but it is in Bridges's play where her brother Clitus, a Christian convert, is burned to death by Nero's order under the pretense that the Christians set fire to Rome. She is particularly effective in her tirade against Nero just before her death:

I know thou fear'st. Then who is most thy foe?
Whom first to kill? That I can tell thee, Caesar:
For none of all thou see'st, or ever saw'st,
Or wilt see again, nay, not thy murdered mother,
Thy poisoned brother, thy beheaded wife,

Whose bloody ghosts watch on the banks of hell
To mark thy doom, none hateth thee as I,
Defieth thee as I, curseth thee as I.
O emperor of the world, thine hour is come.
Within thy cankered soul dwell side by side
Remorse and vanity to drive thee mad:
The grecian furies hound thee, the christian devils
Dispute for thee. Fly to thy dunghill, Caesar,
Where thou must perish. . . .

(*Nero 2*, 5.2.2389–402)

The most perceptive criticism of the Nero plays to date is that of Hopkins in his letters to Bridges and that of Albert Guérard. Hopkins's comments are confined to *Nero 1*, for he did not live to see the completion of *Nero 2*. Hopkins wrote to Bridges, "Nero is a great work, it appears to me, breathing a true dramatic life," and he particularly admired the lines describing the awful silence just preceding the murder of Agrippina:

None answered, and awhile
Was such delay as made the indivisible
And smallest point of time various and broad.[34]

Guérard considers the plays to be equal in achievement to *The Testament of Beauty,* although he faults *Nero 2* for its loose structure. Guérard's analysis of Seneca and his relationship with Nero is particularly discerning.[35] Seneca is a man of principle who swims with the tide; he is weak and cowardly, and he often relies on the judgement of others, particularly on Burrus and Thrasea. By his casuistical reasoning he winks at the murder of Britannicus, and, by pretending that things are not so bad as pictured by Nero's enemies, he justifies to himself his refusal to join Piso's conspiracy. "The characterization of Seneca in the two plays seems to me one of the most profound in dramatic literature."[36]

Palicio

Palicio, "A Romantic Drama in Five Acts in the Elizabethan Manner" as the subtitle of the first edition (1890) describes it, was, with the exception of *Nero 1,* Bridges's earliest drama, being completed in 1883. Bridges himself thought well of it, for he wrote to Sir Henry Newbolt on February 5, 1902, nine years after its composition, "I was rather pleased with Palicio when I went through the proofs, which was more than I expected. I found it quite exciting."[37]

As Bridges points out in his note to the first edition, the play, which takes place in and near Palermo in 1500 during the Spanish occupation of Sicily, is only quasi-historical. It is primarily a romantic story of love and intrigue in the noble brigand tradition with a historical background adjusted to suit dramatic needs. Bridges's chief interest seems to be in the partly historical, partly legendary (and indeed, in Bridges's view, almost mythological) character of Giovanni Palicio, who led a band of brigand patriots against the tyrannical Spanish administration The title page of the first edition carried a fragment from Aeschylus that, says Bridges, "suggests a truly ancient origin for the family of Palicio." The fragment of four lines (of which Bridges quotes the last two lines) is from Aeschylus's lost play *The Women of Aetna*, which was based on the story of the Sicilian maiden named Aetna who after an affair with Zeus prayed that the earth would swallow her up to protect her from Hera. Her prayer was answered and she went underground, but when her twin boys were born the earth opened up to deliver them. They were called *Palici* because they had come back. Bridges's hero Palicio also "comes back" from the darkness of the dungeon to the light of freedom and a happy marriage. The Palici, incidentally, were worshipped as gods near Aetna. Bridges tells us in his 1894 note that the Palicio family, after centuries of distinguished history, degenerated and became associated with the Mafia. He conjectures that the last of the Palicio family may have been the half-witted anarchist lynched by a New Orleans mob in March 1891 for his part in the killing of the head of police.

Here in summary is the plot of Bridges's play. Margaret, sister to Manuel who is chief justiciary of Sicily under the Spanish Viceroy Hugo, secretly sympathizes with the rebel Sicilian patriotic movement and falls in love with their leader under the most romantic of conditions. Palicio, the last descendant of an ancient and semidivine noble Sicilian family but now an outlaw, escapes after being wounded from prison in the guise of a maiden, and is secretly given shelter and administered to first by Manuel and then by Margaret, who discovers him in a room in her brother's palazzo. She has his wounds treated by a young surgeon (in love with her), and her solicitude for Palicio is known by and welcomed by her brother Manuel who wrongly believes her to be in love with the surgeon. Margaret arranges the escape of Palicio and joins him and his rebel band in the hills above Monreale. But although Margaret loves Palicio, she has nothing but contempt for his brigand associates, and, while sympathizing with the cause of Sicilian freedom, she does not think Palicio and his gang of cutthroats are the right people to govern Sicily. Consequently, she extracts a promise from Palicio that if his conspiracy to take Palermo in the next few days fails, he will give up his revolt and settle down to another way of life as her husband. Then she betrays the leaders of the conspiracy to the Spanish viceroy but without mentioning Palicio's name. The conspirators are immediately apprehended and Palicio, breaking his word to Margaret, voluntarily joins them in prison so they will not think that he has betrayed them. In the conflict between love and honor it would seem that love had lost. But Bridges arranges a happy conclusion by means of a political *deus ex machina*. Margaret visits Palicio in prison and admits her betrayal of Palicio's friends. He rages and almost kills her, but, after Margaret has fainted and been revived, the lover in Palicio gains the ascendancy and he begs her forgiveness. He escapes from prison once again. In the final scene the news arrives in Palermo that the old king (as rumored) is dead; a new king, Frederick, has been crowned. Manuel, the brother of Margaret, is named the new ruler of Sicily. He hastens to give amnesty to Palicio and his men and blesses the forthcoming marriage of Margaret and Palicio.

The main story is complicated by various subplots, the most important being the love affair between Manuel and Constance in which Sicilian patriotism also leads to difficulties. Constance is the daughter of Hugo, the corrupt and tyrannical viceroy whom Manuel despises yet up to a certain point must protect because of his love for his daughter, which is threatened by the arrival of Duke Philip, the Spanish commissioner, a former lover of Constance who had abandoned her. Upon his arrival in Palermo he falls in love with her again (or at least thinks he does), becomes jealous of Manuel, and plots to destroy him while attempting without success to make love to Constance.

When the Duke discovers blood on the carpet in Manuel's palazzo, he suspects (correctly) that Manuel has been concealing the wounded Palicio and denounces him for treason before the viceroy who orders him to be sent to Spain for trial and commands his daughter to break off her engagement and marry the Duke. But again a happy denouement is arranged. Manuel, reported dead by drowning when the ship carrying him to Spain ran afoul of the French fleet, actually escapes and enters Palermo disguised as a friar, in which disguise he listens to Duke Philip (who it seems is a just man at heart) confess that he had destroyed his friend Manuel and made love to Manuel's fiancée. With the news of King Frederick's ascension, Manuel throws off his friar's garments, becomes ruler of Sicily on command of the king, and plans to marry Constance on the same day as Margaret and Palicio's wedding.

The play has all the trappings of romantic drama with two love affairs, two disguises, a repentant villain (the Duke), and an unrepentant villain, Blasco, who betrays various characters at moments most convenient to the plot. The critics (even Bridges's friends) have been severe with this play. However, if it is read, as Bridges intended it to be read, as a tale of romantic love, intrigue, and adventure with possible mythological overtones but with no real philosophical nor psychological depth, it seems to me fairly successful. The story has action and suspense, and there are many passages of satisfactory poetry, particularly in the love scenes between Palicio and Margaret. Perhaps the best poetry in the play occurs in the scene between Margaret and Palicio in the hills above Monreale (act 3, scene 4). Palicio is troubled because of a dream that Margaret has turned against him, which in a way is partly true (because of her betrayal of the conspirators), with news of their capture imminent. To distract him and herself from somber thoughts she begins a fanciful speech on the subject of why a certain kind of flower will grow in one place and not in another:

> The spirits of good men allowed to wander
> After their death about the mortal sites
> Where once they dwelt, there where they love to rest
> Shed virtue on the soil, as doth a ray
> Of sunlight: but the immortal qualities
> By which their races differ, as they once
> Differed in blood alive, with various power

Favour the various vegetable germs
With kindred Specialty. This herb, I think,
Grows where the Greek hath been. Its beauty shows
A subtle and full knowledge, and betrays
A genius of contrivance. Seest thou how
The fading emerald and azure blent
On the white petals are immeshed about
With delicate sprigs of green? 'Tis therefore called
Love-in-a-mist.

(3.4.1774–89)

This is Shakespearean pastiche, of course, but very competent pastiche, and not inappropriately addressed to a hero whose family name may derive from the Palici, the Chthonic earth-gods.

The Return of Ulysses

In *The Return of Ulysses* (completed 1884) Bridges took great care in transforming his epic Homeric material into what he hoped would be a successful actable play and in planning in considerable detail how the drama was to be performed, costumed, and staged. In a note, dated 1884, to the first edition (1890) he gave detailed instructions for the setting of the last three acts during which Ulysses confronts and finally slays the suitors of Penelope, and in the McKisson Library copy of the 1890 edition of *Ulysses*, presented to Lionel Muirhead May 24, 1890,[38] there are two elaborate pencil drawings realizing Bridges's directions for the stage setting described above. *The Return of Ulysses* has never been acted, and what reputation it has comes from reading only. But a "closet" drama was not the intention of the author.

The play opens on the seashore of Ithaca, thick with mist, through which Ulysses can barely be discerned asleep under a tree. In the foreground the goddess Athena addresses the audience in dignified and measured tones, recounting how Ulysses, returned to his native Ithaca after twenty years of war and wandering, was landed on the shore and loaded with gifts by friendly mariners. Ulysses awakens, not knowing where he is because of the mists, and not recognizing Athena who is disguised as a youth. In the subsequent dialogue Ulysses (after making up a fictitious story about his past to deceive the unknown youth) discovers Athena's identity and where he is. He is wary of returning immediately to his wife Penelope because of what happened to the returning Agamemnon, who was murdered by *his* wife. He is reassured by Athena that Penelope is faithful, that his son Telemachus is well, but that his house is besieged by riotous suitors intent on despoiling him of his property and on forcing Penelope to marry one of them. Athena insists that, with the aid of Telemachus now returning from Lacedaemon where Athena had sent him to save him from the wooers who were planning his murder, Ulysses should slay all of the suitors for violating her laws of domesticity and hospitality. He vows to do so with the promise of Athena's help and, disguised as a beggar, awaits Telemachus in the hut of the faithful swineherd Eumaeus, a former king who now governs only swine. The beggar-Ulysses (unrecognized by Eumaeus), after learning further details of his wife's situation from the swineherd, assures him that Ulysses is still alive, that he has met him, and that he will return to Ithaca. Eumaeus is doubtful, considering the best hope to be in Telemachus, who now enters, tells of his escape from the suitors who had planned to ambush his ship in the straits, and sends the swineherd to Penelope to announce his safe return and to warn her against this beggar whom he had just met and who claimed to know Ulysses. When Athena temporarily transforms Ulysses to himself, Telemachus, at first thinking he is a god but recognizing him as his father, agrees with his father that because of the command of Athena all the suitors must be destroyed. Ulysses, resuming his disguise as a beggar, accompanies Telemachus to the court of Penelope.

The last three acts take place in the great hall of the house of Ulysses, described in the stage directions quoted above. The safe return of Telemachus is announced to the discomfiture of all the suitors and especially of Antinous, their ringleader. (Only Amphinomus had refused to take part in the plot against the life of Telemachus.) They are upbraided by Penelope for plotting against her son, who then enters and tells Penelope of his visits to the courts of Nestor and of Menelaus and Helen and of his meeting with a beggar who had recent news of Ulysses and who will be brought to the hall so that he can tell his story to Penelope. When Ulysses (as beggar) enters with Eumaeus, his uncouth presence draws insults from Antinous and others, but he is allowed to remain under the protection of Telemachus. Their brawling is interrupted by Penelope who accepts gifts from the leading suitors, retires, and then reenters to still renewed outcry against the presence of Ulysses. She is left alone with Ulysses. who tells a fictitious story of his past life and moves the queen with an accurate description of Ulysses as he was dressed twenty years ago. She tells him of the device of weaving and unweaving the shroud for Laertes in order to delay the necessity of choosing a husband and of her dream of the twenty geese destroyed by an eagle who proclaimed he was Ulysses killing the suitors. But she doubts the veracity of the dream and admits to Ulysses that she has decided to accept the suitor who will win the archery contest the next day—the one who can most easily string the bow of Ulysses and send an arrow through twelve ax heads. Ulysses tells her to stage the contest and to await the arrival of her husband. In the final act the ax heads have been set up but loosened on their handles so they cannot be used as weapons by the suitors. (A precautionary measure introduced by Bridges but overlooked by Homer. But then perhaps, as Bridges's friend Butler claimed, the author of the *Odyssey* was a woman.) All of the weapons have been taken from the walls, ostensibly for cleaning. Penelope (unawares) gets the plot in motion by announcing that she will marry the winner of the archery contest, the gates of the outer court have been locked by the neatherd informed of the plot—Eumaeus too has been informed—and Ulysses with his three allies is now ready to spring the trap. All who try fail to bend the bow, and Penelope is prevailed upon to retire. Ulysses takes the bow, strings it, and shoots Antinous without warning. Then he jumps onto the raised dais where he is joined by Telemachus, the neatherd, and Eumaeus. He reveals himself as Ulysses. In the resulting melee Eurymachus is killed on stage, and the rest fly and are slaughtered offstage in the courtyard. The battle is reported on stage to Penelope by the maids who describe the transformation of Ulysses from a beggar into a godlike figure in golden armor. At the end of the play Ulysses and Penelope embrace. Athena in a final speech orders Ulysses to purify his house, seek atonement at the oracle, and return Eumaeus to his native kingdom, all of which he promises to do.

Bridges's play is derived from Books 13–23 of the *Odyssey*, with much of the material reduced and some digressive scenes omitted for the sake of dramatic unity. Also, some incidents, such as the shooting of an arrow by Ulysses through the twelve axes, have been deleted, probably because of the difficulties of stage presentation, and several violent scenes have been deleted, probably for the sake of decorum. Bridges went to great pains to construct a heroic drama faithful to the Greek spirit with the essential elements of the story of the return of Ulysses intact and yet possessing the unity of structure and tone necessary for a successful play. He preserved a kind of decorum necessary to avoid shocking a Victorian audience, and he ended his play with his hero engaged in a generous act (not in Homer), the restoration of the swineherd to his native kingdom. Because the play has never been acted it is difficult to guess at its probable success or failure as stage drama.

As to the quality of the poetry, Bridges has told us in his note to the play that he made use of the translation by S. H. Butcher and Andrew Lang, and, of course, he was thoroughly familiar with the original Greek. Actually, Bridges's blank verse owes little to this translation. In writing to Samuel Butler February 21, 1900, Bridges said:

> I expect that I do not quite agree with you about "Elizabethan English." I hate the sham of it, such as Lang writes. I can't read it. Your translation of the Iliad seems to me much more Elizabethan than his Odyssey. My difference is thus—The English of 1600 is the unalterable and familiar basis of our speech. It is fixed by Shakespeare and the translation of the Bible. Later styles, as Pope & Macaulay, age very quickly and have little behind them—good style must always have a relation to Shakespeare—Then poetry implies some idealization of language, and this is most aptly supplied by the old tradition.[39]

In this letter Bridges admits that he dislikes Lang's sham Elizabethan English, that he admires the true Elizabethan English of Shakespeare, and that good style must always have some relation to Shakespeare, particularly in its idealization of language, and he defends his own occasional use of archaic expressions because of their pleasing sound. One of the best passages in the play is that spoken by Ulysses in disguise as a warning to one of the more admirable suitors, Amphinomus:

Of all that moves and breathes upon the earth,

Nothing is found more unstable than man.
Awhile his spirit within him is gay, his limbs
Light, and he saith, No ill shall overtake me.
Then evil comes: and lo! he beareth it
Patiently, in its turn as God provides.
So I too once looked to be ever happy,
And gave the rein to wantonness, and now—
Thou seest me . . . Wherefore, say I, let no man
Be lawless, but in quiet and reserve
Possess whatever good the gods have sent.
And this I witness 'gainst the deeds I see,
These wooers, full of mischief, making waste,
And doing such dishonour to a lady,
Whose lord not long will tarry: nay, I tell thee
He is very near,—ay, near. May thy good genius
Withdraw thee soon, lest thou shouldst meet his wrath
When he returns: for not without blood-spilling
Will they be sundered, these infatuate wooers
And he, when he comes stepping thro' his house.

(4.1754–73)

The speech is lucid and dignified and in keeping with Ulysses'
generous heroic character—he is giving Amphinomus fair warning
of disaster. The style is sparse and lean yet dignified and subtle,
but without the kind of poetic beauty that makes for so many
quotable passages in Bridges's *Prometheus* and *Demeter* and
Achilles in Scyros. There is a passage in an unpublished letter
to Henry Newbolt that reveals how carefully Bridges worked
with his source materials. After thanking Newbolt for his favorable review of *Ulysses*,[40] he writes: "I can't imagine the return
of Ulysses without that long interview with Penelope. I thought
when I wrote it that I had converted the Epic into Drama with
almost imperceptible touches. The result is that no one sees the
difference."[41] Bridges, obviously, was quite conscious of the
necessity of modifying Homer's epic material to make it suitable
for drama. What he meant by "almost imperceptible touches"
is brought out in the sentences that follow in his letter to
Newbolt. He is talking about the passage quoted above in which
Ulysses warns Amphinomus, and particularly these lines:

Nothing is found more unstable than man.
Awhile his spirit within him is gay, his limbs

Light, and he saith, No ill shall overtake me.
Then evil comes: and lo! he beareth it
Patiently, in its turn as God provides.
So I too once looked to be ever happy,
And gave the rein to wantonness, and now—
Thou seest me . . . Wherefore, say I, let no man
Be lawless, but in quiet and reserve
Possess whatever good the gods have sent.

(4.1755–64)

Bridges explains that his word *unstable* is closer to the Greek in spirit and in meaning than the words chosen by other translators, including the *feebler* of Butcher and Lang, and he points out that the phrase "and now—/Thou seest me" is his own addition to and improvement of Homer for dramatic purposes, as indeed it is, for there are Jamesian depths of irony in the phrase. Amphinomus sees him as a beggar fallen in fortune, as an example that man's lot is unstable. Yet he doesn't really *see* him for what he is—the hero in disguise who will soon demonstrate to Amphinomus that man's fortune is indeed unstable, for Amphinomus, at that moment the most favored of the suitors and on the verge (he thinks) of marrying Penelope, is, in fact, very close to death at the hands of the man who is warning him. Here is Bridges's comment: "Even in the speech of Ulysses to Amphinomus the addition of 'and now—thou seest me' strikes no one—and I doubt if any translator has ever seen the point of ἀκιδνότερον in that speech XVIII. 130. But I don't know the translators well. But Butcher & Lang have 'feebler.' Butcher (with all his pretences) has 'vainest.' Pope 'vain.' Cowper 'weak.' All missing the point, which is one of the biggest things in the whole of poetry—."[42]

As was true of all of Bridges's plays, *Ulysses* was not widely noticed. William Butler Yeats's critique (published in 1896) must therefore have been especially welcome. He singles out for praise the introduction of Athena during the slaughter of the suitors:

Ah! now what can I see?
Who cometh? Lo! a dazzling helm, a spear
Of silver or electron; sharp and swift
The piercings. How they fall! Ha! shields are raised

In vain. I am blinded, or the beggar-man
Hath waxed in strength. He is changed, he is young. O strange!
He is all in golden armour. These are gods
That slay the suitors.[43]

(5.2688–95)

Yeats comments on this passage as follows:

> The coming of Athene helmed in "silver or electron" and
> her transformation of Ulysses are not, as the way is with the
> only modern dramas that popular criticism holds to be dramatic,
> the climax of an excitement of the nerves, but of that unearthly
> excitement which has wisdom for fruit, and is of like kind with
> the ecstasy of the seers, an altar flame, unshaken by the winds
> of the world, and burning every moment with whiter and purer
> brilliance.[44]

The Feast of Bacchus

*The Feast of Bacchus, A Comedy in the Latin Manner &
Partly Translated from Terence* was (according to the author's
note to the first edition) completed at Yattendon in June 1885,
and first published in a privately printed edition by Daniel in
1889. Subsequent editions have only very minor differences from
the first. Bridges always thought that this play was actable and
that it would have audience appeal. He wrote to Yeats on June
30, 1899, "I don't expect or really wish to see a play of mine on
the stage, but I feel confident that when the 'Feast of Bacchus'
gets there, it will stay."[45] A few months later in a letter to Samuel
Butler he said, "If you sh^d read my 'Feast of Bacchus' tell me if
its broad humanities interest you."[46]

The play takes place in a suburb of Athens close to the house
of Chremes, a retired merchant, and his neighbor Menedemus,
an elderly Athenian gentleman turned farmer. The time is second
century B.C. The duration of the action is a few hours. The
Aristotelian unities of time, place, and plot are preserved. In
the opening conversation the reader discovers that Menedemus
(according to his solicitous and officious friend Chremes) is
working himself to death with manual labor. Why? When he is
obviously rich? Menedemus (he is the self-torturer of Bridges's
source, Terence's *Heautontimorumenos, The Self-Torturer,* which

Terence probably translated or adapted from a lost play of
Menander) is punishing himself for his harsh conduct toward
his son Clinia brought on by a love affair with the poverty-
stricken Antiphila and resulting in Clinia's running away six
months previously to fight with the armies of the king of Persia.
Thus the major theme of the play is introduced, which is also
that of Terence's *Heautontimorumenos* as defined by Gilbert
Norwood: "The whole work is a comment on this—the trouble
caused by lack of confidence between father and son, in families
where restraint is in the atmosphere."[47] The grief-stricken father
has sold his large house and his furniture and has moved to the
suburbs. Chremes sympathizes with his neighbor and explains
that he too, fifteen years previously, lost a daughter in Ephesus
by kidnapping. He attempts to cheer Menedemus up by inviting
him to a double celebration at his house—a birthday party
and the feast of Bacchus. Menedemus declines the invitation.
Pamphilus, son of Chremes, and Clinia who has just returned
secretly from Persia enter, Clinia's return being motivated by his
decision to marry Antiphila. Clinia is astonished to learn that
his father is now in a modest house living the life of a farmer.
He is concerned about two things—what is his father's present
attitude toward him and has Antiphila been faithful to him? In
a conversation between Chremes and his son Pamphilus the
reader discovers that Chremes takes the side of Menedemus in
his treatment of his son. Fathers should maintain strict discipline
and their sons should obey them. Thus the meddlesome and
somewhat tyrannical Chremes is a foil for the now repentant
Menedemus, the one representing strict discipline in the father-
son relationship, the other permissiveness. Pamphilus, because of
this attitude of his father, is hesitant to introduce his friend
Clinia to him in his real person and introduces him under the
name of Clitipho. Chremes takes an instant liking to him.
Pamphilus now arranges to have Antiphila, Clinia (disguised as
Clitipho), and his own mistress, the extravagant and vulgar
Gorgo, invited to the feast of Bacchus at his house. Chremes is
curious to see Clinia's sweetheart who has caused all the trouble.
Philolaches, friend of Pamphilus and an actor eager to exhibit
his histrionic skill, now enters the scene and starts complicating
matters. He wants to go to Menedemus, disguised as a Persian,
tell him he has news of his son Clinia, and ascertain the father's
present attitude toward Clinia and his proposed marriage. He

may even tell Menedemus his son is dead and watch his reaction
to the news. Pamphilus is elated with the idea and decides
that he will act as a Persian chief with Philolaches as interpreter.
Then, one more complication is introduced. Chremes will be told
that Gorgo is Clinia's sweetheart and that Antiphila is Pamphilus's
girl. Chremes will probably let Antiphila alone and concern
himself with Gorgo as he meddles in Menedemus's affairs. Thus
the disguised Clinia can have Antiphila to himself and pursue
his romance without interruption. All of this seems complicated
in summary—but it is less so than Terence's play—and it would
probably be clear enough on the stage.

In the second act, Philolaches assures Clinia that he has
visited Antiphila and that she is faithful, so that when the two
girls, Gorgo and Antiphila, enter, Clinia is ecstatic with joy as
is Antiphila. But they persist in their disguises, and Chremes,
concentrating on Gorgo as the supposed sweetheart of Clinia, is
shocked beyond words at her vulgarity and capacity for his best
wine. He makes up his mind to warn Menedemus against her
and he is annoyed with his son for bringing her into the house.
Philolaches now has another brilliant idea. Pamphilus has been
having difficulty in satisfying his mistress Gorgo's love of money.
Why not trick the stingy Chremes into giving her fifty pounds
as a bribe to renounce her supposed boyfriend Clinia? Thus
(Chremes will be told) if Clinia returns he will be rid of the
girl and reconciled with his father. Chremes will have ingratiated
himself with his rich neighbor and will surely be repaid by him.
Gorgo, who is of course aware of the deception, falls in with the
plot and succeeds in collecting forty pounds from Chremes by
giving him a signed paper renouncing her supposed sweetheart
Clinia forever.

In the third act, Philolaches and Pamphilus, disguised as
Persians, approach Chremes and tell him of the supposed death
of Clinia (Chremes pretending he is Menedemus in order to
extract information). Chremes believes the story and is stunned.
He has to pretend grief at the death of his supposed son, while
in fact he is really irritated with the awareness that Menedemus
will not now refund the forty pounds. He tells Menedemus the
news of his son's reported demise, but Menedemus is skeptical.
He had had a look at the "Persians" and had heard some of their
gobbledygook, which, he assures Chremes, was not Persian. However, he says that if the story turns out to be true he will settle

his money on Clinia's girl; if the news is false and his son returns
he will bless the marriage. Chremes, worried about his forty
pounds, tries to convince Menedemus that his son's sweetheart
is worthless and shows him the paper that Gorgo signed.
Menedemus agrees to go to Chremes' house and look his son's
girl over (whom, of course, he had never met), and Chremes
goes off in search of the "Persians."

In act 4 Sostrata, Chremes' wife, enters with the news (not
entirely unexpected by the audience or reader) that Antiphila
is their long lost daughter as evidenced by jewelry in her possession. The story is checked, turns out to be true, and Clinia (still
disguised as Clitipho) is overjoyed. Now nothing can stop his
marriage with Antiphila. The rest of this act and act 5 are
taken up with the wrath of Chremes. He realizes that he has
been deceived several times over. The "Persians" were actually
his own son and Philolaches, Clinia (whom he had reported as
dead) was in fact under his roof all of the time disguised as
Clitipho, the vulgar Gorgo is the mistress of his own son and
not the sweetheart of Menedemus's son, and the appeal to his
generosity on behalf of Menedemus has resulted in the loss of
forty pounds, which his son's mistress has gone off to spend.
His only solace is the discovery of his lost daughter Antiphila
whom he is happy to see married to Clinia. As for his own
son, Pamphilus, he disinherits him and orders him out of the
house. The combined efforts of his wife, Philolaches, Clinia,
Menedemus, and Pamphilus himself do not shake his resolve.
Only when Antiphila calls him father for the first time and pleads
for Pamphilus does he relent on condition that his son marry
a respectable woman, which Pamphilus agrees to do. Menedemus
promises to refund the forty pounds lost to Gorgo.

Bridges spent considerable effort on the versification of *The
Feast of Bacchus*. In a note he explains his employment of the
principles of stress prosody that were later elaborated and defined
in his essay "On the Prosody of Accentual Verse" (first published
in 1893, final version published in 1921). He says in his 1885
note to *The Feast of Bacchus*:

> The metre is a line of six stresses, written according to the
> rules of English rhythm; and its correspondence with the Latin
> comic trimeter is an accident. A stress never carries more than
> one long syllable with it,—the comic vein allowing some

license as to what is reckoned as long;—but as there are no conventional stresses (except sometimes in the sixth place; or in the third, where the mid-verse break usual in English six-stressed verse is observed, or that place is occupied by a proper name), the accompanying syllables may have any relation of place to their carrying stress. Where four or more short unstressed syllables come together, a stress is distributed or lost: but this distributed stress can only occur in the second, fourth, and fifth place, on account of the rules which govern the other places. Any infringements of these laws are faults or liberties of rhythm: and it will be evident that the best has not been made of the metre. A natural emphasizing of the sense gives the rhythm.

By the phrase *no conventional stresses* Bridges meant that (with certain exceptions he notes) every accented syllable in the scansion would be naturally accented in speaking the line aloud. The result is easy, free-flowing lines each of which usually has six speech accents. The number of syllables is undetermined and the pattern of feet is undetermined—"the accompanying syllables may have any relation of place to their carrying stress." At its best this verse has the flexibility of normal speech with the aesthetic advantage of a discernible rhythm. At its worst the verse is indistinguishable from prose. The following is a fair sample of the verse. In act 1 Clinia is characterizing the meddle-some Chremes. He does not want him prying into his love affair with Antiphila:

Now save me from my friends! Indeed this Pamphilus
Will be my ruin: I wish to heaven I had never met him.
He'll tell his father next, this old Ionian huckster,
Sponge-mongering Chremes; the gods defend me from him,
And his family feast, and his prosy wisdom! I thought to spend
This day of my return with sweet Antiphila:
And here I am, caught by the ears. And yet my troublesome friend
Means well: I should not hurt his feelings; but at any cost
I must go clear, and in one matter I cannot yield:
I will not have Antiphila brought to the judgement seat
Of this suburban oracle. What has he to do
With me and mine, my father or her—to push his nose
Into our affairs?

(1.365–77)

In structure and in characterization *The Feast of Bacchus* seems to me somewhat superior to the source play by Terence. As for its style, Bridges's experimental stress versification is successful, that is, it makes for easy and pleasant reading, and it is of considerable interest to those concerned with the development of Bridges's prosody. The subject matter is somewhat less trivial than Bridges's only other comedy, *The Humours of the Court,* and for that reason may be considered superior to that play.

The Christian Captives

The Christian Captives, written in 1886 and first published in 1890, is, according to Bridges's note at the end of the play, "on the same subject as Calderón's *El Principe Constante,* from which the little common to both plays is directly taken." As this comment suggests, Bridges's work is substantially different from its source, the most obvious change being the transformation of the heroine. Calderón's Fénix, the beautiful daughter of the king of Fez, is a weak character dominated by her father. Although she is in love with General Muley, she agrees to marry Tarudante, king of Morocco, at the command of her father who needs his troops in his war against the Portuguese. At the end of the play, the living Fénix (together with Muley and Tarudante) is exchanged for the body of the Christian Fernando, the constant prince, the implication being that Fernando dead is worth more than Fénix alive. That is, spiritual values, as represented by the prince, are superior to worldly values, as represented by Fénix. It has been argued that there may be some erotic attraction between Fénix and Fernando;[48] however, her love, such as it is, is for Muley. Bridges's heroine, renamed Almeh, has, on the other hand, an overwhelming love for Ferdinand that is stronger than her religious faith, for she is converted to Christianity, and indeed stronger than life itself, for she dies of grief and self-imposed starvation upon discovering the body of Ferdinand. The central theme of Calderón's play is the triumph over its enemies of the Roman Catholic church as represented by Fernando, the constant prince, whose steadfast faith is unshaken by either the vicissitudes of fortune or cruel imprisonment. The title of Bridges's drama (it is named after the chorus) indicates the importance of the victory of Christianity in that play also, for it is the singing of the captives that first attracted the Moorish princess Almeh to the Christian religion and to Ferdinand. However, it is the love of Ferdinand and Almeh that overcomes the barriers of race and faith that is the central concern of Bridges's play, or at least its chief source of appeal to a British audience. Calderón's *Constant Prince* is primarily a religious drama written to appeal to a Catholic, Spanish audience. Bridges's *Christian Captives* is primarily a love play written to appeal to a British, Protestant audience. Both plays are strongly nationalistic, for obvious reasons in the case of Calderón. But the triumph of Portuguese arms also had its appeal to the British, who have been allied to Portugal for centuries. Furthermore, as Bridges points out in his note, "the whole story has this claim on English attention, that the Portuguese Regulus, *Ferdinand,* and his brother *Henry,* 'the *Navigator*' of more solid renown, were grand-children of *John of Gaunt,* through his daughter *Philippa,* who married *King Joam I.*"

The two plays are based on historical events. In 1415 the Portuguese took the town of Ceuta from the Moors. In 1437 they sent an unsuccessful expedition against Tangiers (a city not far from Ceuta) led by Henry the Navigator (Enrique) and Ferdinand (Fernando). The Moors, after surrounding the Portuguese, demanded the surrender of Ceuta in exchange for their lives. Ferdinand was left with the Moors as hostage; Henry left for Portugal to arrange terms for the surrender of Ceuta, which the Portuguese eventually refused. Ferdinand remained captive until his death in Fez in 1443. Relics of his body were brought to Portugal in 1451; his remains were recovered in 1471 and buried in the Monastery of Batalha.[49]

By the time Calderón wrote his play in 1628, Fernando had become a legendary figure, a saint and martyr who alone was responsible for the refusal to surrender Ceuta to the Moors (whereas, in fact, the responsibility was elsewhere). In the first act, which takes place near the sea in the gardens of the king of Fez, the daughter of the king enters to the sound of the Christian captives singing. She is melancholy and no longer pleased by the sea or by the gardens. She is in love with Muley, the king's nephew and a general, but she soon learns that she must marry Tarudante, king of Morocco and a military ally of her father. She accepts his portrait from her father reluctantly. General Muley enters with the news of a large Portuguese fleet off Tangiers. His long poetic description of the fleet is famous, and Bridges adapted a passage from it in his own account of the Greek fleet in *Achilles in Scyros*. Muley then sees Tarudante's picture in Fénix's hands and departs angry and jealous. In the ensuing battle of Tangiers, the Portuguese under Fernando and Enrique are at first successful. Muley is captured by Fernando and then is released by him in a generous act of chivalry when he learns that Muley is in love. Muley vows to repay the debt, and this is the beginning of a major motif in the play—the conflict of loyalty between chivalric friendship and duty to the king. In a second engagement Fernando and Enrique are captured, and Enrique is sent off to negotiate the return of Ceuta to the Moors in exchange for the royal prisoners. Fernando, however, insists that Ceuta must not be given up, and here begins the central conflict between Fernando and the king of Fez over Ceuta. Both are equally stubborn and steadfast.

At the opening of the second act, Fénix is troubled by the prophecy of an old hag that she will be the price of a corpse. Muley believes that the corpse will be himself, slain by Tarudante, but actually this is foreshadowing of the exchange of the living Fénix for the dead Fernando at the end of the play. Fernando at this point is treated courteously by the king, but when Enrique enters with news that the king of Portugal is dead and that Ceuta should be yielded in exchange for the prisoners, the situation changes. Fernando tears up the paper bearing the command and vows that he will never allow himself to be exchanged for a Christian city. The enraged king of Fez orders him loaded with chains and cast into a dungeon by night and deprived of all food and water except what he can beg, and he is forced to do menial tasks by day. Thus begin the trials of the constant prince. Muley, moved by compassion because of his genuine admiration for Fernando, vows to repay his debt. Fernando is discovered by Fénix going about his daily routine as a beggar. He offers her flowers and compares the unstable life of man to the evanescent flowers; Fénix replies, comparing the lot of man to the stars that disappear every day. These flowers and stars sonnets are among the most famous passages in the play. Muley now informs Fernando of an escape plan he has arranged, but the king, suspicious of Muley, puts him in personal charge of the prisoner. This is the first of Muley's moral dilemmas. Should he remain faithful to the chivalric code (his debt to Fernando) or to his king? He decides in favor of his friendship for Fernando, but Fernando refuses the escape plan arguing that loyalty to the king must have precedence with Muley.

In the third act Muley and Fénix plead with the king to alleviate Fernando's suffering, but the king replies that it is Fernando's own fault. Let him yield Ceuta if he wishes better treatment. Alfonso, the new king of Portugal, enters with ransom money for Fernando but is refused. Only Ceuta will ransom Fernando. He quarrels with Tarudante before leaving and promises to meet him on the field of battle. Tarudante offers himself again to Fénix and is again accepted by her father who then entrusts Fénix to Muley's care until the wedding. Thus for a second time Muley is in a moral dilemma. Should he obey his king and preserve Fénix for Tarudante or should he press his own suit? Meanwhile Fernando is dying from starvation. No one dares help him, not even Fénix. He asks to be buried in his religious cloak and his grave marked so that his body may be ransomed. In the final scenes the Portuguese under Alfonso are led to victory by the ghost of Fernando dressed in a religious cloak and carrying a torch. Tarudante, Fénix, and Muley are made prisoners and are exchanged for the body of Fernando, thus fulfilling the prophecy that the living Fénix would be the price of a corpse. The captives are released and the king of Fez promises to marry Fénix to Muley as stipulated by Alfonso because of Muley's friendship for the dead Fernando.

The play gains its emotional effect from the triumph of the Portuguese faith and of Portuguese arms over the Moors, from the steadfastness of Fernando in his faith and that of Muley in his concept of the chivalric code, and from the quality of several poetic speeches, particularly the flower and star sonnets spoken by Fernando and Fénix, the speech of Muley in the first act describing the Portuguese fleet, and the rhetorical description by Fernando of the first engagement in which he captures Muley.

In Bridges's play at the opening of the first act Almeh (Calderón's Fénix) immediately shows her moral and spiritual superiority to Calderón's character by expressing compassion for the Christian captives as well as admiration for their singing. She persuades her father to give them liberty once a day so she can see and hear them. Like her prototype, Fénix, she tends to be melancholic, and she fancies herself leading a solitary life attended by the captives as singing minstrels. As in Calderón's play, she is commanded to marry Tarudante, accepts his picture, and tells Sala ben Sala (Calderón's Muley) that she will obey her father in spite of Sala's insane jealousy. When she hears of Ferdinand's chivalric gesture in freeing Sala, her interest is aroused, and it is evident that her attraction to the Christian prince will be stronger than Fénix's.

In act 2 Almeh is so impressed by the singing of the captives that she persuades them to tell her the story of Jesus, the subject of their hymns. When Almeh's father enters with Tarudante and the captive Ferdinand, he promises his daughter in marriage to Tarudante, but Almeh has eyes only for the chivalrous Christian prince. Here begins the conflict between love and loyalty to her father, her faith, and her country. Ferdinand in an aside expresses his astonishment at Almeh's beauty and says that she has stolen his soul. It is a case of love at first sight. The king of Fez informs the princes that only the surrender of Ceuta will ransom Ferdinand, although Sala tries to intervene on Ferdinand's behalf. The relationship between Sala and Ferdinand is the same as in Calderón. At the end of the act Ferdinand is begged by the captives and by Almeh to yield Ceuta, but he refuses.

In act 3 Ferdinand continues to refuse Almeh's pleas to surrender Ceuta. Sala offers Ferdinand a plan of escape because of the debt he owes him and also because he wishes to get rid of his rival in love. Thus Sala's motives are mixed and his behavior is less admirable than it is in Calderón. Ferdinand promises to escape, but on learning that Sala has never been betrothed to Almeh and that Almeh does not love him, he decides to remain. The king of Fez, indignant at the delay in Almeh's marriage to Tarudante, tells Sala that he will turn over Ferdinand and the captives to Almeh to release them if she wishes the moment she marries Tarudante. From this point on the love story comes to the fore, and Bridges's play takes a turn quite different from Calderón's. Almeh is informed that if she marries a man she dislikes, the man she loves and the captives she pities will go free. If she refuses, the prince and the captives will die unless Ceuta is surrendered. She promises her father she will obey him, but when Ferdinand enters, they exchange vows of mutual love, kiss, and are discovered by the king, Tarudante, and Sala. The enraged king orders Sala to imprison Ferdinand, and when Almeh begs for his life and confesses her love for him, the king drives his daughter from his presence. He wishes to execute Ferdinand, but that would mean the loss of his last hope to regain Ceuta and so he decides to starve him into submission.

In the next act the reader discovers Almeh starving herself in protest against the treatment of her lover. News from an intercepted love letter of her baptism as a Christian and of the approaching death of Ferdinand from starvation reaches the astonished king of Fez. He decides that Ferdinand's life must be preserved, at least until he yields Ceuta, which is in his power to do, for the king of Portugal is dead and Ferdinand is regent. Ferdinand is brought to the king, food is placed before him, and the temptation scene commences. Ferdinand is told that if he will eat and live he and the Christian captives will be freed and Almeh will wed him in Christian marriage. Ferdinand reaches for the food, asking "And Ceuta"? The king replies, "That is mine, her price." Ferdinand rejects the food, and the enraged king stabs him to death across the table. This dramatic scene in which Ferdinand is forced to choose between Ceuta and Almeh (together with his freedom and that of the captives) is not in Calderón. After Ferdinand's death, his ghost appears on the darkened stage to the king, who tries again to kill him, much to Sala's disgust. When Sala discovers the murdered body of Ferdinand, he expresses his contempt for the King's unchivalrous conduct.

The final act of Bridges's play is also substantially different from Calderón's. There is no exchange of the dead Ferdinand for the living Almeh. Instead, against a background of battle sounds, the emaciated Almeh thinks of death and dreams of eventual union with Ferdinand in a Christian paradise. When she discovers the body of her lover in the arbor, she dies on his corpse after a distraught speech. The king of Fez is killed by the Christian captives as the Portuguese army advances; Sala too is captured but, because of his chivalrous conduct, is freed, and terms of peace are arranged by which the Moors and Christians retain the territories each is holding at the time. The bodies of Ferdinand and Almeh receive Christian burial in Ceuta, and Sala is given perpetual permission to visit their graves. Enrique vows never again to draw sword but to spend his life in peaceful pursuits.

It should be noted that the basic conflict in both Bridges's and Calderón's play is over the possession of a city, but the desire to possess the city is motivated by religious and not secular concerns. Ceuta takes precedence over everything else in both

the king of Fez's and in Ferdinand's mind. In Bridges's play
the king of Fez is willing to give his daughter in marriage to a
Christian prince to gain it. Ferdinand gives up the woman he
loves and his own life in order to retain it for Christian Portugal.

Bridges's play achieves its dramatic effect from this struggle
of wills over Ceuta, an effect that is augmented by the love story.
The love element in Calderón's play is relatively slight. Questions
of staging and acting aside, Bridges's play as a work of dramatic
literature is probably better than Calderón's. By ennobling the
character of Almeh, converting her to Christianity, and having
her fall in love with Ferdinand (a love that is self-sacrificing and
spiritual as well as physical), and then forcing Ferdinand to
choose between her and his religious principles, Bridges sharpens
the dramatic conflict and makes Ferdinand even more the constant
prince than does Calderón.

As for the quality of the poetry, Bridges's verse appears to
be comparable to Calderón's—perhaps even better. A tone of
dignity and solemnity without grandiloquence and appropriate
to tragedy is maintained throughout. One or two of Almeh's
speeches describing the effect of the singing of the captives on
her are among the best in all of Bridges's plays. Here is Almeh
speaking in the first act:

> 'Twas last night, Sala, as I lay long awake
> Dreamily hearkening to the ocean murmur,
> Softer than silence, on mine ears there stole
> A solemn sound of wailful harmony:
> So beautiful it was that first I thought
> This castle was enchanted, as I have read
> In eastern tales; or else that 'twas the song
> Of people of this land, who make the sea
> Their secret god, and at midnight arise
> To kneel upon the shore, and his divinity
> Trouble with shrilling prayer: or then it seemed
> A liquid-voicèd choir of spirits that swam
> Upon the ocean surface, harp in hand,
> Swelling their hymns with his deep undersong.
> That was the Christian captives.

(1.332–46)

The cadences of this blank verse are done with remarkable
skill, and the second line quoted above with the trochaic

substitution in the first foot, the light extrametrical syllable in the third foot, and the feminine ending in the fifth foot is beautifully expressive of the sound of the ocean and is obviously the work of a master prosodist.

Achilles in Scyros

Achilles in Scyros, completed in August 1887[50] and first published in 1890, dramatizes an event in the early life of the Greek hero. As the play opens, the goddess Thetis, mother of Achilles, explains in a prologue that she is on the isle of Scyros to watch over her son Achilles, who has been disguised as a maiden and brought up in the court of Lycomedes, king of Scyros, to keep him concealed from the Greek army that needs him in the expedition against Troy, for it has been prophesied that without Achilles the Greeks could not be victorious. Thetis, knowing that it had been ruled by fate that her son would either live a short life and die gloriously in battle or live a long life of inglorious ease, has persuaded Achilles out of love for her to accept the life of inglorious ease on Scyros. Ulysses, who has been informed by his spies of Thetis's stratagem, has arrived in Scyros to search for Achilles. In a dialogue with Diomede he explains his plot—to disguise himself as a pedlar, gain access to the maidens, and discover Achilles. In the ensuing scene between Deidamia, daughter of King Lycomedes, and Achilles (disguised as Pyrrha) it is clear that they love each other, although innocently on Deidamia's part because she believes Pyrrha to be a maiden. The girls play at being Amazons, and Deidamia suggests that they take over the island and rule it as an Amazonian kingdom after the death of her aged father, Lycomedes, who is annoyed when he discovers the reason for Ulysses' visits. He thinks his honor has been impugned. When Achilles overhears Diomede making insulting remarks on his lack of courage for hiding as a girl in Scyros while the Greeks go off to fight, Achilles is about to reveal himself and join the Greeks, but Thetis persuades him against it.

Ulysses, disguised as a peddler, shows his wares of maiden gear to Deidamia and the other maidens and then to Achilles, who has accepted the gift of a brooch from Deidamia reluctantly. Achilles sees a sword that Ulysses uncovers among the trinkets and snatches it, thus revealing himself. Ulysses pulls off his peddler's beard, discovering his identity to Achilles. Achilles throws off his robe, revealing his magic garment presented him by Thetis, which appears to be shining armor. They exchange insults, but eventually Achilles promises to join the Greek army. Lycomedes, upon discovering that Pyrrha is Achilles and that he is in love with Deidamia, readily accepts him as his future son-in-law, and Deidamia also realizes that she loves him as a man. But then Achilles states his dilemma. Should he marry Deidamia and live a life of ease in Scyros or should he obey the call to duty and honor and fight the Trojans. He leaves it to Deidamia to decide and she tells him that he must choose the way of honor. The wedding is solemnized that night and Achilles and Deidamia will have a few days together before Achilles departs.

Only one stage production of *Achilles in Scyros* has been mounted. This was done by the Guild of the Cheltenham Ladies College with music by Cyril B. Rootham and a dance composed by Gertrude Matthews.[51] There were performances on June 27 and 29, 1912, one of these being attended by Bridges. Bridges wrote to Henry Bradley that after receiving an honorary degree in letters at Oxford commencement he went down to Cheltenham,

> . . . where the girl students were giving my Achilles in Scyros with new music by Dr Rootham of Camb. There was a deal of cheering and bestowing of bouquets at the end: but the thing was a failure. I felt at first somewhat depressed at the flatness of it until it struck me that since the girls did not (with exception of Deidamia who looked and acted well) in any way appear like the persons whom they represented, and since one could not hear exactly what they said the effect was natural. As for your friend Lycomedes—I remember your liking him— he was converted into a light comedy part! The fact is that the girls could not get near masculine personation of any kind, and their little shrill argumentative voices w^d have dispelled any ocular illusion if it had existed. However my play was in everyone's hands, and that saved me from discredit.[52]

Twenty years previous to the Cheltenham performance, Bridges in a letter dated September 15, 1892, expressed discouragement at the reception of his plays. He wrote:

> I am afraid that there is not much chance of my plays getting printed—for I told my publisher to send Achilles to all the

writers—that is nearly 2 months ago and there has not been a single notice of it, so unless it sells itself, which can hardly be expected, the experiment is a failure—.[53]

There are a number of references to the Achilles in Scyros story scattered throughout Greek and Roman literature.[54] Bridges may have used some or all of them, but he made important changes in the source material. First, he greatly amplified the story, for his is the longest account extant of Achilles' adventures in Scyros. Also, he changed the character of Achilles. The classical sources[55] state that Achilles had a liaison with Deidamia that produced a child named Pyrrhus or Neoptolemus. In some accounts the device of the trumpet blast was introduced. As the peddler's gear was spread before Achilles and the maidens, Ulysses causes a trumpet to be blown. Achilles, thinking the island is under attack, seizes a shield and spear from among the maiden trinkets, thus discovering himself.[56] The trumpet is omitted in Bridges's play. The magic garment that Thetis gives Achilles to wear under his robe appears to be an innovation of Bridges. The most important modification introduced by Bridges was his decision to make the relationship between Deidamia and Achilles innocent. Deidamia does not discover that her beloved Pyrrha is a man until near the end of the play, and Achilles abstains from any overt lovemaking. The innocence of this relationship is in keeping with the pastoral and masquelike tone of Bridges's drama and enables him to introduce the conflict between love and honor at the end. Achilles must decide between a life of pleasure with Deidamia in Scyros or a glorious death in battle against the Trojans. It is characteristic of Bridges's Achilles, who is not the stern warrior of Homer, that he should leave the decision to a woman.

By contrast, the Achilles of Statius's version is much closer to Homer's conception of the Greek hero. He is an extremely virile and somewhat immoral young man who uses his disguise to ravish Deidamia, and in doing so, he explains that he obeyed his mother's command to disguise himself in order to be near Deidamia whom he secretly loved. A son is born of this union, whom Achilles rather defiantly presents to Lycomedes when his disguise is revealed. When Achilles notices a shield and spear among the maiden trinkets, his response in Statius's rather florid account is much more marked than in Bridges's play:

. . . he shouted loud and rolled his eyes, and his hair rose
up from his brow; forgotten were his mother's words, forgotten
his secret love, and Troy fills all his breast. As a lion, torn
from his mother's dugs, submits to be tamed and lets his
mane be combed, and learns to have awe of man . . . yet if
but once the steel has glittered in his sight, his fealty is
forsworn and his tamer becomes his foe.[57]

When the trumpet blast sounds,

. . . from his breast the raiment fell without his touching,
already the shield and puny spear are lost in the grasp of his
hand ("consumitur," *consumed* by his hand) . . . and he
seemed to surpass by head and shoulders the Ithacan and the
Aetolian chief: with a sheen so awful does the sudden blaze
of arms and martial fire dazzle the palace-hall.[58]

Much of the amplification that Bridges gives his material
consists of poetic descriptions of the pastoral setting and lyrics
sung by the chorus. Two or three of Calderón's plays may have
influenced the pastoral passages, and one play, Calderón's *El
Principe Constante,* was the source of the description of the
Cretan fleet, one of the finest passages in all of Bridges and,
in all probability, considerably superior to its source. Lycomedes
is telling Abas, servant to Ulysses, that he is well aware of the
formidable force mounted against the Trojans and recalls his
sight of the Cretan fleet at dawn:

> Twas such a breathless morning
> When all the sound and motion of the sea
> Is short and sullen, like a dreaming beast:
> Or as 'twere mixed of heavier elements
> Than the bright water, that obeys the wind.
> Hiring a fishing-boat we bade the sailors
> Row us to Aulis; when midway the straits,
> The morning mist lifted, and lo, a sight
> Unpicturable.—High upon our left
> Where we supposed was nothing, suddenly
> A tall and shadowy figure loomed: then two,
> And three, and four, and more towering above us:
> But whether poised upon the leaden sea
> They stood, or floated in the misty air,
> That baffling our best vision held entangled
> The silver of the half-awakened sun,

Or whether near or far, we could not tell,
Nor what: at first I thought them rocks, but ere
That error could be told, they were upon us
Bearing down swiftly athwart our course; and all
Saw 'twas a fleet of ships, not three or four
Now, but unnumber'd: like a floating city,
If such could be, with walls and battlements
Spread on the wondering water: and now the sun
Broke thro' the haze, and from the shields outhung
Blazed back his dazzling beams, and round their prows
On the divided water played; as still
They rode the tide in silence, all their oars
Stretched out aloft, as are the balanced wings
Of storm-fowl, which returned from battling flight
Across the sea, steady their aching plumes
And skim along the shuddering cliffs at ease:
So came they gliding on the sullen plain,
Out of the dark, in silent state, by force
Yet unexpended on their nightlong speed.

Henry Bradley compared the original description in Calderón with Bridges's: "I read . . . *El Príncipe Constante*, which gave me real pleasure. But the passage about the ships strikes me as tinged with bombast, and rather dragged in, while your imitation in Achilles in Scyros is surely much finer than the original, and seems to be in its natural place. What I mean is that for your gentle untravelled meditative island-king it is appropriate—indeed one might say necessary—that he should apprehend the sight and describe it in that way; but how a seasoned commander should see and speak so is what I do not understand."[59]

Achilles in Scyros has some of the finest poetry in all of Bridges's plays, and for this reason it is successful as a pastoral masque; but it is lacking in profound and original characterization and in dramatic conflict, and as an actable play that will hold audience interest it must be considered unsatisfactory.

The Humours of the Court

The Humours of the Court (written in 1888, first published in 1893) is the only play by Bridges that was produced on the London stage. It had performances by the Oxford Dramatic Society at the Arts Theatre in London on the evening of Sunday, January 5, 1930, and on the afternoon of the following Tuesday.[60]

Bridges elected to remain in Oxford, but his wife attended the Tuesday matinee. Bridges wrote to Logan Pearsall Smith on January 7: "I ought to be in town today to show my gratitude and respect for the people who are acting in my play. I wish very much that you c^d have attended it and sent me your account of it. Considering the disrepute of poetic drama it is almost inconceivable that a play of mine sh^d please: but the unexpected happened and this experiment interests me."[61] And in a letter to Mrs. Daniel, January 9, 1930, Bridges said that his wife saw the matinee and, although he did not see it, he was "tickled" by newspaper accounts.[62] Edith Evans (later Dame Edith Evans), who took the part of Diana, became one of the most famous actresses of the century. Robert Speaight, who played Frederick, also has had a distinguished career. The *Times* reviewer describes the play as "a highly artificial comedy of gallantry and intrigue" and calls Edith Evans's performance "gentle though still quick in its humour and brilliant in its transitions from raillery to light sentiment." Robert Speaight (as Frederick) was "in black hat and cloak, a trifle too much like the Fifth of November" but "full of spirit and humour." As the reviewer says, the play is indeed extremely light, artificial comedy. One could imagine it as a libretto for a Mozart opera. Brilliant acting could make it successful. It does not have the importance of *The Christian Captives* or of *Nero* when read as closet drama.

The plot is derived from Calderón's *El Secreto a voces* (*The Secret in Words*) with one scene (act 3, scene 1) taken from Lope de Vega's opening scene of *El perro del hortelano* (*The Gardener's Dog*). In Calderón's play the action takes place in Parma in or near the palace and grounds of Flerida, the Duchess of Parma, whose strict rule is that there will be no sub-rosa love affairs at her court kept secret from her. She herself, however, is secretly in love with her secretary, Frederick. But Frederick is hopelessly in love with one of the Duchess's ladies, Laura, who, returning his affection, becomes involved in secret communications and meetings with him, some of their communications being carried on by means of a code under the very eyes of the Duchess. The lovers plan an elopement to Mantua, aided by Frederick's friend, Henry, the Duke of Mantua, who is present in Parma in disguise to pursue his seemingly hopeless suit of the Duchess. The chief line of action of the play consists of Flerida's attempt to discover Frederick's secret mistress. She has as her aide Fabio, Frederick's faithless servant, whom she bribes. Frederick's love affair with Laura is further complicated by Lisardo, who considers himself betrothed to Laura and is supported by her father Arnesto, Governor of Parma. When in the final act the planned elopement of Laura and Frederick is discovered by the Duchess herself in conversation with Frederick on the night of the elopement (Frederick, mistakenly believing he is talking with Laura), the Duchess, remembering her social position, rises above her passion and anger, gives her secretary and her lady Laura her blessing and favors the now undisguised Duke with hope of a happy outcome of his suit. A good deal of the humor arises from Frederick's supposed journey to Mantua and back to carry messages between the Duke of Mantua and the Duchess, whereas, actually, he has only to go to his rooms in Parma to deliver them to his friend, and also from Frederick's and Laura's success in eluding the prying eyes of the Duchess. Forbidden to meet openly, they meet in secret and set up a code consisting of the first few words preceding the pause in each line they speak to the Duchess so that many of their speeches consist of double talk with one meaning for the Duchess and another for themselves. This device is probably amusing when well acted. It makes tedious reading, and Bridges mercifully omitted it in his adaptation of Calderón's plot.

There are other changes made by Bridges. The Duchess of Parma is renamed Diana, Countess of Belflor, where the action takes place. Henry becomes Richard, Duke of Milan instead of Mantua, and Frederick's servant is renamed Tristram. The two lovers retain the same names, but Laura is Diana's adopted sister, rather than her lady. Laura's father is renamed Sir Gregory, and he is Diana's majordomo instead of being governor. Laura's suitor is renamed St. Nicholas. In Bridges's version, the Duke of Milan is somewhat less admirable than Calderón's Duke. He furthers the love affair of Frederick and Laura not so much out of friendship for Frederick but rather for his own interests. He wants Frederick out of the way and disgraced in the eyes of Diana so that he can turn Diana's passion away from Frederick and toward himself. He states quite bluntly:

> The very thing
> I plot to save myself, most helps my friend.

> (1.782–83)

In Bridges's play the action takes place at the Court of Belflor, where the countess, Diana, has imposed a rigid code of ethics, forbidding all intrigues and secret love affairs. The love situation is similar to Calderón's. Diana secretly loves her secretary, Frederick; the Duke, Richard of Milan, is enamored of Diana whom he idealizes; Frederick and Laura (the Countess's adopted sister and trusted confidante) are mutually in love and resolve (with the aid of the Duke) to fly to Milan where they can wed and Laura can escape the marriage imposed on her by her father Sir Gregory to the fop St. Nicholas. Also, as a subplot, Tristram, servant to Frederick, and Flora, maid to Diana, are mutually in love. The most impressive poetry in the play occurs in the first act—the lyrics sung in honor of Diana (see "Fire of heaven whose starry arrow"[63]), and Richard's idealized description of the gardens of Belflor, which seem to him like paradise because of the presence of Diana:

> All this hour
> I have seemed in Paradise: and the fair prospect
> Hath quieted my spirit: I think I sail
> Into the windless haven of my life
> To-day with happy omens: as the stir
> And sleep-forbidding rattle of the journey
> Was like my life till now. Here all is peace:
> The still fresh air of this October morning,
> With its resigning odours: the rich hues
> Wherein the gay leaves revel to their fall;
> The deep blue sky; the misty distances,
> And splashing fountains; and I thought I heard
> A magic service of meandering music
> Threading the glades and stealing on the lawns.

(1.101–14)

By the end of act 1 Diana has revealed (to the audience) her love for Frederick, and Frederick and Laura have arranged their rendezvous at night in the garden to plan their escape. During this act there is an interesting Court of Love scene in which the Countess presides over a debate on the question of "Why love is called bitter-sweet." The best speech in this debate is given by Frederick, who argues that the greatest pain occurs when fate separates two preordained lovers. In act 2 Frederick and Laura meet in the garden. Laura tells Frederick that the Countess is in love with him and that she would make him a better match than herself, but Frederick successfully convinces Laura of his geniune love for her. In lines reminiscent of Shakespeare he urges her to waste no more time:

> Then waste no more the precious moments, Laura,
> To question the great blessing we enjoy.
> Our hours will all be as this hour tonight;
> Either to step with in eternity
> Towards our perfection with unwavering will,
> Or with a questioning purpose let it slide,
> And leave us far behind.

(2.1.1051–60)

Frederick promises to carry her off within two days, and to forestall the immediate signing of the marriage contract between Laura and Nicholas by drawing it up himself with flaws that will require delay and revision. Diana in the meantime continues with bribes to Tristram her attempts to discover the identity of Frederick's secret lover, little dreaming that it is her trusted adopted sister. In act 3 Frederick and Laura successfully begin their flight to Milan, while Nicholas is detained from discovery and pursuit by Tristram's locking him in the cupboard. Sir Gregory eventually finds his daughter's glove in Frederick's room, unlocks the rejected suitor Nicholas from his cupboard, and informs Diana of the elopement. As in Calderón, Diana rises above her passion for Frederick, and when the eloping lovers are captured by Nicholas and brought before her, she forgives them, orders their immediate marriage, consents to the marriage of Tristram and Flora, and implies to the Duke, after a series of impressive love speeches by him, that she will marry him. Thus social decorum is satisfied. Each marries according to his rank, and only Nicholas is left disappointed.

Before writing *The Humours of the Court*, Bridges had been studying Lope de Vega's *The Gardener's Dog* (c. 1618) as well as Calderón's play, and in his note of acknowledgment to the Spanish playwrights he said that both plays "appeared to me to be variations of the same story." The heroine of Lope's play is Diana, Countess of Belflor; one of her suitors is the Marquis

Riccardo, and the servant of the secretary, Teodoro, is named Tristran. Thus Bridges derived the names of at least three characters from Lope's drama. In Lope's opening scene, Tristran and Teodoro are discovered intruding into Diana's quarters where Teodoro had an assignation with Marcella, Diana's Lady in Waiting. They escape as Tristran douses the lamp with his hat. Diana then calls on each of her ladies in turn to question them about the male intruder. Bridges derived most of his first scene in act 3 from Lope's scene. As for the rest of Lope's play, there are marked differences, as well as a few similarities, with Bridges's *Humours of the Court.* In *The Gardener's Dog,* Diana is in love with her secretary, Teodoro, and eventually marries him, overcoming their difference in rank by promulgating a story (which she knows to be false) of the discovery that Teodoro is actually the long lost son of the noble Lodovico, a trick arranged by Teodoro's servant, Tristran. In Bridges's play the Countess relinquishes her secretary to her rival and marries the Duke. The main story line in Lope's play is Diana's jealous passion for Teodoro, a man beneath her social station. She can't bear to see him happily married to Marcella; she can't bear to marry him herself because of the disgrace of his low birth. She is, as Teodoro says, the "gardener's dog," who will not eat herself or let others eat. The tone of Lope's drama (as Bridges points out in his notes) is at times farcical, with Diana's quick changes of attitude toward Teodoro, first encouraging him so that he turns away from Marcella, then rejecting him so that he goes back to Marcella again. And there is an unbelievable and farcical assassination plot in which Tristran is hired by two of Diana's suitors to assassinate Teodoro, the would-be assassins not knowing that Tristran is Teodoro's servant. The stock device in which Lodovico is immediately and too easily convinced by Tristran (disguised as a Greek) that Teodoro is his long lost son is also farcical. The tone of Bridges's play, on the other hand, is considerably more sophisticated—an ironic portrayal of a petty tyrant moved by passion and jealousy and shamed by pride who eventually accepts the inevitable. Furthermore, the depiction of Frederick and Laura's mutual love and of the Duke's idealized love for Diana is expressed in poetry that is considerably superior to anything in de Vega's play. In fact, at its best, Bridges's blank verse reminds us of Shakespeare—particularly of *Twelfth Night.* The Duke of *Twelfth Night* has some affinity with Bridges's

Duke, as does Diana with Shakespeare's Olivia. Also, Bridges's Tristram talks like a typical Shakespearian clown, and St. Nicholas is a Shakespearean fop who reminds one somewhat of Osric. John Garnett Underhill in his comments on *The Gardener's Dog* says that Lope's play in tone and locale (Italy) reminds him of *Twelfth Night*.[64] But to me, *The Humours of the Court*, in style, characterization, and tone appears much closer to Shakespeare than does *The Gardener's Dog*. Also it is known that Bridges read *Twelfth Night*, whereas Lope de Vega probably did not.

There are, as previously noted, a few passages of superior blank verse (as well as two beautiful lyrics) written in a fairly elevated style. The greater part of the play, however, is in blank verse that successfully approximates normal conversation without altogether losing its iambic rhythms. In a letter to Butler, Bridges wrote:

> In the "Humours of the Court" I have I think succeeded in making blank verse do a great deal of comic ordinary business without flatness which I don't think has ever been accomplished before. If I have succeeded, it is merely by dint of technical devices of extreme elaboration tho' of course hidden.[65]

Bridges, like Eliot years later, was quite conscious of the problem of making poetry on the modern stage acceptable to an audience used to prose, and in this instance Bridges's own evaluation of his success may be correct.

Bridges's house, Chilswell, Boar's Hill, Oxford, where he resided from 1907 until his death in 1930. *Courtesy of Elizabeth Daryush.*

Robert Bridges in 1925 at Chilswell. *Photograph taken by V. Sackvill- West. Courtesy of Elizabeth Daryush.*

Robert Bridges seated in his library at Chilswell. *Courtesy of Elizabeth Daryush.*

The poet seated beside the Dolmetsch clavichord given to him by friends on his eightieth birthday. *Courtesy of Elizabeth Daryush.*

Photograph of Bridges taken by Percy Withers, biographer. *Courtesy of Elizabeth Daryush.*

Another close-up of the poet. *Courtesy of Elizabeth Daryush.*

Three photographs of the poet in old age, dates unknown. *Courtesy of Robert Bridges.*

The Philosophical Poet:
The Testament of Beauty

The Development of the Text

The Dates of Composition. According to the testimony of Mrs. Bridges, the first few lines of *The Testament of Beauty* were written on Christmas Day 1924.[1] I have found no other evidence for this early date. According to the dating of the trial text (discussed below), the first draft of Book 1 was completed by December 24, 1926; Book 2, in first draft, was finished by July 1927; the first draft of Book 3 was finished by March 1928; and the first part of Book 4 (through line 1,135 of the trial text) was completed by December of 1928. According to Simon Nowell-Smith,[2] the conclusion of Book 4 was finished by July 15, 1929. An unpublished letter from Bridges to A. E. Housman substantiates Nowell-Smith's date. Bridges wrote to Housman on June 4, 1929, "I am hoping to send my long poem to press next month, it is heavy work correcting and finishing but it is done."[3]

It is probable that most of the writing of Book 1 was done during the year 1926. By March of that year Bridges was already hard at work on it; the first draft was finished by Christmas and set up in proof for the trial text by January of 1927. This first book was entered at Oxford Press as "Philosophical Verse" and was soon being referred to by Bridges and by the press as *De Hominum Natura* (or D. H. N.) after Lucretius's *De Rerum Natura*.[4] In the final version of the poem Bridges gave each book a heading (1. Introduction, 2. Selfhood, 3. Breed, 4. Ethick), but these headings do not appear in the trial texts.

The Printing of the Trial Text. As shown above, the writing of the first draft of Book 1 was completed by Christmas of 1926. Bridges sent this book to the Oxford Press shortly thereafter and received proof in January 1927.[5] Twenty-five copies were printed in February. Book 2 was printed in September 1927, Book 3 in May 1928, and the first 1,135 lines (as numbered in the trial text) of Book 4 were printed in February 1929. All of these were in "editions" of twenty-five copies. Four copies of the conclusion or "tail" of Book 4 were presented unexpectedly to Bridges on his birthday, October 23, 1929. In order to prevent this final section of the trial text from becoming an exceedingly rare collector's item, Bridges requested that further copies be printed. Seventeen were printed in October 1929. This tail section was set up from uncorrected proof of the 1929 edition (regular issue) and not from manuscript.[6]

Circulation of the Trial Text. Bridges sent copies of the trial text to friends whose opinions he valued. If serious criticism was not forthcoming, Bridges was offended. Edward Thompson, for example, spent an uncomfortable afternoon with the poet laureate after he had failed to make suggestions for the improvement of Book 2.[7] Bridges took his friends' suggestions seriously and adopted some of them; and when errors in his prosody were pointed out he rectified them. Among those receiving this private edition were R. C. Trevelyan, Stanley Morison, Edward Thompson, Logan Pearsall Smith, Kenneth Sisam, and, of course, Mrs. Bridges.

Correspondence Concerning the Trial Text. Letters exchanged between Bridges and R. C. Trevelyan, Stanley Morison, and others furnish some information on the composition and revision of the poem. Trevelyan received a copy of Book 1 of the trial edition in June 1927, and a lively correspondence with the poet ensued.[8] Trevelyan wrote enthusiastically on July 1:

. . . it seems to me an exceedingly fine poem, even in its present unfinished state. . . . It has all the qualities that I have admired so much in "Come si quando," with perhaps even greater mastery of the difficult metrical technique. . . . I do not feel quite clear about your metrical intention; [in certain lines] e.g. line 26 "had made fair-order'd husbandry of that native Pleasaunce," which seems to be a thirteen syllabled line. Also I suppose that line 13, "With like surprise of joy as oft a traveler feels," is a decasyllabic verse, though you have not indented it, as you have done in several cases later on. [P. 9]

Bridges was delighted with the letter and responded immediately on July 2, asking Trevelyan to enter his criticisms in the margins of his copy before returning it, and stating that Book 2 would be printed "next month." (Actually, it was completed in July but not printed until September.) Bridges mentioned his intentions in the first two books: "This 1st is a sort of general orientation which will serve for definition of terms. Section II attacks the Instincts." He commented on Trevelyan's discovery of the thirteen-syllable line: "I remember your discovery of a misprint in 'Come si quando.' Now this 13 syllable line is a useful find. I looked it up in the MS and find it comes of a correction."

This line, which became number 24 of the final text, was revised to read "a fair-order'd husbandry of that native pleasaunce," which reduces the line to twelve syllables.

Trevelyan wrote again on July 13 to Bridges. He was still very enthusiastic about Book 1, although he had some difficulty at first in understanding the organization and structure:

At first I found the transitions and the sequence of ideas rather difficult, especially in the first part. But I now see a more obviously coherent design would probably have not been so suitable for your material, which requires to be treated freely and discursively. Anyhow the main ideas come out quite clearly. Perhaps I admire the last two hundred lines most of all; but everywhere there are wonderful passages of really great poetry; and the thought, too, is of a kind that I find myself very sympathetic to.

As to the metre, there can be no doubt that it is admirably suited in movement and emotional effect to the subject matter. [P. 11]

Trevelyan did, however, have difficulty in understanding the meter of a few lines that (apparently) he marked in his copy of the trial text. Trevelyan went on to say:

> My wife, who does not pretend to understand the metre, enjoyed the poem immensely, without troubling herself about the scansion. Perhaps this is the wisest thing to do; yet I do not myself get the fullest enjoyment out of a poem that is so distinguished for its metre, unless I fully understand the metre as I read it. [P. 12]

Bridges replied on July 21, thanking Trevelyan for his criticisms and expressing the hope that Book 2 would be in type by August and Book 3 finished by Christmas of 1927. On September 23 Bridges sent him the trial text of Book 2 with the comment, "I fear that as I get on I shall have more philosophy—and therefore perhaps less poetry—but I find it all very amusing." Trevelyan replied with detailed comments for which Bridges thanked him on October 15th with interesting remarks on his concept of elision and his treatment of the word *spiritual*:

> . . . I will observe my treatment of "spiritual," but my varieties in that word are not metrical conveniences. If there was any definite uniform propriety I should have welcomed it, but it would be a dreadful word if it were confined to any one of its possibilities.
>
> The first half is contractible, and the second half is like unto the first and should be elided before a vowel, but when for instance the word is an important predicate at end of sentence it almost requires its full syllabizing, though that would deform it when it had no sort of emphasis.
>
> I have always attempted to determine "elisions" by natural speech values and these vary with the diction and rhythmical collocution. [P. 15]

At the close of his letter Bridges remarks that he has finished about five hundred lines of Book 3, "which is of course on Breed-sex." Bridges wrote again on February 8, 1928, saying that he had intended to finish Book 3 by Christmas of 1927 but illness and the cold weather had prevented it. "I can't guess what the Book will be worth but I do not think it will be condemned for lack of saltation." He finally sent the trial text of Book 3 to Trevelyan

on May 25, 1928, saying, "It has escaped from the Press today.
I have no notion what it is like. It gave me pleasure writing it."
Trevelyan's reply is not available, but evidently he pointed out
a number of metrical errors, for on June 7, 1927, Bridges wrote:
"But really I didn't know there were so many metrical flaws. . . .
Your friendliness will save me a deal of the most tedious kind
of correction."

Bridges by this date had finished about 200 lines of Book 4:
"I think that the subject (ethic) will enable me to say all that
I wish to say and more than anyone will care to read."

On May 2, 1929, Bridges sent Trevelyan the trial text of Book
4 with the comment: "This Book IV is still unfinished. I lost
two months of my time last year. I sent what I had done to the
Press at Christmas and my plan was to set to work again on
St. David's Day."

Trevelyan's reply is not available, but Bridges was immensely
pleased with his criticism. He wrote on March 16:

> My sense of indebtedness to you is so overwhelming that I do
> not know how to express my gratitude or my shame for having
> imposed this task on you. Your notes will save me an immense
> amount of labour—that is of tedious attention to these partic-
> ular points of scansion, and they serve to expose to me the sort
> of slovenliness that this manner of writing induces. [P. 24]

On October 24, 1929, the date of publication of *The Testament
of Beauty,* Bridges wrote to Trevelyan promising him a copy and
also a copy of the "tail," as Bridges called it, of Book 4, which
Oxford Press had printed (four copies in September, seventeen
in October) uniform with the rest of the trial text. Trevelyan
thanked him on October 27th: "It is a most rare piece of good
fortune when a difficult poem that has not aimed at popularity,
all the same becomes popular, as seems likely to happen here."

Excerpts from Bridges's correspondence with Stanley Morison
concerning the trial text of *The Testament of Beauty* have been
published for the first time in Nicolas Barker's *Stanley Morison.*
As shown above, Morison first met Bridges when the great
typographer called on the poet at Boar's Hill, Oxford, November
8, 1923.[9] This was the meeting that eventually resulted in Morison's designing of Bridges's collection *The Tapestry* (1925). When
Bridges completed the first book of the trial text of *The Testament*

of Beauty he wrote to Morison January 17, 1927, asking him to pay another visit to Boar's Hill: "Come as soon as you can. . . . My poem is in type so that you will be able to take it away with you—& you will be interested in it if nobody else sh^d be."[10]

For the next two and a half years, as the four books of the trial texts were completed, Morison read them carefully and offered his criticism. He commented on Book 1 in a letter to Mrs. Bridges dated March 10, 1927:

> I found the new poem intensely interesting. I read it as a testament and I have derived much religious consolation from it. I do not easily "Ask what is reasonable" though I hope I have a humble mind. But such piled up horrors as that mining accident set me to re[ad] the poem again and I seemed to feel that the conclusion was a little abrupt and the acceptance of Christianity—even of private interpretation—a little unexpected, as scarcely being implicit in the body of the text. I half expected something like a more explicit reference to the determinist tone of certain earlier passages. [P. 216]

At this time the poem had no title, although Bridges referred to it as his philosophical poem or as *De Hominum Natura.* Morison's comment "I read it as a testament" may have suggested the final title. Although not sympathetic with Bridges's rather undogmatic Christianity, the Roman Catholic Morison found the *Testament* a poem of religious consolation as did, several years later, a Unitarian minister at Bristol who preached a course of sermons on it.[11]

About two years after he first read Book 1, Morison learned that Book 4 was nearing completion. He wrote Bridges on February 23, 1929:

> . . . your news about the 4th Book of the Poem is most exciting to me. I read and re-read the parts already printed and have gained enormously from it. I look forward to seeing what you have done with a most urgent appetite for the questions you are tackling give my mind little rest and it is a very great consolation to be able to turn to your poem. [P. 253]

In April of the same year Bridges, impatient at not hearing from Morison about Book 4, wrote "I sh^d be sorry to miss the advantage of any criticism—and attach great importance to matters in which you w^d find obscurity or offence."[12] Morison replied immediately with particular reference to the famous passage in which Bridges criticized his young Jesuit friend Hopkins for not accepting a peach because it would give him too much pleasure:

> . . . I much enjoyed the Poem, I am greatly helped by several portions of it (the section dealing with Pleasure for example, though I have more sympathy with that Jesuit than you feel; wasn't he just in training? Remember that celibacy may necessitate a greater discipline of the appetites in some than in others) but I found difficulties in the lines which treat of Good Disposition. I suspect my mind is still affected by touches of Pauline theology—but it was precisely a distrust of my own natural "Disposition" which turned my attention to Christianity with its doctrine of a human nature warped by concupiscence. [P. 255]

A few days later, April 19, 1929, Morison sent Bridges his critique of Book 4, which I quote entire:

> Is it possible to distinguish in the sense of Duty: between the *I Must* of the Individual and the *I Must* of Society? You dramatically challenge the inflexibility with which the Church outfaces the Prophet and Poet, but have we not to deal with a sharper struggle than merely that of the Bureaucrat with the Individual i.e. the People against the Man whose sense of Duty is at variance, as they think, with the comfort of the State.
>   The lines dealing with the development of conscience which transfigureth the instincts are good; and I have found y^r treatment of Pleasure most suggestive and valuable. At line[s] 225–9 you well say that "Duty instill'd with order . . ." and elsewhere that Virtue is a matter of conduct rather than of doctrine. But I suppose Virtue can be subjective only and the lover of the beauty of social order demands objective Virtue— hence the prayer of the psalmist *Da mihi intellectum.* I note that y^r acc^t of the development of Conscience stresses the view that it is Reason functioning in Morals & isn't a sense *in se*— the truth as it seems to me, a concomitant of that *habitus* of Virtue in the reflective and well-disposed man. Line[s] 700 sqq are admirable and when at 780 you tackle the mystery of Knowledge your words are most penetrating; y^r contention that *Reason* is a means towards, & not the *Creator* of the Idea of Beauty is squarely and beautifully expressed. But, throughout, the passage of y^r thought is superbly easy to

follow and your argument though condensed is so happily wrought as to win its way into the understanding. I very much like the downright forcefulness of lines like 910 & 949–50 and you come at 1099 to the only answer possible

Bonitatem et disciplinam et scientiam doce me!

I think your conclusion has great verity and grandeur . . . and I turn, as I have turned before, to re-read the Poem. It is easy to read yet it is not easy to read more than three or four pages at a time—so, at least, is my experience, as the subject and y^r solemn treatment of it are the matter and form almost of a sacrament. I am most grateful for your having done this work; those tens of thousands of perplexed in this and future generations who ponder the tremendous problems you tackle will be unspeakably grateful for your teaching, for your courage & for your poetry. I look forward with enormous interest (and necessity) for your concluding—and then it must be printed in appropriate form. . . .
P.S. I think the criticism of Socialism is harsh; wd B^d Shaw allow that he preached Class hatred as the enlightened gospel of Love? Marx does not desire Class hatred—he only points out that A will hate B if B's wealth is accumulated at A's expense or by the organisation of a number of men like A who will starve if they don't enter B's service at the wage profitable to *him*. [Pp. 256–57]

It was natural that, as a Catholic Socialist, Morison would object to Bridges's occasional snide remarks about the Jesuits and to his lifelong contempt for socialism. The postscript refers specifically to these lines:

Thus 'tis that levellers, deeming all ethick one,
and for being Socialists thinking themselves Teachers,
can preach class-hatred as the enlightened gospel of love.

(270–72)

These lines are followed by the account of Sir Leonard Woolley's excavations at Ur, lines beautiful and moving as poetry but hardly effective as an argument against socialism.

Within a few weeks after these letters, Morison set about designing the quarto deluxe edition of *The Testament of Beauty*.

The Revisions of the Trial Text. For a number of years after Bridges's death the trial text was not available for study. However, with the acquisition of Stanley Morison's copy by the British Museum, and of a copy owned by Simon Nowell-Smith by the Bodleian library, it is now possible to study the revisions made by Bridges in the *Testament of Beauty.* The Bodleian copy is completely free of markings. In Morison's copy Book 1 is heavily corrected in Bridges's own hand. Books 2, 3, and 4 have no corrections. However, boxed with the trial text is a typescript of the final lines of Book 4 (lines 1,136 to 1,459 as numbered in the trial text—lines 1123 to 1446 as numbered in the final text of the 1953 Oxford collected edition). This typescript has been corrected in Bridges's own hand. As Nowell-Smith has explained, this final "tail" section of Book 4 was set up from uncorrected proofs of the first 8vo edition of *The Testament of Beauty,* and therefore the printed "tail" section does not have the status of a first draft as does the rest of the trial text.[13] The typescript is, probably, a first draft. Using it, therefore, in conjunction with Books 1, 2, 3, and the first part of Book 4, one can, by comparing the privately printed text and the typescript with the final text as it appears in the Oxford collected edition of 1953, study the changes Bridges made in *The Testament of Beauty.*

There are numerous variants in spelling and punctuation that I am disregarding in this study, which examines only the changes in wording. These changes fall into three categories: (1) the revision of a word or brief phrase to make a line conform to the prosody of the poem—twelve syllables to a line except for indented lines, which have ten syllables; (2) the revision of a word or phrase to improve style and/or precision of meaning; (3) rather substantial alterations of several lines or more for stylistic improvement, alterations that sometimes change the meaning and intention.

In the first book there are four passages substantially altered. At the beginning of his "Introduction" Bridges is describing in one of the most moving passages in the poem the feeling of a "new birth," of a childlike wonder that came to him late in life, an experience that was probably one of the motivations of *The Testament of Beauty.* Lines 8–18 in the final text read:

'Twas late in my long journey, when I had clomb to where
the path was narrowing and the company few,
a glow of childlike wonder enthral'd me, as if my sense
had come to a new birth purified, my mind enrapt
re-awakening to a fresh initiation of life;
with like surprise of joy as any man may know
who rambling wide hath turn'd, resting on some hill-top
to view the plain he has left, and see'th it now out-spredd
Mapp'd at his feet, a landscape so by beauty estranged
he scarce wil ken familiar haunts, nor his own home,
maybe, where far it lieth, small as a faded thought.

In the corresponding passage in the trial text the original version
reads:

'Twas late in my long journey, when I had clomb to where
the path was narrowing and the company few,
a glow of childlike wonder enthral'd me, as if my sense
had come to a new birth purified, my mind enrapt
re-awakening to a fresh initiation of life;
with like surprise of joy as oft a traveler feels
who resting on a hill has turn'd about to view
the plain he has left; and seeth it now outspredd
a landscape of far beauty, forest field and stream
mapp'd in perspectiv harmony, and he stands agaze
at pains to recognise his long familiar home
by beauty estranged, merging the stiff outlines of space
as the hard throbs of Time are blent in memory's mist.

It will be seen that in the final version a line has been lost,
but, stylistically Bridges has improved this passage in revision.
The vague phrase "perspective harmony" has been deleted, and
the unsatisfactory harsh final two lines of the original version
give place to

he scarce wil ken familiar haunts, nor his own home,
maybe, where far it lieth, small as a faded thought,

which contain one of the most memorable similes in the entire
Testament. A few lines later Bridges is contrasting the purely
materialistic-scientific concept of bird-song, "a light disturbance
of the atoms of air," with the poet's response to bird music.
Without the poet's ear, the trial text reads:

> . . . sound would have no report
> Nature have no music; nor would there be for thee
> any better melody in the April woods at dawn
> than an old stone-deaf labourer lying awake
> cheerless and lorn of life may perchance be aware of
> when a whole plague of rats run a mock in his thatch?

(84–89)

This has been revised to:

> . . . sound would hav no report,
> Nature hav no music; nor would ther be for thee
> any better melody in the April woods at dawn
> than what an old stone-deaf labourer, lying awake
> o'night in his comfortless attic, might perchance
> be aware of, when the rats run amok in his thatch?

The revision improves on the rather bathetic phrases "cheerless and lorn of life" and the hyperbolic "whole plague of rats."

When Bridges takes up the problem of the appearance of mind in the scheme of life consciousness (or, as he calls it, *conscience*), he rejects the notion that mind appeared accidentally,

> that whatsoever grew and groweth can be unlike
> in cause and substance to the thing it groweth on

and accepts the concept of Leibniz's "monad-atoms with mind." In the trial text occurs this passage:

> Though in the schools 'tis held a contradiction in terms
> to assert that Mind can exist, if incapable
> of their verbal dialectic to argue things out
> on the method whereby Mind itself is reduced
> to a chaos that calleth on the Creator afresh.

(433–37)

This has been completely revised to read in the final text:

> tho' in our schools of thought "unconscious mind" is call'd
> a contradiction in terms; as if the embranglements
> of logic wer the prime condition of all Being,
> the essence of things; and man in the toilsom journey

from conscience of nothing to conscient ignorance
mistook his tottery crutch for the main organ of life.

In both passages Bridges is attacking the verbal games of contemporary logicians, the importance of purely discursive reason.
The revision is somewhat easier to follow and much less prosaic
in style than the original.

In a vivid passage on the influence of Eastern culture on
Western thought, Bridges (no doubt remembering his own travels) wrote in his trial text:

> The best part of our lives we are wanderers in Romance:
> Our fathers travel'd Eastward to revel in wonders
> of pyramid and pagoda and picturesque attire,
> the outlandish reliquaries of nebulous time,
> as they dug Mammoths out, and Ichthyosaurian-bones
> from cliff or frozen scarp; but now will the Orientals
> make westward pilgrimage, like the Magi of old,
> and flock to gape at our unsightly novelties,
> factories, machines, and scientific tricks—they have seen
> the electric light in the West, and come to Worship.
> All things in turn have glory: Glory is opinion,
> the one doxology wherewith man praiseth God.

(499–515)

This was revised to:

> The best part of our lives we are wanderers in Romance:
> Our fathers travel'd Eastward to revel in wonders
> where pyramid pagoda and picturesque attire
> glow in the fading sunset of antiquity;
> and now wil the Orientals make hither in return
> outlandish pilgrimage: their wiseacres hav seen
> the electric light i' the West, and come to worship;
> tasting romance in our unsightly novelties
> and scientific tricks; for all things in their day
> may have opinion of glory: Glory is opinion,
> the vain doxology wherewith man would praise God.

The revised passage is undoubtedly superior—the harsh lines
about the Mammoths and the Ichthyosaurian bones have been
replaced by a single line, "glow in the fading sunset of antiquity,"
and the ugly phrase "flock to gape at" by "tasting romance in."

Of the briefer revisions, a number have been made for metrical reasons. All lines in *The Testament of Beauty* are twelve syllables except a few indented ten-syllable lines. Extra syllables are always in a context where they may be elided out. Thus line 416 of the trial text reads:

Thus I saw Conscient Reason as a natural flower-bud.

This has fifteen syllables without elision, fourteen syllables with the elision of *ur* in natural. It was revised to:

Thus I saw Conscience as a natural flower-bud,

which has twelve syllables with elision. Following are two other examples of revision for metrical reasons. The first is line 237 of the final text:

cumber'd him with servility, and his memory,

which as line 239 of the trial text read

cumber'd him with their servility, and his memory.

The original line had thirteen syllables (*or* of mem*o*ry is elided), the revised line twelve. Similarly line 319,

is Man's generic mark. A wolf that all his life,

originally read

is Man's generic essence. A wolf that all his life.

The revision of *essence* to *mark* reduces the line to twelve syllables. In fact, most of the revisions of Book 1 that involve only one line were made for metrical reasons although, of course, other stylistic matters were sometimes involved. A comparison of the original readings cited in the appendix of this chapter shows that in at least twenty-six cases a revision brought the syllable count from a line of more or less than twelve syllables to the proper amount. These lines, besides those already mentioned, as they are numbered in the final text are: 24, 43, 54, 67, 155, 179, 213, 217, 361, 371, 373, 474, 572, 579, 590, 671, 724, 747, 749, 758, 762, 767, and 771.

In Book 2 the most obvious revision is the deletion of twenty lines that originally appeared at the end of the book. Edward Thompson refers to this deletion and takes some credit for persuading Bridges to drop the entire passage.[4] (The passage will be found in the appendix.) Why did Bridges and Thompson dislike it? The quality of the poetry appears to be not inferior to much of the *Testament*. Probably Bridges had second thoughts about his fierce attack on the "Tyger" Clemenceau and the ungenerous peace terms of the Treaty of Versailles—an attack that was perhaps too narrowly political for a philosophical poem.

Another interesting revision occurs beginning with line 909 of the final text (see appendix for original reading). In both versions Bridges is stating his disagreement with Aristotle's philosophy as being too coldly intellectual, but the revised version is just a shade more moderate in tone and the striking lines

I have shrunk from the Arctic cold of Aristotle's heav'n
& the snow-image of his pensive deity

have unfortunately been dropped.

In the passage beginning with line 509 of the final text Bridges warns against the spiritual catastrophe that may result from a loss of religious faith and surrender to "the fury of Man's self-destructive passions." In his original draft Bridges succumbed to the temptation to overwrite—and there is the somewhat exaggerated picture of man without spiritual faith:

no pestilence so poisonous as his hideous sins,
no parch'd Sahara barren as his sour follies are,
no sorrow bitter as his vain tears, no abyss deep
as his despair, no death like to his ghostly fear.
Then will men, fashioning idols, kneel to monstrous gods
abstractions of oblivion and terror, devils
born in the shadow of negation—and will "look
to death's benumbing opium as their only cure,"
or even seek proudly to ennoble Melancholy
by embracement and make a last Wisdom of Woe.

(521–30, trial text)

This was fortunately revised to:

no pestilence so poisonous as his hideous sins.

Thus men in slavery of sorrow imagin ghastly creeds,
monstrous devilry, abstractions of terror, and wil *look
to death's benumbing opium as their only cure,*
or, seeking proudly to ennoble melancholy
by embracement will make a last wisdom of woe.

(520–25, final text)

Toward the end of the book Bridges refers to the massacres of
World War I and the "savage self-defence of England's peaceful
folk." As is to be expected, the point of view is that of the Allies,
but in the first draft there was a direct personal attack on the
kaiser that was eventually deleted:

But we who hav seen, constrain'd to teach our peaceful folk
to fashion, and wield, new instruments of death, to stem
the mass'd onrush of scientific savagery
wherewith the Prussian warlord would have swept the world. . . .

(970–73, trial text)

There are numerous other changes in the text, mostly minor,
and some for purely metrical reasons, that are entered in the
appendix.

In Book 3 the most extensive revision occurred in the passage
affirming the truth of the Platonic doctrine of love (lines 780–808
of the final text, 783–804 of the trial text). The revision is
perhaps somewhat superior to the original draft in cadence and
diction and is a bit stronger than the original in its attack on
purely carnal desire. There are a great many minor revisions
of single lines, chiefly for metrical reasons, throughout Book 3.

One of the most remarkable passages in *The Testament of
Beauty* occurs in Book 4 (lines 284ff. of the final text) and
describes the discoveries of Charles Leonard Woolley in Meso-
potamia. Bridges draws an unforgettable picture of ancient life
and conveys the intense interest of the English of the 1920s in
archaeological discoveries. The passage was supposed to be an
attack on socialist theories of the natural goodness of man. But

in fact, the passage is a digression that could stand as an independent poem. The trial text shows a number of stylistic changes in this passage designed to improve the cadence and make the tone slightly more elegant—for example, "he dug out from the dust" becomes "they shovel'd from the dust" and "each liegeman spear in hand,/ his head crush'd in his helmet" becomes "each liegeman spear in hand,/ in sepulchred attention." The most marked change in this passage is the deletion of these nine lines following line 337 of the final text:

> Standing now in the very arena of that terror,
> Envisaging the scene of human sacrifice,
> the explorer was dismay'd and griev'd moreover of heart
> because by script and cypher he had unriddled this folk
> to be the teachers of thatt great Sumerian Race
> whence Aryan culture sprang, himself their British heir
> (in lineage so remote it might be twentyfold
> thousandth generation) and he piously had held
> his proud Sumerian kin free of that Scythian crime.—
>
> (338–46, trial text)

These lines make Bridges's intentions in the Ur passage perfectly clear, and it was, perhaps, a mistake to omit them. Bridges has just described the glory of the court of the ancient warrior king and the splendor of the artifacts and jewelry and art work found in his tomb—and then the shock of the discovery of the slaughtered grooms and bodyguard who were sent to the other world along with their master. The point is that even in a great culture the evil in human nature is close to the surface and cannot be disregarded as (according to Bridges) it is disregarded by some socialist theoreticians. In the deleted passage Bridges makes the point clear, and the whole episode is therefore better integrated with the poem. I suspect that Bridges may have omitted it because it seemed to him and to some of his friends an unnecessary admission of weakness in Aryan-British culture. As in the previous books, there are numerous small stylistic changes—all of which are listed in the appendix.

Because the "tail" of Book 4 was set up from proof of the 8° volume and not from Bridges's corrected trial text, it is necessary to examine the changes Bridges made in the typescript of this section to ascertain his revisions of the original draft. These changes are listed in the appendix. All of them were made for minor metrical and stylistic reasons and do not require comment.

Vision and Reason

As all readers have noted, *The Testament of Beauty* is not a logically constructed philosophical poem. Rather, a few principal themes are stated, then developed by illustrative and sometimes digressive material, then restated with variations. The procedure suggests that of musical composition (music "whereby our art excelleth the antique" was one of the poet's strongest interests) ; yet, Bridges does not follow any specific kind of musical composition as Eliot did in constructing each of his *Four Quartets* according to the pattern of a late Beethoven quartet.

Book 1: Introduction. The first seven lines of the *Introduction* state an idea recurrent not only in the *Testament* but in Bridges's earlier poetry—that "Our stability is but balance." The reasoned life, or, as Bridges's friend Santayana called it, *The Life of Reason,* is precarious and under the constant threat of subrational and "demonic" forces in the individual and in society. There is a break after the seventh line and a change in tone that tend to substantiate the memory of Mrs. Bridges that the first seven lines were written as a unit and at a time considerably earlier than the rest of the poem.

With the eighth line the tone changes from one of calm deliberation to one of mystical transport as the poet recalls a moment of spiritual vision. Moments of vision, of mysterious and perhaps supernatural joy, had been the occasion for some of Bridges's most eloquent lines in his earlier poetry, and it is the subject of one of his finest lyrics, "Joy, sweetest lifeborn joy, where dost thou dwell?" (written 1879) :

> Then comes the happy moment: not a stir
> In any tree, no portent in the sky:
> The morn doth neither hasten nor defer,
> The morrow hath no name to call it by,
> But life and joy are one,—we know not why,—
> As though our very blood long breathless lain
> Had tasted of the breath of God again.

(43–49)

The moment of vision that appears to be the central motivating experience of the entire *Testament* occurred, the poet tells us, late in life:

> a glow of childlike wonder enthral'd me, as if my sense
> had come to a new birth purified, my mind enrapt
> re-awakening to a fresh initiation of life.

> (1.10–12)

The vision, a spiritual rebirth, suffused everything with a strange beauty, like a familiar landscape seen now from a different and higher perspective:

> . . . a landscape so by beauty estranged
> he scarce wil ken familiar haunts, nor his own home,
> maybe, where far it lieth, small as a faded thought.

> (1.16–18)

So far, the procedure in describing this experience has been allegorical and general. Bridges now compares it to and illustrates it with a trip he took on a day in June on the South Downs where he came upon a wild garden planted years before. He longed to "lie there ever indolently and undisturbed" to watch "the common flowers":

> each type a faultless essence of God's will, such gems
> as magic master-minds in painting or music
> threw aside once for man's regard or disregard;
> things supreme in themselves, eternal, unnumber'd
> in the unexplored necessities of Life and Love.

> (1.32–36)

These moments of vision may give not only the individual life but the culture of an entire society significance and value, as he says later of the Greeks:

> And every divination of Natur or reach of Art
> is nearer attainment to the divine plenitude
> of understanding, and in moments of Vision
>   their unseen company is the breath of Life.

> (1.688–91)

These visions, although they may give one an insight into eternity, are by their nature transitory. Most of our time is taken up with the business of ordinary living, which may best be conducted according to reason. Reason—its necessity, virtue, and limitations —is the countertheme of Book 1 of *The Testament of Beauty*.

Bridges is not very consistent in his use of the term *reason*. Sometimes it seems to mean consciousness or mental power. Sometimes it means sanity, common sense, good judgment. Sometimes it means the ability to construct intricate logical argument. Sometimes Bridges seems to be using the term in the Kantian sense—reason is the faculty by which we attain the knowledge of first principles. The context usually makes Bridges's intentions clear.

Reason, Bridges tells us in the passage beginning with line 57, is in "insolvency to sense" and "without alliance of the animal senses reason has no 'miracle'." There follows a lovely but somewhat digressive passage on the beauty of birds and of bird music, which without our senses would have no significance whatsoever. This passage is the first of many expressing Bridges's philosophy of monism—that the ideal spiritual world is indissolubly linked with and grounded on the material world as perceived by the senses. Even man's highest attainment, the response to the occult influence of Beauty that at the highest intensity becomes the moment of vision, is grounded on and impossible without the animal senses.

The limitations of reason and of man (who is distinguished from the animals by his faculty of reason) is surveyed in a passage beginning with line 129. Man's reason may be capable of discovering reality and what is. It is probably not capable of discovering the origins of things or the why of things. Furthermore, it should be remembered that man's reason in the entire scheme of nature is a "small and tickle . . . thing," and to the vast unconscious mind of man or of God it is merely a surface veneer. Furthermore, organic life itself, which makes reason possible, is an extremely small part of the physical universe.

Nevertheless, reason has its uses. Besides being a guide to conduct, it may in the act of contemplation give us the pleasure of seeing objects in their spiritual significance, and, furthermore, it is the faculty that makes poetic vision possible:

> . . . if **Reason's** only function were

to heighten our pleasure, thatt wer vindication enough.

(1.202–3)

Bridges's attitude here seems to be that of the refined intellectual hedonist, although in a later passage he claims that he rejects hedonism.

The major theme, vision, is picked up once again. Vision gives us an awareness of a "diviner principle implicit in Life" that transcends reason. There follows an account of visionaries and of moments of vision in history with particular reference to St. Francis and to Aquinas. Francis is praised as a mystic who had

> . . . but one garment—
> and scorning intellect and pursuit of knowledge
> liv'd as a bare spirit in its low prison of flesh.

(1.253–55)

Aquinas is somewhat less favorably depicted. His *Summa* was derived from a false premise, the fall of Adam, "the myth of a divine fiasco." Aquinas as a schoolman created a monstrous scheme of "illachrymable logic." However, he succeeded in transcending human reason and dogma:

> . . . his vision at Mass
> —in Naples it was when he fell suddenly in trance—
> was some disenthralment of his humanity.

(1.485–87)

After the vision, Aquinas found his own dogmatic writings of small worth.

Between these accounts of two religious visionaries there is a beautiful passage of pure description of a rural scene that begins as follows:

> The sky's unresting cloudland, that with varying play
> sifteth the sunlight thru' its figured shades, that now
> stand in massiv range, cumulated stupendous
> mountainous snowbillowy up-piled in dazzling sheen. . . .

(1.277–80)

These lines are not merely digressive, however. They illustrate another kind of mystical experience, outside Christian dogma and possible to the non-Christian:

> This spiritual elation and response to Nature
> is Man's generic mark.

(1.318–19)

This intellectual wonder, first revealed to savages and children, is the foundation of art, religion, and science:

> Thus Rafael once venturing to show God in Man
> gave a Child's eyes of wonder to the baby Christ.
> .   .   .   .
> 'Tis divinest Childhood's incomparable bloom,
> the loss whereof leaveth the man's face shabby and dull.

(1.331–32; 335–36)

Bridges returns to further metaphysical speculation and to a further critique of reason. Nature's purpose in creating man with "conscient" (i.e., conscious) reason was to arouse and satisfy a desire for knowledge. But is there will or purpose in nature itself? Man, in searching for the answer to this question, should remember that he himself is a part of nature and of its will and purpose, if there is a will and purpose. After a brief but respectful glance at Heraclitus and Leibniz, a comparison of instinct and reason (reason is superior—"Tis the Reason of man that is the exception and marvel"), and a further criticism of the limits of reason in the search for reality—

> this picklock Reason is still a-fumbling at the wards
> bragging to unlock the door of stern Reality—

(1.463–64)

Bridges describes the mystical trance of Aquinas previously discussed. At this point in the poem it appears that the answer to the metaphysical question will be found in the mystical experience that is ineffable.

There is next a brief historical survey that illustrates the misuse of faith and reason in the dark ages, followed by a consideration of ancient times. Egyptian and Grecian culture are compared. In Greece, conscient reason under the influence of divine "moments of Vision" reached its highest achievements:

> By such happy influence of their chosen goddess
> the mind of Hellas blossom'd with a wondrous flow'r,
> flaming in summer season, and in its autumn fall
> ripening an everlasting fruit, that in dying
> scatter'd its pregnant seeds unto all the winds of heav'n:
> nor ever again hath like bloom appear'd among men.

(1.692-97)

We can never again hope for the overall perfection of Greek culture, although our own Western world is superior to the Greeks in mathematics, music, and science.

The Greeks declined because they overesteemed "fleshly prowess" as in the Olympic games, a fault that led to an overesteem of the prowess of combat in war and to the empire of Alexander who overreached himself. Christ's empire of peace following that of Alexander was more admirable and more lasting, but it too has fallen into decay, and "the old lion's voice roareth o'er all the lands."

The moment of vision, of spiritual elation in response to beauty, is the highest experience possible to the individual man. It transcends reason, yet reason is necessary for the conduct of men in society and for the creation of culture. The greatest cultural achievements are the result of the operation of reason inspired by moments of vision. The poem *The Testament of Beauty* is itself a work of art inspired by such a moment.

Book 2: Selfhood. The book opens with the vision of Socrates (as recorded by Plato), who saw the spirit of man as a chariot speeding between heaven and earth drawn by two horses. The charioteer, Bridges tells us, is reason. The two horses, used, driven, and controlled by reason, are selfhood and breed. (In Plato they are called spirit and appetite.) Both selfhood and breed are animal instincts, but both are capable of development into higher forms of human experience and activity. Book 2 is primarily an analysis of the origin, development, and variations of the instinct of selfhood, together with a discussion of the charioteer reason, his virtues and limitations, and his relationship to selfhood. The theme and countertheme of Book 1 (reason and vision) receive further development. Usually, vision is considered to be higher than reason because it is capable of responding to the unseen powers, influences, and essences (Plato's Ideas) that profoundly affect our lives.

The origin of selfhood, the essence of self, which goes back to the atom, is evident in plants, which are examples of absolute selfhood, and in children, who at first as babies are as absolute in their instinctive selfhood as plants. What is the proper attitude of reason, the charioteer, toward the complete autarchy of the steed selfhood? He denounces it. But although it is reason's duty to govern this horse, nevertheless "Selfhood had of itself begotten its own restraint—." Beasts of prey, for instance, who hunt in packs for material benefit, show selfhood's own restraint in a very rudimentary form. Parental concern of birds and animals for their offspring and mother love in human life that puts constraints on absolute selfhood have their origins in instinct rather than in reason, and this love in its highest form seems to be a kind of mystical experience that has little to do with reason. These moments of mystical bliss that are like "a divine dream in the vaulted slumber of life" fashion "a new selfhood of spirit . . . in the redemption of beauty." Love and the response to the occult influence of beauty transform absolute selfhood and make it more responsive to the control of reason.

There follows a consideration of how nature operates without mother love, as in the life of bees and ants. His description of bee life here (as in the earlier "Epistle to a Socialist") leads him into a digressive attack on socialism and then to a comparison of the cells of a man's body with a colony of bees—both cells and bees operate instinctively without reason or love, although nature herself, in using bees to maintain the life of flowers, appears to be undertaking an unconscious "labor of love":

> or when, tho' *summer hath o'er brim'd their clammy cells*
> the shorten'd days are shadow'd with dark fears of dearth,
> bees ply the more, issuing on sultry noons to throng
> in the ivy-blooms—what time October's flaming hues
> surcharge the brooding hours, till passionat soul and sense

blend in a rich reverie with the dying year;—
when and wherever bees are busy, it is the flowers
dispense their daily task and determin its field;

.   .   .   .

Unwitting tho' it is, this great labor of love
in such kindly intimacy with nature's workings
hath a genial beauty.

(2.355–62; 365–67)

The individual bee, however (like the individual human being
in a socialistic society, according to Bridges), is of small worth
except for what it contributes to the welfare of the colony, and
his life without emotion or reason is extremely limited. This
comment on the bees leads to a reconsideration of "Conscient
Reason, the channel of man's spiritual joy" but also the channel
of bodily suffering in animals and men and of mental and spiritual
suffering in man. The child, especially, though in his innocence
he is "ever our nearest picture of happiness," is also particularly
susceptible to mental torments and terrors. There follows a
consideration of the problem of evil for which Bridges offers
two conventional solutions—evil is a challenge that stimulates
the virtue of courage: "good warriorship welcometh the challenge
of death." Second, as the chariot of the spirit of man speeds
toward heaven it needs not only reason to govern it but faith
to sustain it. Faith will overcome evil and prevent men from
looking *"to death's benumbing opium as their only cure."*
   The view that evil may stimulate courage leads to long
discussions of war as an expression of selfhood and art as an
expression of selfhood. In his much criticized comments on war,
Bridges seems to develop a perfectly ambivalent attitude. War is
good because it springs from disciplined selfhood and gives rise
to the virtues of courage, heroism, and self-sacrifice. Furthermore, war is entrenched in human psychology and history, it
has been exalted by poets, and it will probably always be with
us. On the other hand, when Bridges considers the horrors of
World War I, war appears to be bad. It arises not from disciplined
selfhood but from uncleanness of soul. It is a plague that has left
Western civilization sick in spirit. Between these two unresolved
and contradictory attitudes toward war, Bridges considers another
important expression of selfhood—art. Art is unreservedly praised

as the redeemer of man's spiritual life, inspired by experience beyond the reach of reason, that is, inspired by vision. It is a higher form of expression of man's spirit than philosophy or ethics. Art is both a response to the occult influence of beauty and a creation of new forms of beauty. Bridges's definitions of beauty and art are a key passage of the *Testament:*

> Beauty is the highest of all these occult influences,
> the quality of appearances that thru' the sense
> wakeneth spiritual emotion in the mind of man:
> And Art, as it createth new forms of beauty,
> awakeneth new ideas that advance the spirit
> in the life of Reason to the wisdom of God.

> (2.842–47)

Bridges, in considering the relationships of reason to war and to art, develops further his view that reason is a strictly limited faculty. He quotes Aristotle—

> Being (saith he) lieth in the unbroken exercise
> of absolute intellect—

> (2.911–12)

and disagrees with him "because the arch-thinker's heav'n cannot move my desire." Both beauty and love that is inspired by beauty are superior to reason. God himself is love, and the highest achievement of selfhood is

> . . . thatt mystic rapture, the consummation of which
> is the absorption of Selfhood in the Being of God.

> (2.926–27)

Reason, however, still has its uses in disciplining the spirit of selfhood in the warrior and in achieving a harmony between abstract intelligence and spiritual perception in the artist:

> For spiritual perception vague and uncontroll'd
> being independent of the abstract intelligence,
> he is disconcerted twixt their rival promises
>   . . . I conclude

that man's true wisdom were a reason'd harmony
and correlation of these divergent faculties.

(2.813–15; 817–19)

Book 3: Breed. Before taking up the second and "younger"
prime instinct of man, breed (that is, sex), Bridges treats the
reader to a 120-line digressive attack on the epicure who, with
the aid of reason, perverts a basic drive of selfhood, hunger, with
the false aesthetic of the gourmet. The epicure's obsession with
food and wine to the exclusion of higher pursuits "rotteth and
stinketh/ in the dust-bin of Ethick." The poet repeats briefly
his assertion that war, like hunger, comes from selfhood rather
than sex, and then begins his discussion of breed, which "is to
the race as SELFHOOD to the individual."

Nature's purpose in the differentiation of sex is the enrichment of species through the instinctive preference for beauty—
because of "love of Beauty," "our happiest espousals are nature's
free gift." As for the origins of sex, they lie "in thatt darkness/
wherein all origins are"—yet Bridges attempts to trace them.
He can ascertain no sex differentiation in the lowest forms of
life; he finds some in plants; in the higher animals he finds
considerable differentiation with periodic appetite and "mutual
attraction/ sometimes engaging Beauty." In man, sexual differentiation is most marked. His sexual experience consists of mutual
attraction, beauty, and constant conscious passion—all transformed
by reason to altruistic emotion and spiritual love. Examples of
spiritual or idealized love are to be found in Dante, Lucretius,
and Shakespeare. Love at first sight (which is for many the only
experience that approaches the miracle of mystical vision) inspired Dante to the highest expression of ideal love ever achieved
in poetry:

it happ'd to Dante, I say, as with no other man
in the height of his vision and for his faith therein:
the starry plenitude of his radiant soul,
searching for tenement in the bounties of life,
encounter'd an aspect of spiritual beauty
at the still hour of dawn which is holier than day:
as when a rose-bud first untrammeleth the shells
of her swathing petals and looseneth their embrace,

so the sunlight may enter to flush the casket
of her virgin promise.

(3.227–36)

Lucretius's "frenzy of Beauty" caused him to leave "his atoms
in the lurch" and fall to worshipping "Aphroditè, the naked
Goddess of man's breed." He was moved mainly by a contemplation of physical beauty. In Shakespeare's sonnets, on the other
hand, there is a balanced vision of beauty that is both spiritual
and physical. Bridges argues that "high beauty of the spirit,"
although it starts from physical beauty, is finally not dependent
on it

> but absolute in its transmittal of power and grace
> maketh a new beauty of its own appearances.

(3.286–87)

Purely physical love, he goes on to say, usually ends in despair
and melancholy, whereas "love's true passion is of immortal
happiness" of which the Greeks had some knowledge, but the
immortality of love is primarily a Christian concept.

After this excursion into Platonic and Christian concepts of
love and beauty, Bridges returns to his meditation on the lure
of purely physical beauty (the subject, incidentally, of "Eros,"
[see chap. 1] one of the most powerful of his short poems) :

> But think not Aphrodite therefor disesteem'd
> for rout of her worshippers, nor sensuous Beauty
> torn from her royal throne. . . .

(3.316–18)

The pleasure arising from a contemplation of physical beauty,
he considers superior to the pleasure arising from virtue. The
allure of bodily beauty is more active in the male but more
predominant in the female, "more deeply engaging life." Bodily
beauty, now considered to be primarily a feminine attribute,
was once considered to be a male attribute, primarily in the
hunting period of man's history. But as men turned to farming,
male beauty declined. There follows a digression on the develop-

ment of farming from team plowing to machinery—each method
producing a poetry of toil:

> How was November's melancholy endear'd to me
> in the effigy of plowteams following and recrossing
> patiently the desolat landscape from dawn to dusk,
> as the slow-creeping ripple of their single furrow
> submerged the sodden litter of summer's festival!

(3.354–58)

Farm machinery, however, also has a beauty of its own:

> Or what man feeleth not a new poetry of toil,
> whenas on frosty evenings neath its clouding smoke
> the engin hath huddled-up its clumsy threshing-coach
> against the ricks, wherefrom laborers standing aloft
> toss the sheaves on its tongue; while the grain runneth out,
> and in the whirr of its multitudinous hurry
> it hummeth like the bee, a warm industrious boom
> that comforteth the farm. . . .

(3.374–81)

Bridges now returns to a discussion of male and female beauty.
After a reference to the superior beauty of the male among
birds, he points out that it was man who finally ascribed beauty
to women and celebrated it in art and song, for men are superior
to women in the creation of art:

> . . . that the fair Muses
> should hav masculin wooers was Apollo's will.
> .   .   .   .
> Today if any lady in her boudoir rhymeth,
> she is drowned in man's tradition. . . .

(3.397–98; 403–4)

The Troubadours were the first to raise the worship of female
beauty to a kind of religion. The woman in the love relationship,
on the other hand, has a purpose deeper than the man. She is
driven by the instinct of motherhood, for

> . . . love's call to woman
> is graver and more solemn than it can be to him,
> by reason of her higher function and duty therein.

(3.449–51)

Because of the importance of motherhood it naturally follows
that lesbianism is a serious vice even when it results in the poetry
of Sappho, and for the same reason an overemphasis on asceticism
in certain religions is to be deplored.

Extreme denial of sex and of self occurred in the two "Wars
of the Essenes." (Bridges uses the name of the ancient monastic
Jewish sect to refer to perverse asceticism or Puritanism.) The
first war was against "the poetry/of SELFHOOD," that is, the
poetry of battle, the sagas and epics that celebrated the battles
of the dark ages during and following the destruction of the
Roman empire. The "Essene" (i.e., Catholic) priests denounced
these bards of battle and attempted to turn their attention to
Christian religious subjects—Bible stories, saints' lives, mystery
plays. Even British Arthur and his knights were Christianized.
The second war of the "Essenes" was against "the young poetry
of BREED," specifically the love poetry of the Troubadours who
created a new ideal of womanhood and wrote in

> a fine phantasy of spirit with light fabric of art;
> so the faint dream of chivalry, as it took-on form,
> tripp'd delicately with the delicat music
> of the tentativ language . . .

(3.652–55)

so that "Provence seemed to mankind the one land of delight,—"
comparable to Hawaii, Samoa, Kashmiri, and several other earthly
paradises that Bridges lists in a passage of Miltonic name-dropping
that includes a number of Troubadour towns in Provence. However, this land of peace and love harbored the Manichees, heretics
who believed the visible world to be the work of the devil.
Pope Innocent III proclaimed the Albigensian war against them,
and the Manichees were destroyed along with the culture of
Provence, although many Troubadours escaped the slaughter and
fled to Italy where the devotees of the New Learning gave them
asylum and where their idealization of woman combined with

the Church's worship of the Mother of God assured the Christian consecration of marriage.

There follows a meditation on the importance of the vision of beauty in redeeming the selfhood of man, for

> . . . mankind's love of life
> apart from love of beauty is a tale of no count.

(3.748–49)

This same vision of beauty also redeems sex, which in man would have been mere animal pleasure "had he not learn'd in beauty to transfigure love."

This vision of beauty is real, even though the scientist as scientist can know nothing of it. "How should science find beauty?" The philosopher Leibniz thought he had solved the problem by setting up two independent worlds of matter and mind that move in preestablished harmony. The world of matter would be the proper object of scientific knowledge. Beauty, which belongs to the world of mind, would be the proper province of the philosopher and artist. Although Leibniz's doctrine is irrefutable (it cannot be proved or disproved), Bridges seems to reject it as "a pleasant freak of man's godlike intelligence." Indeed, Leibniz's dualism is inconsistent with the fundamental monism of Bridges's philosophy.

In the passage that follows, Bridges appears to be arguing that one knows beauty to be real by the experience of one's response to it in nature and in women. Just as wonder is the chief motivation of intellect, so beauty is the principal "mover and spring" of man's soul. It is beauty in the opposite sex that leads to Christian marriage, a bond that in spite of its too frequent disillusionments, is necessary for complete love. Happiness in marriage depends chiefly on the proper correlation of spirit and mind. This the Jews understood in their concept of mating as symbolized in the creation of Eve from the rib of Adam. (Nowell Charles Smith points out quite correctly that Bridges's interpretation of this myth is not at all clear.) The notion of marriage as a purely spiritual and intellectual companionship was carried to extremes by the Puritans. After a brief reference to "vestiges of his strong asceticism" in man's archaic prehistory, Bridges holds up as an ideal the institution of marriage as it is practiced among the British aristocracy in which woman with her "potency/ of spirit stored in flesh" by intuition draws man's earthly passion to spiritual love, "From blind animal passion to the vision of Spirit."

This evolution of mind that is caused by a love of beauty leads from the poet's consideration of sex to a discussion of art as "the true and happy science of the soul." No plastic art can wholly escape its earthly medium, but music and poetry can achieve suprasensuous vision. The art of painting, striving for portrayal of spirit, made use of symbolism that proved to be inferior to the appeal to direct feeling. For example, in Titian's *Women at a Well*, the idealized naked feminine figure of earthly love is more effective than the "draped Uranian figure" of celestial love. Any attempt to portray pure spirit in plastic art is bound to fail. Symbolism and allegory in painting become merely fanciful and removed from reality, as the child in Titian's painting of the women at the well sees the reflection of the female figures rather than the figures themselves as he gazes in the well and confuses their identity by stirring the water with his hand and mingling their reflected images.

Book 4: Ethick. In the first ninety lines, which treat mainly of beauty, the reader finds once again the joint theme of vision and reason. It is the function of reason to harmonize the soul's visions of beauty, which are strongest in the child but which may recur, usually for moments only, in the adult:

> . . . these intimations come to be understood
> and harmonized by Reason in the conduct of life.

(4.78–79)

"Ethick" is the science of the conduct of life under the control of the charioteer of Plato's myth, that is, under the harmonizing discipline of Reason. But the principal motivation, the driving force of life, is Beauty, which

> attempteth every mortal child with influences
> of her divine supremacy. . . .

(4.4–5)

Beauty like

> the red blood floodeth into a beating heart
> to build the animal body

(4.8–9)

and at the same time it can

> flush his spirit
> with pleasurable ichor of heaven.

(4.10–11)

Response to beauty is strongest and most spontaneous in the child. Childlike spirituality has been fittingly symbolized in the infant Jesus. In the adult this spiritual experience as a result of awakened sexual impulses may degenerate into lust. On the other hand, these impulses under the guidance of reason may lead to virtue, that is, to good conduct.

The science of conduct, Ethick, implies a sense of duty. From lines 91 to 361 Bridges considers the meaning and significance of the term *duty*. It is "Necessity become conscient in man" that closes the Ring of Being:

> The Ring in its repose is Unity and Being:
> Causation and Existence are the motion thereof.
> Thru'out all runneth Duty. . . .

(4.123–25)

The origin of the sense of duty may be found in the instinct of birds and animals. The black ouzel building a nest "under the Rosemary on the wall" in a primitive way is carrying out a compulsive duty by instinct. In higher animals the instinctive sense of duty is modified by experience and education. Duty enters the moral field when man's conscience transforms selfhood to affection and sex (breed) to spiritual love. The sense of duty in man gives rise to social codes, but these become outmoded and repressive.

Teachers, "men of inborn nobility," "saviours of society," are needed to lead and educate men in the two kinds of Ethick—social and spiritual. Levelers and socialists, "Sticklers for equality," will not follow such spiritual guides although they may accept a social Ethick that is merely legalized virtue. After his attack on Socialists for preaching the doctrine of "class-hatred as the enlighten'd gospel of love" (Bridges expressed a similar dislike of Socialism twenty-seven years previously in his "To a Socialist in London"), there follows the brilliant and moving account of Sir Leonard Woolley's excavations in Ur. It is one of the finest passages of poetry in the *Testament,* yet misapplied for it proves nothing. Bridges is attempting to illustrate the failure of social Ethick as legalized virtue by citing four examples of barbarous brutality within a seemingly civilized society. The first is Woolley's discovery of the massacre of the king's body-guard, harem, and servants at Ur. After the excavators had

> shovel'd from the dust
> the relics of thatt old monarch's magnificence—
> Drinking vessels of beaten silver or of clean gold,
> vases of alabaster, obsidian chalices,
> cylinder seals of empire and delicat gems
> of personal adornment, ear-rings and finger-rings,
> craftsmen's tools copper and golden, and for music a harp—

(4.293–99)

Woolley discovered the evidence of the massacre-sacrifice committed in honor of the king:

> his spirit, dazed awhile
> in wonder, suddenly was strick'n with great horror;
> for either side the pole, where lay the harness'd bones
> of the yoke-mated oxen, there beside their bones
> lay the bones of the grooms, and slaughter'd at their post
> all the king's body-guard, each liegeman spear in hand,
> in sepulchred attention; and whereby lay the harp
> the arm-bones of the player, as there she had pluck'd her dirge,
> lay mingled with its fragments; and nearby disposed
> two rows of skeletons, her sisterly audience
> whose lavish ear-pendants and gold-filleted hair,
> the uniform decoration of their young service,
> mark'd them for women of the harem, sacrified
> to accompany their lord, the day when he set forth
> to enter into the presence of the scepter'd shades
> congregated with splendour in the mansions of death.

(4.322–37)

A second illustration of the savage immorality possible within
a strict social code is taken from the Hindu Suttee where

> the mild Hindus hav burnt
> their multitudinous girl-concubines alive.

(4.344–45)

The third example is the execution of the wives of Henry VIII
who, in Bridges's opinion, was (because he was supposedly
Christian and a defender of the faith) more despicable than the
old monarch of Ur. The final example is the callous treatment
by British society of

> the London poor
> in their Victorian slums lodged closer and filthier
> than the outraged alien; and under liberty's name
> our Industry is worse fed and shut out from the sun.

(4.357–60)

The discussion of duty is followed by a long meditation on
pleasure (362–594). Bridges rejects out of hand "pure Hedonism"
and "spiritual Hedonism" because hedonists do not distinguish
between good and bad pleasures. It is the prime task of Ethick
to make such a distinction. Pleasure arises from selfhood, from
"Life-joy," from "the grace and ease of health alike in body and
mind" and is not necessarily bad but, indeed, may be a positive
good. Pleasure, therefore, is not necessarily contrary to virtue.
The saints were wrong in their abnormal fear of pleasure, as
was Gerard Manley Hopkins in his refusal of a peach for fear
of the pleasure it would give him:

> when the young poet my companion in study
> and friend of my heart refused a peach at my hands,
> he being then a housecarl in Loyola's menie,
> 'twas that he fear'd the savor of it.

(4.434–37)

The saints fear pleasure because it distracts from holiness; yet,
the mystical communion of the saint with God is a kind of
pleasure. Pleasure then cannot be rejected in toto, even by the
saints. Another kind of pleasure that is a positive good and not

contrary to virtue is the response to the beauties of nature, and to illustrate the point Bridges in a fine descriptive passage (463–506) recalls the pleasure he feels in the colors, shapes, and perfumes of flowers:

> The imponderable fragrance
> of my window-jasmin, that from her starry cup
> of red-stemm'd ivory invadeth my being,
> as she floateth forth, and wantoning unabash'd
> asserteth her idea in the omnipotent blaze
> of the tormented sun-ball, chequering the grey wall
> with shadow-tracery of her shapely fronds; this frail
> unique spice of perfumery, in which she holdeth
> monopoly by royal licence of Nature,
> is but one of a thousand angelic species,
> original beauties that win conscience in man.

(4.466–76)

Man, "vain of his Reason," sometimes mistakenly uses his reason to make a distinction between pleasure and happiness, but Bridges rejects this distinction as false, arguing that

> The name of happiness is but a wider term
> for the unalloy'd conditions of the Pleasur of Life.

(4.533–34)

As man develops, the quality of his pleasure will change from mere "animal life-joy" to what Aristotle called "the Perfect Happiness" achieved by a combination of spiritual, mental, and animal pleasures.

Man's spiritual advancement in achieving the habit of virtue depends on good disposition and right education. Mimicry, an inborn faculty in man, is important in achieving good disposition. The inborn love of beauty and the tendency to imitate will establish the well-bred child in the habit of virtue for he will naturally imitate beautiful things and good actions. Love of beauty and response to beauty are most important in the growth of the spiritual life in the child; hence (the implication is) a child brought up in a good environment among beautiful surroundings will have an advantage over the child brought up amid ugliness and poverty. The ability to absorb spiritual things precedes the intellectual faculty. In stressing the importance of a beautiful environment in the early development of spiritual growth, Bridges is implying the importance of the established, wealthy, aristocratic family. A poor child in a bleak environment may have great native intellectual ability, but his spiritual life may be permanently stunted at an early age, and his intellectual training may therefore be fruitless.

After a passage dealing with spiritual combat and with the question of who has the more virtue, a person who leads a good life without inner conflict or a person who achieves virtue only after struggle, Bridges comments on Socrates' doctrine of *know thyself,* that is, to banish ignorance by turning reason inwardly upon the mind. There follows a long analytical discourse (781–1137) on the nature of the mind. All terrestrial life is "logically correlated in action under some final cause." These "co-ordinations" may be conscious with reasoned purpose as when one learns to play a musical instrument; they may be innate as in the spontaneous flight of birds; they may be altogether unconscious as cellular coordination in plants or the digestive processes in man, which "proudly stand off from conscience." But although these "unify'd organities" may be unconscious, they are, nevertheless, stimulated by thought as well as by sensation. The "corporate mind" that governs action is partly mental and partly physical. There is no boundary between mind and matter.

Spontaneous life "oweth nought to Reason" nor do the ideas of Beauty, Courage, Mirth, Faith, Love, Poetry, or Music. Reason's property is the idea of order. Its special provinces are mathematics, science, and philosophy, but reason's scope is not universal. Again Bridges is emphasizing the limitations of reason.

Socrates has told us to know ourselves, that is, our minds. What is mind? Every man is a personality consisting of body and mind, which are inseparable. Every man is the unique creation of and evolved consciousness of "Universal Mind." The intellect of every man is formed of the essential ideas with which he has come into contact by means of the senses. The number of ideas in the intellect of the individual man is strictly limited by his environment both personal and national. (The Christological heresy of the Armenians, for example, has been maintained because of their narrow isolated nationalism.)

Nobility of soul consists not in the number of ideas in the soul, but in what Bridges calls a *harmony of Essences.* Harmony between man and nature is also important and possible because, when man engages in artistic creation, it is nature itself that is functioning in the creative faculty. The ideas of the artist start from nature and draw their imagery from nature. Furthermore, art (particularly poetry) is the intimate echo of the artist's own life. The artist fixes his hold on joy by expressing "some mintage of himself." Thus the old dichotomies between art and nature and art and life are rejected. It is evident from this passage that Bridges finds the most nearly perfect harmony of essences, and hence the greatest nobility of soul, in the poet.

What, then, is the true function of reason? Reason can diagnose and sometimes cure disharmony of ideas in the mind. Once the mind has achieved harmony of ideas with the aid of reason, the will can act for good. However, when ideas are in disharmony, or when there is a tyranny of one idea, the action of the will may be bad.

Bridges has now described the growth of the mind from unconscious existence to spiritual consciousness through the guiding aid of reason. As man matures, reason orders the attitude of the soul as it seeks self-realization in the vision of God. This brings the reader back to the theme of reason and vision introduced in Book 1. Reason is inferior to vision; yet reason has the important function of *preparing the soul for vision.*

The proper relationship between creature and creator, between man and God, is called religion. And just as in the past religion frequently degenerated into superstition, so today in the midst of scientific materialism and a physical environment made ugly by industrialism, man, in his "hankering after lost Beauty," has frequently succumbed to superstition and false religions.

Because man is a spiritual animal (an appellation, says Bridges, nearer the truth than rational animal) he feels the need of prayer, "the heav'n breathing foliage of faith." Prayer has been neglected by moral philosophers; yet it is an exercise as necessary to the soul as physical exercise is to the body, and when properly conducted redeems for the soul the beauty of holiness. It is this beauty of holiness that saves mankind from the vulgar irrationality of the herd, the common folk who are often driven by the obsession of a fixed idea like a crowd at a football game. Even the philosopher may be carried away by the irrational fixations of the mob. Yet it is appropriate for the philosopher to respond to and join the prayer of the common folk, which has a special dignity and humility. Prayer implies fellowship, and even the solitary ascetic mystic enjoys a mysterious communication with fellow mystics in the communion of saints.

As to the central idea of many religions, immortality, Bridges rejects the concept of the resurrection of the body. As for the mind, it too perishes with the body unless

> the personal co-ordination of its ideas
> hav won to Being higher than animal life.

> (4.1263–64)

A trancelike vision of beauty inspired by a sunset leads the poet to consider again the relationship between vision and reason:

> Verily by Beauty it is that we come at WISDOM,
> yet not by Reason at Beauty.

> (4.1305–6)

Reason (with an ironic comment on its use in scholastic theology in constructing a hierarchy of angels between God and man) is again relegated to a faculty inferior to the capacity for responding to beauty.

The final lines of the poem (1314–1446) are concerned with love as it occurs between mother and child, man and woman, man and Christ, and man and God. This love is

> ONE ETERNAL
> in the love of Beauty and in the selfhood of Love

> (4.1445–46)

or, as Nowell Charles Smith puts it: "God loves the world of men, [and] returns their love which, imperfect though it is, has been won by the vision of his own Beauty."[15]

Prosody and Style

Bridges in *The Testament of Beauty* describes his lines as "my loose Alexandrines," and Dean Inge is reported to have said that he hated loose Alexandrines worse than loose living. The prosody of the poem has been a matter of difficulty to many, even to those most sympathetic to Bridges's poetry. Some, like Trevelyan and Santayana, have considered it to be successful; others, like Yvor Winters, believe it to be much of the time awkward and prosaic.

As shown above,[16] these "loose Alexandrines" were the final result of Bridges's experiments in neo-Miltonic syllabics. Carrying what he considered to be Milton's practice of "freeing" every foot except the last foot one step further, Bridges "freed" every foot in the line and increased the line from five to six feet.

The dictionary definition of an Alexandrine is "a line of poetry of six iambic feet." The "loose Alexandrine" of the *Testament* has the equivalent of six iambic feet—that is, twelve syllables—but the feet are not necessarily iambic. (Occasionally a line has ten syllables. Such a line is always indented.) "Extra" syllables are always reduced by elision. In practice, this verse gave Bridges a great deal of metrical freedom so that he could imitate speech cadences or attempt special effects not possible in strictly accentual syllabic verse. It enabled him to include philosophical and factual material usually reserved for expository prose. The best way to read this poetry is with no attention to scansion (it doesn't scan by any known system), but preserving normal speech accents and rhythms. In most instances, the reader will find the poetry has a cadence appropriate to its subject matter, with a richness of texture derived from various standard devices—alliteration, imagery, vowel and consonant chimes—and given rhythmic emphasis by fairly strong end stops at the conclusion of each line.

Elizabeth Cox Wright[17] was the first to note the importance of the end-stopped line in the rhythms of the *Testament*. She agrees with Guérard that one important aspect of the rhythm is identical syllable count in each line. But she points out that there is no prosodic unit *within the line* since Bridges, by freeing the foot, is left without any consistent pattern of iambs or trochees as a metrical norm. The prosodic unit, according to Wright, is not the foot but the single line—and each line takes an equal time to pronounce. This, she believes, was Bridges's intention—that the line (end paused) is the basic prosodic unit and not the foot or syllable, and she argues that Bridges in effect achieved his intention without ever clearly stating it. Thus there is a metrical rhythm based on the single line that sets up a counterpoint with the rhythm of the speaking voice.

Wright defines and defends the prosody of the *Testament* as follows:

> First, some of the familiar music of accentual metres is allowed to appear from time to time, the use of both accentual pattern and end-pause giving special emphasis to these lines. Second, there is a constant play of variation in the marking of the end-pause comparable in richness to the more usual kind of counterpoint in English poetry. But most important of all, this metre permits the inclusion of all the poem's disparate experience in appropriate idiom and inflection by liberating the speech-rhythms under the discipline of isochronous lines. By this, a voice emerges as the auditory evidence of a dramatic figure, which with range of utterance sufficient to encompass all the material, nevertheless unifies the poem into a kind of interpreted story of mankind.[14]

Bridges, at any rate, whether or not Wright's theory of the isochronous line is correct, devised a medium capable of the most varied effects ranging from the mystical transport of the medieval dream-vision poetry (enhanced by a deliberate use of archaic diction) to discussions of social theory and scientific thought, matters usually reserved for expository prose. A few illustrations of Bridges's skill in achieving special effects may aid the reader in making his own discoveries.

All of his life Bridges had a passion for music, and there are frequent references to music in his earlier poetry. Music in various forms—the song of birds, the sound of bees—echo through the Alexandrines of *The Testament of Beauty*. Some of the most haunting effects, oddly enough, use references to music to enhance a feeling of entranced silence, such as these lines that introduce the intricate silence of abstract speculation on "ethic lore":

> tho' no lute ever sounded there nor Muse hath sung,
> deviously in the obscure shadows. . . .

(4.765–66)

Anyone familiar with Elizabethan love verses sung to the lute will recognize the aptness of "deviously." Again to suggest en-

tranced moments of silent, spiritual bliss Bridges combines sound
with visual effects:

> As when a high moon thru' the rifted wrack
> gleameth upon the random of the windswept night;
> or as a sunbeam softly, on early worshippers
> at some rich shrine kneeling, stealeth thru' the eastern apse
> and on the clouded incense and the fresco'd walls
> mantleth the hush of prayer with a vaster silence,
> laden as 'twer with the unheard music of the spheres;
> —nay, incommunicable and beyond all compare
> are the rich influences of those moments of bliss,
> mocking imagination or pictured remembrance,
> as a divine dream in the vaulted slumber of life.

(2.166–76)

The passage should be read aloud, unrhetorically, in a normal
speaking voice for a full appreciation of the richness of sound
texture.

Bridges was, quite naturally, interested in the songs of the
troubadours, and he makes a skillful use of dentals in this passage:

> so the faint dream of chivalry, as it took-on form
> stripp'd delicatly with the delicat music
> of the tentative language. . . .

(3.653–55)

The hum of bees, the sound of rural streams, bird music
echo through *The Testament of Beauty*. The sounds are evident
in describing a threshing machine:

> and in the whirr of its multitudinous hurry
> it hummeth like the bee, a warm industrious boom;

(3.379–80)

or a Greek landscape:

> Long had the homing bees plunder'd the thymy flanks
> of famed Hymettus harvesting their sweet honey.

(1.653–54)

or an English landscape:

> valleys
> vocal with angelic rilling of rocky streams.

(1.312–13)

The mazy dreams that come to him in the Muse's "garden of thought" are compared to bats in several very beautiful lines:

> as when
> the small bats, issued from their hangings, flitter o'erhead
> thru' the summer twilight, with thin cries to and fro
> hunting in muffled flight atween the stars and flowers.

(4.1283–86)

And the following passage is typical of Bridges's constant attention to bird music:

> Lov'st thou in the blithe hour
> of April dawns—nay marvelest thou not—to hear
> the ravishing music that the small birdës make
> in garden or woodland, rapturously heralding
> the break of day; when the first lark on high hath warn'd
> the vigilant robin already of the sun's approach,
> and he on slender pipe calleth the nesting tribes
> to awake and fill and thrill their myriad-warbling throats
> praising life's God.

(1.63–71)

The passage is not too obviously onomatopoeic like Tennyson's "the moan of doves in immemorial elms," yet liquid *l*'s and *r*'s and vowel sounds subtly suggest the music of birds throughout.

Bridges's daughter, Elizabeth Daryush, testifies to the poet's knowledge of flowers; he knew the names of all the wild flowers around Oxford and taught them to her. This love of flowers appears frequently in his poetry. One of the finest passages occurs in Book 4 of the *Testament*:

> The imponderable fragrance
> of my window-jasmine, that from her starry cup
> of red-stemm'd ivory invadeth my being,

as she floateth it forth, and wantoning unabash'd
asserteth her idea in the omnipotent blaze
of the tormented sun-ball, checquering the grey wall
with shadow-tracery of her shapely fronds; this frail
unique spice of perfumery, in which she holdeth
monopoly by royal licence of Nature,
is but one of a thousand angelic species,
original beauties that win conscience in man . . .
                    Legion is their name;
Lily-of-the-vale, Violet, Verbena, Mignonette,
Hyacinth, Heliotrope, Sweet-briar, Pinks and Peas,
Lilac and Wallflower, or such white and purple blooms
that sleep i' the sun. . . .

                                   (4.466–77, 481–85)

The quoted lines are but part of a long passage that achieves
an amazingly rich texture of sight and smell.

Clouds, as shown above, often move Bridges to landscape
painting in verse:

The sky's unresting cloudland, that with varying play
sifteth the sunlight thro' its figured shades, that now
stand in massiv range, cumulated stupendous
mountainous snowbillowy up-piled in dazzling sheen,
Now like sailing ships on a calm ocean drifting,
Now scatter'd wispy waifs, that neath the eager blaze
disperse in air; Or now parcelling the icy inane
highspredd in fine diaper of silver and mother-of-pearl
freaking the intense azure. . . .

                                   (1.277–85)

Contrasting sound and movements in lines 4, 5, and 6 of this
quotation, which suggest the varying texture and movement of
the clouds, are particularly effective.

The poem, of course, abounds in apt similes and metaphors.
One of the best occurs early in Book 1. The poet is climbing a
hill and has reached a point where he can look back and see his
native landscape, which he thought he knew well, but is now
changed by a new beauty. The journey up the narrowing path
is itself a symbol of his advance into old age. Within this extended
metaphor or symbol is the fine simile comparing his home seen
at a distance to a faded thought:

          a landscape so by beauty estranged
he scarce wil ken familiar haunts, nor his own home,
maybe, where far it lieth, small as a faded thought.

(1.17–18)

A few lines further on, two similes are combined to illustrate
this rebirth of spiritual life in response to beauty:

      as if in a museum the fossils on their shelves
      should come to life suddenly, or a winter rose-bed
      burst into crowded holiday of scent and bloom.

(1.41–43)

Bridges throughout his career made good use of the extended
simile in the manner of Dante and Milton. The following, which
illustrates the subjective versus the objective view of the outer
world, is a good example:

      As a man thru' a window into a darken'd house
peering vainly wil see, always and easily,
the glass surface and his own face mirror'd thereon,
tho' looking from another angle, or hooding his eyes
he may discern some real objects within the room—
some say 'tis so with us, and also affirm that they
by study of their reflection hav discover'd in truth
ther is nothing but thatt same reflection inside the house.

(1.350–57)

Bridges in *The Testament of Beauty* employs an extremely flex-
ible verse form that enables him effectively to illustrate a few
themes and recurrent motifs with a wealth of material brought
together from widely divergent fields of science, exploration,
art, music, philosophy, history, religion, and so forth, all of this
material being expressed by means of standard poetic devices
yet given freshness and vitality because of the poet's mastery of
the language.

Bridges and Santayana

George Santayana, after resigning his professorship at Harvard in 1912, spent the rest of his life abroad. During the war years (1914–18) he was in England. By 1915 he had met Bridges and was lunching with him at Oxford. Bridges wrote to Logan Pearsall Smith on December 20, 1915, "Santayana has been to lunch with me twice at C.C.C. I like him very much, and hope to see more of him."[19] Their relationship, however, began by correspondence at a much earlier date. About the turn of the century a friend showed Bridges Santayana's *Interpretations of Poetry and Religion* with the remark, "Here is somebody whose philosophy seems to be much like yours."[20] Bridges, after reading the book, wrote Santayana an appreciative letter.

According to George Howgate, "Bridges was one of Santayana's most intimate friends in England, and long conversations upon philosophy and life served to bring out the discoveries and insights they held in common."[21] In 1918 Smith was planning his *Little Essays Drawn from the Writings of George Santayana* (published in 1920): Bridges, in corresponding with Smith about his book, indicated that he had read only two or three of Santayana's volumes but intended a further study of the philosopher:

> I feel that it is a very responsible work, and I sh^d not like to have any of the responsibility without reading a good deal more of the books. I happen to have read two of them lately and I might be of some use concerning them. As far however as your bk. will represent his philosophy, so as the reader might understand his system of the universe & his metaphysick, I sh^d be quite useless. Especially as I do not understand metaphysics.[22]

Again in 1920 Bridges indicated he would be glad to review Smith's selection for the *London Mercury* but, he wrote, "I must keep away from his philosophy or I may get into trouble."[23] Four years later Bridges is still referring to Santayana in his letters to Smith:

> I had a long letter from Santayana the other day. I wrote to him because I was enjoying his books so much. I like his Vol. in *American thought* [*Character and Opinion in the United States*] most of all—also *Egotism* [*Egotism in German Philosophy*] is full of good matter—his reputation has got very high with writer[s] but I find the philosophers are puzzled and reluctant to praise him. I wish he wd come back to Oxford

—But his Latin feelings are intensifying, and he says that England reminds him of America. I thought very well of the Americans.[24]

On January 24, 1926, when Book 1 of *The Testament of Beauty* had already been started, Bridges told Smith of his daily reading of the Spanish philosopher:

You are locally nearer Santayana than I am, and I hope you will see him. Lately he has been my daily companion, for I have made and am making an effort to work through his "system."—I find him difficult but except in certain emotional attitudes, I agree with him so entirely when I think that I quite understand him, that I have the exquisite patience to wrestle with his dialectic: which is often profoundly embarrassing, & I confess that I sh^d be inclined to disregard it if I were not always hoping to discover—and sometimes I do discover—by his byeways the actual footing of his mind. In spite of his wanton indulgence in metaphysical gymnastics (which are those of an expert and graceful acrobat) the more I read him the better I like him. He confirms me in my own heresies: and I could not overstate my wonder at the unfailing and solid riches of his rhetoric.[25]

Of all Santayana's works, *The Life of Reason* (1905–6) probably had the greatest influence on the *Testament*. Dr. Benjamin Rand, after a visit with Bridges, is reported to have said that the poet took down his volumes of *The Life of Reason* from the shelf and read passages that paralleled *The Testament of Beauty*.[26] And of course Bridges refers to this work by title in Book 4, line 1088.

Santayana, on his side, liked and admired the poet laureate. In *Soliloquies in England* he refers to "the hospitable eminence of Chilswell,"[27] and in his autobiography he speaks of Bridges's natural, unpretentious manner and says that this was one of the very few cases in which he had a close friendship with an older and famous man. The Latin philosopher was particularly impressed with the Anglo-Saxon's physical stamina:

Robert Bridges, the most complete of Englishmen, at the age of eighty, used to take his cold bath every morning in the lounge-hall of his house, before a roaring wood fire. Here was Sparta rather than India transported to the chilly North.[28]

Bridges, on his part, returned the admiration and in 1919 made a serious attempt to persuade Santayana to settle down in Oxford because he "had things to say that the English needed to hear." Bridges persuaded the Head of Corpus Christi to offer Santayana membership for life in the Common Room and at High Table. Santayana politely refused, saying he was in danger of losing his "philosophical cruelty and independence," and moved on to Paris.[29]

Bridges began studying Santayana seriously when the philosopher's reputation was very high, at home and abroad. Howgate says, "Never, except perhaps now [1938] has he been so much before the public eye as in the period from 1920–1923."[30] During these years appeared *Character and Opinion in the United States, Little Essays Drawn from the Writings of George Santayana, Soliloquies in England, Scepticism and Animal Faith,* and a reissue of *The Life of Reason.* All evidence points to *The Life of Reason* being the major influence of Santayana on Bridges, although the early *Sense of Beauty* and Santayana's famous doctrine of essences—developed systematically in *The Realm of Essence* (1927) —foreshadowed in earlier books also played a part.

Bridges's review of *Little Essays* is of help in any analysis of the influence of the philosopher on the poet. Bridges praises Santayana's craftsmanship, diction, and style as well as his philosophical system. "The book has, therefore, two claims, literary and philosophical."[31] Of his style Bridges wrote, "Indeed it has been said that George Santayana has imperilled the recognition of his philosophy by the fine robes in which he has consistently presented it."[32] As to Santayana's thought, Bridges likes Santayana's attack on the philosophers who construct dialectical systems, and he refers with approval to his remark that such philosophers do not proceed as honest searchers for truth but rather as lawyers who labor to make the best of a case to which they are professionally committed. In his own "system" Santayana, says Bridges,

> recognizes Spinoza and Democritus for his immediate masters, and his philosophy might perhaps be describ'd as a building up of idealism—that is, the supremacy of the imagination— on a naturalistic or materialistic basis.[33]

This building up of idealism by means of the imagination on a materialistic basis is also the procedure of Bridges in *The Testament of Beauty*. Bridges also mentions, apparently with approval, Santayana's concept of reason as the faculty that "harmonizes the various instincts and impulses, and establishes an ideal of good"— a concept similar to Bridges's figure in the *Testament* of reason as the charioteer that controls the instincts of self and breed. He compliments Santayana in his view of religion as "something humane and necessary . . . and the source, perhaps, of the best human happiness"[34] but objects to his assertion that Protestantism's connection with Christianity was purely accidental. On the contrary, Bridges asserts, "protestant London in the nineteenth century was more essentially Christian than Catholic Rome was in the fifteenth."[35]

Bridges further describes Santayana's philosophy as a system that "sets out to establish a high spiritual ideal of life on the basis of the emotions" and that it takes "its most persuasive support from the idea of beauty."[36] As to the sources of the arts, Bridges agrees with Santayana that it is a "vision of perfection." He quotes Santayana: "Accordingly as this harmony is induced in a man, he will clarify his ideals, and may even come to a vision of perfection. Such moments of inspiration are the source of the arts, and a work of art is the monument of such a moment."[37] Bridges refers to Santayana on the function of poetry: "It is Mr. Santayana's opinion that it is the function of poetry to emotionalize philosophy; and that the great poem must be the esthetical exposition of a complete theory of human life, so far as that is understood."[38] And Bridges agrees with Santayana's praise of Lucretius and Dante.

This review essay was written in 1920. When, a few years later, Bridges was writing the *Testament* he was, in Santayana's sense, emotionalizing philosophy and attempting an aesthetic exposition of a theory of human life. In the *Testament* Bridges developed attitudes toward reason, beauty, and vision consonant with those attributed to Santayana in the review essay.

Albert Guérard has provided one of the best discussions of Bridges and Santayana yet in print.[39] He believes that this philosopher was the greatest single influence on *The Testament of Beauty* and that Book 1 of the *Testament* seems to have been modeled on *Reason in Common Sense*. Furthermore, the analysis of love in Book 3 owes much to *Reason in Society,* and the passages on the relationship of existence to perception, the dualism of reason, the continuity of mind and nature, and the ideality of nature may be direct paraphrases from Santayana. Bridges's letter to Logan Pearsall Smith, which indicates that as he was writing Book 1 the books of Santayana were his daily companion, reinforces Guérard's statements. Guérard also points to the influence of Santayana's doctrine of essences, developed most fully in *The Realm of Essence* (published in 1927) and therefore available to Bridges before he completed Book 4. This influence appears most clearly in Bridges's description of the Ring of Being:

> The Ring in its repose is Unity and Being:
> Causation and Existence are the motion thereof.
> Thru'out all runneth Duty, and the conscience of it
> is thatt creativ faculty of animal mind
> that, wakening to self-conscience of all Essences,
> closeth the full circle, where the spirit of man
> escaping from the bondage of physical Law
> re-entereth eternity by the vision of God.
>
> (4.123–130)

These essences, according to Santayana, are the object of all thought, experience, and imagination. They are the "character or identifiable property of anything that is or might be, whether sensory, ideal, material, or wholly imaginary."[40] Bridges takes over the term from Santayana without realizing (apparently) the profound skepticism of Santayana's doctrine—for Santayana believed that essences are appearances, illusions, and that there was no necessary connection between essence and existence, between what things appear to be and what they are. Arnett says of Santayana's essences: "For the doctrine of essence assumes that there is no demonstrable or actual relation at all between what is experienced or thought and what exists. Essence . . . is only the formal condition of appearance."[41] But, whether Bridges fully understood Santayana or not, the influence of certain aspects of Santayana's thought on *The Testament of Beauty* is clear and demonstrable.

Although there are affinities of thought between Bridges and Santayana, there are also marked differences, some of which have been pointed up by Santayana himself in letters and commentary published after Guérard's book. According to Willard Arnett,

the thought of George Santayana must . . . be characterized

finally as *a philosophy of ultimate disillusion.* In the last analysis, he claimed, neither the senses, nor science, nor art, nor religion, nor philosophy can provide any genuine or trustworthy clues to the ultimate character of existence.[42]

George Howgate quotes Santayana: "disillusion was my earliest friend."[43] Disillusionment is, of course, not the tone of *The Testament of Beauty,* nor is a philosophy of skepticism and disillusionment attributable to Bridges in general. Accompanying Santayana's profound skepticism is, at times, a note of rather facile hedonism:

> The weather has got into our bones; there is a fog in the brain; the limits of our own being become uncertain to us. Yet what is the harm, if only we move and change inwardly in harmony with the ambient flux? Why this mania for naming and measuring and mastering what is carrying us so merrily along? Why shouldn't the intellect be vague while the heart is comfortable?[44]

There is a good deal of hedonism in Bridges, too, some of it, perhaps, derived from Santayana, but the tone is less casual, less skeptical. In the passage just quoted, Santayana may be ironical, or may be not. It is often difficult to determine the exact amount of irony in Santayana's prose. But in the following passage Santayana is stating seriously his own attitude without question. The quotation is from the essay "At Heaven's Gate":

> Of myself also I would keep nothing but what God may keep of me—some lovely essence, mine for a moment in that I beheld it, some object of devout love enshrined where all other hearts that have a like intelligence of love in their day may worship it; but my loves themselves and my reasonings are but a flutter of feathers weaker than a lark's, a prattle idler than his warblings, happy enough if they too may fly with him and die with him at the gate of heaven.[45]

Bridges might have written this passage up to the semicolon, but not the portion following it. The difference is that between a more-or-less Christian theist who is by temperament usually optimistic and whose response to beauty is joy and love (Bridges) and a skeptic who is not a theist in any Christian sense but who is also sensitive to beauty and responds with joy and love, but without forgetting that his response is momentary and meaningless (Santayana). The profound difference between the skeptic Santayana and the theist Bridges is clearly evident if one compares the passage just quoted from Santayana with the conclusion of *The Testament of Beauty*:

> and in the fellowship of the friendship of Christ
> God is seen as the very self-essence of love,
> Creator and mover of all as activ Lover of all,
> self-express'd in not-self, without which no self were.
> nor space nor time; nor any fault nor gap therein
> 'twixt self and not-self, mind and body, mother and child,
> 'twixt lover and loved, God and man: but ONE ETERNAL
> in the love of Beauty and in the selfhood of Love.

(4.1438–46)

In the spring of 1928 Bridges offered to send Santayana the trial text of *The Testament of Beauty,* saying that the philosopher would find in it a philosophy similar to his own and referring to his recent reading of *The Realm of Essence*.[46] In the fall of 1929 Bridges sent Santayana a copy of the *Testament*. Santayana replied with a critique of the poem, expressing his admiration for its poetic quality—"saturation, abundance, picturesqueness, colour"—and for its prosody, which "carried me along buoyantly."[47] He then makes an acute analysis of certain fundamental differences between himself and the poet with particular reference to the Ring of Being, to the transformation of his essences into what Bridges called influences, and to Bridges's anti-Catholicism. Santayana rejects the notion that the entire universe moves harmoniously in a Ring of Being:

> . . . if you mean this "Ring" and this pre-established harmony to describe the whole universe, I should decidedly reject that view: because I am convinced that the relation between things natural and things moral is forthright and unreturning. . . . A Harmony sustaining the beautiful . . . is an islet in a sea of indifference.[48]

The difference between Bridges and Santayana is, to repeat, fundamental. Bridges saw spirit pervading and harmonizing the entire universe. Santayana made sharp distinctions between the world of the spirit and the world of nature and, for that matter, the world of intellect. Santayana goes on to say: "I should therefore agree with you completely if it were understood that you were traversing the life of spirit only, and leaving out all physics and logic."[49]

Similarly, Santayana objected to Bridges's changing his "essences" into "influences." As shown above, Santayana considered *essence* to be the formal condition of appearance and to have no necessary relationship with existence. Bridges (according to Santayana) changed *essences* to *influences,* that is, important or guiding ideas. Santayana rejects Bridges's interpretation:

> I should go further and say that . . . they [i.e., Bridges's influences] are not even influences, but only impulses or virtues in ourselves: because no idea or goal would be influential unless we were initially directed upon it. Between those particular chosen essences and the effort of life, issuing in beauty, there is evidently the circularity and reciprocity which you describe: but that is not because they are essences, but because they are chosen, so that the marvel is a tautology.[50]

Santayana concludes his letter by chiding Bridges for his anti-Romanism:

> If you admitted openly, as I do, that the impulses which determine the direction in which the good and the beautiful may be realized are specific, local, and temporal impulses, I think your judgement, for instance, of the Catholic church would be more sympathetic than it is. For why does the church accept a myth (as I agree with you that it is) and pass it off for true-history and eschatology. . . . Because without this supernatural environing world, invented to suit the human conscience, spiritual and moral life would be precarious.[51]

Bridges replied to this critique in a long letter (not at present available) on which Santayana comments in his autobiography, stating their differences clearly and claiming that Bridges never understood him as a philosopher:

> That he was influenced by my philosophy is not admissible. A thinker is seldom influenced by another much younger than himself, and Bridges besides did not *understand* my philosophy. His own position was not clear to me until, with reference to

his *Testament of Beauty*, he asked me expressly to criticise it and then replied, in a long letter, to my criticisms. He agreed with me, or rather with Kant, as to the *necessarily original* form of the mind, in sensation no less than in religion; but he clung to the belief that this inevitable originality was inspired, and revealed a sympathetic moral spirit in nature at large. Now, my position excludes this belief; because morality and spirit, in my view, express specific and contrary vital interests, as in politics.[52]

Again the difference is fundamental. Bridges believed in a "sympathetic moral spirit in nature at large." Santayana did not. It would appear from this exchange of letters that although Bridges thought that *The Testament of Beauty* incorporated much of the philosophy set forth in *The Life of Reason* and in *The Realm of Essence*, Santayana, at least, was aware of certain important differences between himself and the poet.

5

The Critic

Throughout his long career Bridges wrote a number of essays and commentaries in which he set forth his views on certain aspects of the work of well-known English poets including Chaucer, Shakespeare, Keats, Wordsworth, Dryden, Milton, Kipling, and Emily Brontë, as well as lesser known writers like Mary Coleridge, George Darley, Lord de Tabley, Digby Dolben, and R. W. Dixon. He also wrote a brief and controversial commentary on the then-unknown poet Gerard Manley Hopkins and two essays of a general nature on the importance of poetry in the modern world. All of these were written for special occasions. The BBC. wanted a lecture for its National Broadcast series, or his friend A. H. Bullen wished something for his tenth volume of Shakespeare's works, or he requested an introduction to the poems of Keats for the Muses Library Series. Or Bridges himself wished to promote and commemorate the work of dead friends— Digby Dolben, Canon Dixon, and Gerard Manley Hopkins. There is no attempt at systemization of these miscellaneous pieces, and, consequently, when they are read as a single body of criticism, the effect is somewhat scattered. Nevertheless, they are all beautifully written, challenging, and perceptive. Furthermore, a coherent set of critical principles does emerge, and, although the Shakespeare essay and the Hopkins commentary drew much unjustifiable opposition, Bridges's critical evaluations have stood up well over the years, with one important reservation. In the case of several minor poets (Dolben and Dixon, for example), Bridges allowed his friendship and admiration for the personal qualities of the men to color his critical judgment.

Thirty of Bridges's essays were reprinted from 1927 to 1936 in ten volumes of *Collected Essays,* edited at first by Bridges and, after his death, by his wife, and published by the Oxford University Press.[1] They are printed in a system of phonetic spelling with specially designed type, both system and type devised by Bridges to reform English orthography. The system is perfectly rational and can be mastered with a little practice, but it did not catch on, and therefore all readers today find the phonetic type a barrier to an easy reading of the essays, with the possible exception of those in the last two volumes, in which the full phonetic was abandoned for a slight modification of conventional spelling, like that used in *The Testament of Beauty.* It is to be hoped that the principal essays will eventually be reprinted in one volume in conventional type and spelling.

Bridges frequently made critical comments on various poets in his personal letters to friends, many of which are extant although few have been published. In the following pages some of these informal opinions from his correspondence have been used to augment the formally published criticism.

Most of Bridges's essays fall into two categories—those dealing with poetry from the point of view of the literary critic in a rather general sense, and those which formulate and explain theoretical and technical matters. Those in the first category are discussed in the following pages. Those in the second group which are on classical prosody and on English prosody (including the famous prosodic study of Milton) are drawn upon in previous chapters, in which Bridges's experimentalist and traditional poetry is discussed. The essays on music and a few articles that deal only indirectly with literature and a few minor reviews have been omitted, as have Bridges's contributions to the Society for Pure English.

William Shakespeare

The Sonnets. Bridges had a lifelong but increasingly selective admiration for Shakespeare's sonnets. The two "long poems," that is, *Venus and Adonis* and *The Rape of Lucrece,* he called "unreadable" in a letter to John Mackail on March 29, 1910,[2] but "The sonnets of course I need not say I admire. I worked at them once, but the literature about them is of the worst." He may at one time have considered an essay on them, but if so, it was never written. He planned with his friend Logan Pearsall Smith an anthology of English verse that would have contained a careful selection of the sonnets "but gave it up finding that their tastes were too divergent."[3] Near the beginning of his career his early sonnet sequence *The Growth of Love* (1876) shows some Shakespearean influence in its diction; the revised sequence (1889) reveals a greatly increased Shakespearean influence, with numerous verbal echoes and with fifteen sonnets in the Shakespearean rather than in the Miltonic form. His last published work during his lifetime, *The Testament of Beauty*, praises Shakespeare for his expression of idealized love in the sonnets:

Thus Shakespeare, *in the sessions of sweet silent thought*
gathering from memory the idealization of love,
when he launch'd from their dream-sheds those golden sonnets
that swim like gondolas i' the wake of his drama,
fashion'd for their ensignry a pregnant axiom,
and wrote: *From fairest creatures we desire increase*
That thereby Beauty's Rose might never die; wherein
he asserteth beauty to be of love the one motiv,
and thatt in double meaning of object and cause.

(3.263–71)

Bridges's critical estimate of the sonnets is to be found in his letters, particularly those to Samuel Butler and Logan Pearsall Smith. Those to Butler are available.[4] Those to Pearsall Smith have not been published.[5] The first extended commentary there is by Bridges on the sonnets is in his letters to Butler dated December 31, 1899, to January 25, 1900.[6] Butler had sent Bridges a copy of his *Shakespeare's Sonnets Reconsidered* (1899) in which he made two major points: that the sonnets were the product of Shakespeare's youth and were composed between 1585 and 1588; that many of the sonnets were addressed to a young man, Master W. H., whom Butler identified as a certain William Hughes who eventually became a cook in the navy. Bridges accepted the first point but rejected the second with vehemence, and in so doing revealed his own estimate of the sonnets at that stage in his career. Bridges considered them to be an expression of ideal love without sexual implications, an ideal he repeated much later in his *Testament of Beauty,* an idea that Butler scoffed at: "I seem to hear Venus laughing from the skies."[7] Bridges also felt that the sonnets constituted one poem or organic whole (an idea that Butler also rejected), and he believed the sonnets to be the work of Shakespeare's youth, with which Butler, of course, agreed. Both Bridges and Butler felt that the chief stylistic fault of the sonnets, overwriting, could be laid to Shakespeare's youth. (It should be noted, however, that a quarter of a century later Bridges may have changed his mind, for the passage on the sonnets in *The Testament of Beauty* quoted above implies that they were written toward the end of Shakespeare's career and from a memory of youthful love.) But the main point Bridges makes is this:

> My own key to the sonnets has been that Shakespeare saw that ideal love could be heightened by dissociation from sex and feeling for W. H. something of this ideal love he sought to give it poetic expression: and I think it was the absence of sexual feeling which enabled him to use the sexual imagery. This sexual imagery is of universal application in metaphor, and could only be excluded from a treatment of ideal love by secondary considerations of propriety and fear of a misunderstanding which Shakespeare did not fear.[8]

It was this notion of idealized love that is dissociated from sex or transcends sex that is Bridges's chief debt to Shakespeare in his own *The Growth of Love.*

Bridges's letters to Logan Pearsall Smith written several years after those to Butler show a more selective and critical attitude toward the sonnets. On January 28, [1906?] he wrote, "Considered as perfect poems I am not nearly as enthusiastic about Shakespeare's sonnets as I once was." He lists what he considers to be the eleven best sonnets with comments:

> 1. CXXIX "The expense of spirit." I think it the most powerful one that Shakespeare wrote. . . . Except for the commanding diction of the first line, it does not appear to me to have any purely poetic beauty. 2. XC "Then hate me when thou wilt." This sonnet again is not distinguished by any special beauty of diction: but it seems almost of the same value, and direct expression as the last. It is of the most convincing sincerity of passion. 3. XXXI "Thy bosom is

endear'd." I have long thought this the most beautiful in meaning of all the sonnets—and it is through its Platonism allied to the most typical sonnets whereas Shakespeare's usually are supposed to stand apart.

Bridges next mentions four sonnets from Palgrave's anthology that he also likes: XXX "When to the session," LXXI "No longer mourn," LXXIII "That time of year," and XCVII "How like a winter." After these come XCVIII "From you I have been absent," and CII "My love is strengthened." Of this last he says, "The second and third quatrains I think of the greatest beauty, and the whole sonnet convincing." These quatrains are:

Our love was new, and then but in the spring,
When I was wont to greet it with my lays,
As Philomel in summer's front doth sing,
And stops his pipe in growth of riper days:
Not that the summer is less pleasant now
Than when his mournful hymns did hush the night,
But that wild music burdens every bough,
And sweets grown common lose their dear delight.

Bridges then names two more from the *Golden Treasury,* CXVI "Let me not to the marriage" and CXLVI "Poor soul." His interesting comment on the latter is, "This last being the only 'religious' poem that Shakespeare wrote has as much claim to quotation as that other exceptional one 'The expense of spirit.' It also lacks beauty, but the couplet at the end is of extraordinary value in Shakespeare's mouth." In this couplet Shakespeare says of the soul:

So shalt thou feed on death, that feeds on men,
And death once dead, there's no more dying then.

After looking over the sonnets he had selected, Bridges confessed that he was somewhat disappointed:

The sonnets are excellent poetic reading, but they very seldom satisfy one throughout, and it is perhaps for that reason that I have put among those which I select some which in their general strength, argument and intention are complete, although these are deficient in the poetic beauty for which some more imperfect sonnets are conspicuous.

Bridges makes out a second list that he labels "Other of the better sonnets." They are: XII, XXIX, XXXII, LII, LX, LXVI, LXXV, LXXXVII, CIV, CVI, CVII, and CX. LX "Like as the waves" he said was "marred by obscurities."

This letter to Pearsall Smith represents Bridges's mature thinking on the sonnets. He mentions three main criteria—does the poem have coherent structure and meaning, does it have convincing power, does it have poetic beauty? First place goes to "The expense of spirit" for its power, but it lacks beauty; "Thy bosom is endeared" has the most beautiful meaning; the second and third quatrains of CII have the "greatest beauty." But no one poem satisfies all three criteria.

The Influence of the Audience on Shakespeare's Drama. Bridges began to consider seriously the possibility of an essay on Shakespeare's plays early in 1905. On January 15 of that year he wrote to A. H. Bullen (who wished a contribution from Bridges for volume ten of his Stratford Town Shakespeare) to express his hesitation about tackling so formidable a task, but at the time outlining roughly what he might do if he decided to undertake it:

> My notion of my essay was . . . to make a sort of emotional, i.e. not intellectual, analysis of Shakespeare's work, and separate off all that *offended*. Regard this as a chemical reaction. You have an unknown, miscellaneous and extremely elaborate mixture to analyze. You take a single reagent, the quality of which is known and determinate, you test the mixture, which you have to analyse, with the reagent, and you get a definite precipitate.
>
> Now something very definite ought to come of this. The process is simple and (observe) entirely free from the great blemish of testing a great *intellect* by a smaller one.[9]

He was reluctant, he goes on to say, to complete the job for fear that neither Bullen nor his readers would like it. Bridges admired Shakespeare, and yet "there is something very strange about him, and my 'precipitate' would lead me to say some very strange things." His essay would "virtually amount to a tabulation and classification of depths or blemishes which all point one way." The major problem in Shakespeare's drama, he continues, is "his extraordinary mixture of 'brutality' with extreme, even celestial gentleness."

In the essay as it is in its final published form, the "key" or "reagent" seems to be this—Shakespeare was attempting to please an audience a large part of which was insensitive, coarse, and even brutal. This audience craved intense emotion; they expected to get it from the Elizabethan plays as staged (not read). "Shakespeare," wrote Bridges, "aimed at exciting his audience to the limit of their endurance."[10] Such an aim accounts for scenes that displease us today, like the blinding of Gloucester. Furthermore, Bridges said, "Shakespeare sometimes judged conduct to be dramatically more effective when not adequately motiv'd."[11] Coleridge had called attention to what he considered to be Iago's "motiveless malignity," but Bridges finds more glaring examples than Iago. In his constant wish, then, for dramatic effectiveness Shakespeare often very consciously failed to do the job of any competent dramatist—making an action credible by adjusting motive to action—and indeed the proper evaluation of human experience that must occur in all serious literature depends on the writer's and the audience's awareness of the appropriate relationship between motivation and emotional response. This cardinal weakness in Shakespeare's plays was not apparent to the greater part of an Elizabethan audience, and indeed Shakespeare seems to have taken advantage of their impercipience, using it as an opportunity for dramatic effectiveness without risk of incredibility. The weakness is apparent, however, to the modern reader who has the leisure to contemplate and analyze the actions of men like Macbeth. Bridges's essay conceals more dynamite than might appear at first reading, for Bridges draws up a bill of particulars that amount to not only a serious indictment of one aspect of Shakespeare's drama but, by implication, an indictment against all drama that makes immediate appeal to a heterogeneous audience. Drama becomes by this estimation a literary genre inferior to poetry and fiction, which are usually read and contemplated at leisure. It should be remembered, too, that this essay was written shortly after the turn of a century when most Shakespearean criticism was close to idolatry.

Bridges, therefore, expected the essay to be controversial, and indeed he hoped (once he had decided to go through with it) that it would be noted and argued by such critics and creative writers as Shaw, Chesterton, Swinburne, Sidney Lee, Dowden,

A. C. Benson, and A. C. Bradley. He envisaged the possibility of the essay expanded, as the result of such controversy, into a small book.[12] There was, in fact, a critical reaction that lasted for a number of years. An early review that Bullen sent him in a letter was not wholly to his liking. He wrote to Bullen on October 15, 1907:

> He [the reviewer] really does not face the matter, and his assumption that I do not sympathize with Shakespeare and am overlaid with modern refinement is I think wrong. "Refinement" is not modern in the only sense in which it can be alleged that I appeal to it. There were plenty of "refined" minds in Shakespeare's day, and always have been everywhere.[13]

The notion that Bridges himself was too refined in his tastes became a long and commonly held opinion. Augustus Ralli, commenting in the early 1930s on Bridges's essay, said: "But we rather think that Dr. Bridges overvalues what is correct and consistent in poetry."[14] Irving Ribner, in an otherwise judicious discussion of Bridges's essay, voiced another common response to it—that Bridges was woefully misinformed about Shakespeare's audience and would have benefited from a reading of Alfred Harbage's *Shakespeare's Audience,* which was first published in 1941.[15] But was Bridges mistaken in his assumptions about Elizabethan theatergoers? He states in his unpublished letter to Bullen quoted above that "There were plenty of refined minds in Shakespeare's day." Presumably some of them found their way to the Bankside theaters as well as to the more prestigious places where plays were performed, or at least Bridges doesn't deny this. Bridges's point is that Shakespeare found it necessary and, indeed, at times advantageous to appeal to unrefined elements in his audience and to all who, refined or not, craved intense emotions on the stage. How can one otherwise explain certain aspects of Shakespeare's art? Ribner, in his above-mentioned article, points out that "His [Bridges's] views attracted wide attention, and they may have been particularly influential upon E. E. Stoll . . . the father of twentieth-century historical criticism of Shakespeare."[16] Ribner goes on to say that Stoll probably owes to Bridges "the notion that the principal effect of Shakespeare's tragedies is in their power to shock by what Stoll calls 'steep, tragic contrast' revealing a hero performing an act of which the author has conditioned the audience to believe him incapable, such for instance as Macbeth's murder of Duncan or Othello's of Desdemona" (p. 198).

How strong an indictment does Bridges make against Shakespeare, and what is his evidence? Alfred Harbage[17] calls the essay a "furious assault" that "scarcely invites refutation," which is perhaps why he doesn't successfully refute it. He merely dismisses it in cavalier fashion together with a similar view expressed by Muriel St. Clare Byrne in her article "Shakespeare's Audience."[18] Miss Byrne, writing twenty years after the publication of Bridges's essay, merely repeats the poet's main contention. She says, "A strong vein of brutality and an insensitiveness to physical suffering were part and parcel of the mentality of the Elizabethan audience." Indeed, after dismissing Bridges and Byrne, Harbage goes on to substantiate this very point. He writes:

> Each age has its own brutalities. The Elizabethans were forced to live intimately with theirs, and they acceded to the conditions of their existence. Shakespeare's auditors look at Talbot spattered with stage blood; but as they look, they weep. Throngs gather to see the felons hanged at Tyburn, but "the criminals' friends come and draw them down by their feet, that they may die all the sooner." Is this brutality or tenderness?[19]

It is both brutality and tenderness, of course, which is precisely the point Bridges makes in his letter to Bullen quoted above, that a major problem in Shakespeare's drama is "his extraordinary mixture of 'brutality' with extreme, even celestial gentleness." And Bridges's answer to the problem is the same as Harbage's but arrived at thirty-five years earlier than Harbage's, that, in Harbage's words, "the Elizabethans acceded to the conditions of their existence." To dismiss an author and then rephrase one of his main arguments as your own is not a very convincing method of refutation. Harbage doesn't tackle the more subtle and the more profound problem that Bridges raises (and with which Stoll agrees), that of the discrepancy between character and action in a number of Shakespeare's plays.

What are the particulars of Bridges's case against Shakespeare, or, rather, against one aspect of his art—his yielding to the tastes of his audience? There are, first of all, the verbal trifles, bad jokes, and obscenities that are annoying but not serious for the modern reader. He can, according to Bridges, simply skip over them. The obscenities, Bridges points out in passing, taint many of the women in Shakespeare's plays, like Miranda who speculates (for no reason at all except to titillate the Elizabethan audience) on the possible adultery of her grandmother. More serious are what Bridges calls the dramatic improprieties. These include offenses to our feelings such as the murder of Macduff's child, the blinding of Gloucester, and "the piteous moan that Rutland made" (his murder is thus referred to in *Richard III*), as well as errors of manners that range from rudeness to brutality, such as the rudeness of Valentine to Thurio; the grossness of Leontes' language to Hermione, Claudio's to Hero, and Capulet's to Juliet; and the disgusting utterance by Ariel concerning the "filthy mantel'd poole." Furthermore, there are improprieties condemned by instinctive judgment, for example, Valentine's reconciliation with Proteus, the pardon of Angelo, and the reconciliation of Leontes and Hermione. Finally and most serious, there is a whole series of poorly motivated feelings and actions in which people behave inconsistently with their previously established characters for the sake of dramatic surprise and for the sake of arousing intense excitement in an audience incapable of perceiving that they have been deceived. These include the behavior of Angelo, who is changed in a moment from a high principled, stoic self-deceiver to a licentious hypocrite; Macbeth, whose nobility of character would have made him incapable of secret murder, even when set upon by the witches and his wife; and Othello, who is too quickly and too easily made jealous by a villain who (in real life) would never have the reputation of "honest Iago." "The whole thing is impossible," says Bridges. Some of Hamlet's actions, too, such as the murder of Rosencrantz and Guildenstern and the upbraiding of Ophelia, are poorly motivated, Shakespeare obscuring the deception by leaving unanswered the question of Hamlet's madness, whether it is actual or feigned. There are other poorly motivated patterns of behavior besides these: Leontes' jealousy, Falstaff's farcical desecration of Hotspur's body (with the Prince conniving in Falstaff's story of his killing of Hotspur), and Antonio's inordinate love for Bassanio.

Were these contradictions and obscurities careless errors or consciously employed for dramatic effect? Bridges thinks that they were conscious. Shakespeare came to believe that often a poorly motivated but strong action had a more intense emotional effect (because of the element of surprise) than one properly motivated. But they do not have the desired effect on a modern reader with critical discrimination and intelligence.

As Bridges explained in his letter to Bullen, the essay is purposely one-sided. He was trying to analyze and explain Shakespeare's blemishes, taking his great virtues (which had been sufficiently praised during the preceding century) for granted. For Bridges, Shakespeare was still preeminent in spite of his faults. But the faults, Bridges believed, were there, and he makes out a strong case. The essay is the work of an intelligent, perceptive, sensitive, and learned mind, clearly expressed and cogently argued. It cannot be shrugged off as the eccentric effusion of a late-Victorian prude as it has been by Harbage, Ralli, and others. If there is agreement with Jonson that Shakespeare wrote not for an age but for all time, and if it can be shown by analysis that he frequently and consciously yielded to the weakness of his age, then criticism such as Bridges's is justified. If Bridges's essay is wrong, its errors will have to be demonstrated in a better refutation than it has so far received.

John Keats

In the spring of 1894 A. H. Bullen suggested to Bridges that he write a critical essay on Keats as an introduction to a collection of Keats's poems that he wished to publish in the Muses Library series. The idea immediately appealed to Bridges, but his admiration for Keats was so great that he hesitated to undertake the project.[20] "I think J. K. one of the highest gifted poets that was ever born into the world," wrote Bridges to Bullen, "and to give a worthy portrait of his mind, & at the same time a clear philosophical acc^t of his ways towards nature and art etc.—may prove beyond my paces." But by the summer of 1894 he was hard at work on the essay, and by September he was distributing proof to his friends for their suggestions. He sent Bullen the final revised proof October 4, 1894, saying, "I am glad to get it out of the house," and "I have made it as definite and concise as I could, and owing to the generous help of 2 friends it is better than c^d have been expected of me." The collection of Keats's poems with Bridges's introduction was published in a limited edition in 1895 and reprinted several times. Bridges took great pains with it, as revealed not only in his letters to Bullen but also in those to H. W. Garrod in 1929.[21] In his original essay he had called attention to the obscurity of the concluding lines of "In a drearnighted December." Now, before reprinting his essay, he wished to check with Garrod concerning the accuracy of the text of Keats's poem that he had used. He wrote on January 13, "I know that there has been a serious questioning of the text, & some MS authorities for correcting it. Do you happen to know *whether anything was definitely arrived at* [?]" Evidently Garrod sent him some conjectural emendations, for Bridges wrote again on January 15, "I knew only the printed text, and thought that the last stanza (wh: sh[d] have clenched the meaning) broke down. The subsequent attempts to mend it show that its inefficiency is generally recognized. I can make nothing of it."

Bridges paid close attention to detail in the Keats essay because he probably considered it to be his most important critical piece and one that went beyond the subject of Keats's poetry. When Samuel Butler sent him several of his books in 1900, Bridges offered several of his own in return, calling especial attention to the Keats article:

> It is a treatise on poetic forms—in their external aspect—and is I think written in different manner of criticism from that generally used: the manner which I think sound and useful. . . . I think it is really generally interesting not only for its method but its matter.[22]

And in a subsequent letter to Butler, Bridges wrote:

> I sh[d] like you to read my "Essay on Keats." Art is what I most care for, and that tract expresses or at least implies my attitude toward it.[23]

On December 30, 1926, in an exchange of letters with Logan Pearsall Smith, Bridges said, "You have found in my Keats Essay some of the stuff that was my purpose in writing it, for it was intended to convey some of my notions on poetic forms."[24]

Bridges made a brief preliminary summary of his intentions to Bullen on April 16, 1894:

> My notion of an essay on him w[d] be to give
> The bare facts of his life & circumstances &

how they influenced his work.
The models of development of his poetry, etc. etc.
The faults of his work
The special excellencies
but I consider that a stiff job.
As the essay is so short there w^d be no room for
illustrations, nor for complete chronological
treatment of his poems—which w^d have to be
given in a table.[25]

And on April 18 he wrote, "I sh^d wish to get at more interesting and precise generalizations than the literary critics do."[26]

In his essay in its final form[27] Bridges begins with the general opinion of Keats's poetry, that "the best of it is of the highest excellence, the most of it is disappointing."[28] The chief fault is want of restraint. Bridges's purposes will be "to examine Keats's more important poems by the highest standard of excellence as works of art, in such a manner as may be both useful and interesting; to investigate their construction, and by naming the faults to distinguish their beauties, and set them in an approximate order of merit; as by exhibiting his method to vindicate both the form and meaning of some poems from the assumption of even his reasonable admirers that they have neither one nor other."[29] Early in the essay his comment on *Endymion* assures immediately that Bridges's appraisal of Keats will not be undiscriminatingly enthusiastic: "To one who expects to be carried on by the interest of a story, this poem is tedious and unreadable, and parts of it at least merit some of the condemnation which fell on the whole."[30] Less original, perhaps, and less controversial than his essay on Shakespeare, Bridges's essay on Keats is nevertheless a model of its kind, for it leads to a better understanding of and appreciation of the virtues of Keats's poetry. It is both interpretative and evaluative—evaluative, in fact, every step of the way. It ranges from the most detailed analysis of the particulars of style, to questions of structure, to the consideration of the difficult problems of allegory and symbolism, to broad psychological and philosophical matters. It does not neglect sources, influences, and biographical and historical facts when they are relevant. Much of it is so apt and so beautifully phrased that it is difficult to resist frequent quotation.

In his discussion of *Endymion,* Bridges analyzes in tabular form the outward events of the poem and then explains the allegory. His explications of Endymion as man or Everyman; of Cynthia, the moon goddess, as the principle of ideal beauty, the supersensuous quality that makes all desired objects ideal; of the Indian lady as sensuous passion; and of Peona as the simple, ordinary woman (like Keats's sister-in-law) have stood up well enough over the years, as has his analysis of the general scheme of each of the four books representing the four elements. Bridges concludes his discussion of *Endymion* by calling attention to a "lamentable deficiency in Keats's art" that affects much of his work but is particularly prominent in *Endymion,* and that is the "superficial and unworthy treatment of his ideal female characters" that he traces, interestingly enough, to the pictorial basis of Keats's art and to the fact that a satisfactory pictorial basis for an ideal woman did not exist in Keats's time. (Keats died before the Pre-Raphaelite "stunner" was born!.) Bridges elaborates:

> Neither the Greek nor the Renaissance ideals were understood, and the thin convention of classicism, which we may see in the works of West and Canova, was play'd out; so that the rising artists, and Keats with them, finding "nothing to be intense upon," turn'd to nature, and produced from English models the domestic-belle type, which ruled throughout the second quarter of the century, degrading our poets as well as painters.[31]

As another example of Keats's early style, Bridges analyzes "Sleep and Poetry," giving first a summary of the argument and then a more detailed discussion of the passage lines 101–62. "The meaning of it is exactly the same with that of Wordsworth's *Tintern Abbey*" with its three states of mind: animal pleasure, passionate ecstasy in nature, and reflective pleasure in nature. But Keats's treatment of the subject, Bridges explains, is far different from Wordsworth's, for Keats's treatment is what Bridges calls *objective,* that is, the idea is suggested but not clearly defined by a series of images. Keats's poem is therefore more obscure than Wordsworth's. "If the imagery fails to define the poet's thought, it must be remembered that definition is neither desired nor sought." In a highly interesting passage, Bridges analyzes Keats's objective method in terms that foreshadow Pound's theories of imagism and Eliot's objective correlative. Bridges says that Keats was attempting to communicate "those mysterious feelings with which they [people] are moved in the presence of natural beauty," and that he did so by special use of the extended simile as in *Hyperion,* where Keats compares the old gods of Olympus lying out "at random, carelessly diffused," to

> a dismal cirque
> Of Druid stones upon a forlorn moor,
> When the chill rain begins at shut of eve
> In dull November, and their chancel vault,
> The heaven itself, is blinded throughout night.

(2.34–38)

Bridges points out that the effect of this passage is not to heighten the reader's picture of the Olympian gods but to glorify the mystery of Stonehenge or Keswick. The poet, after putting the reader in an appropriate mood created by the story of the poem, takes advantage of that mood, as it were, to communicate his own feelings evoked by a mysterious landscape. Bridges says that "nothing can exceed the force of such a reserved method," but he goes on to point out the chief danger of a method in which the intentions of the poet are concealed, in which intensity of effect takes precedence over clarity of motivation, and therefore over understanding of one's emotions, which is, after all, one of the prime aims of poetry. Keats, Bridges says has succeeded in picturing a mood. "But it is of course much more difficult to picture ideas than moods. . . . the poetic picture requires a statement of intention. . . ," but such a statement is sometimes lacking in Keats's poetry with resulting obscurity. There are vivid pictures and intense feeling, but the reader does not know what the pictures and the feeling are "about." It seems to me that Bridges has put his finger on the limitations of the kind of poetry developed in the imagist movement two decades before doctrinaire imagism came into being and several decades before the final results of imagism in Pound's *Cantos.*

With *Hyperion* Keats moved from his effort to reconstruct English poetry in the Elizabethan manner to his attempt to write an epic in Milton's manner. The substitution of the Miltonic for the Elizabethan influence was a mixed blessing. According to Bridges, the style of *Hyperion* is that of the epic and in places as good as Milton, but the poem "lacks the solid basis of outward event, by which the epic maintains its interest. . . . The failure here is really the same in kind as the fault of *Endymion*: there is little but imagination, and a onesidedness or incompleteness of that; a languor which lingers in the main design, though the influence of Milton is generally uplifting the language."[32]

Before considering the revised *Hyperion,* Bridges notes Keats's rejection of the Miltonic influence and particularly his rejection of Milton's use of Greek and Latin inversions. He then goes on to defend the proper use of the inversion in English poetry, and in so doing he probably had his own poetry in mind as well as the poetry of Milton and Keats: ". . . the first thing that a writer must do is to get his words in the order of his ideas, as he wishes them to enter the reader's mind; and when such an arrangement happens not to be the order of common speech, it may be call'd a grammatical inversion."[33]

In the revised *Hyperion,* Bridges tells us, Keats abandoned the imagistic or objective method described above and "now introduces a character who discusses with the main person the meaning of what is pictured." There are still the images and pictures, but there are also clear statements as to what they mean. Also, Keats returns to allegorizing and in so doing supplies his most masterly attempt at presenting his own personal philosophy. The style is now more austere and powerful than it was in the original *Hyperion,* and for the first time, in its gravity of vision and in its individual touches, it shows the influence of Dante:

> When in mid-day the sickening east-wind
> Shifts sudden to the south, the small warm rain
> Melts out the frozen incense from all flowers.
>
> (1.97–99)

The new poem, as Bridges reads it, is an allegory, a vision of knowledge rather than, as in the original *Hyperion,* of love in which Keats is depicting his own attempts to break out of the selfish isolationism of his earlier worship of beauty. Keats is now trying to identify himself with suffering humanity. He "now valued the life of action and conduct above that of meditation and poetry." But Bridges refuses to consider this a straightforward advance. He points out that throughout his life, Keats vacillated back and forth from one view to another, and that there is evidence of the position defined in the revised *Hyperion* in his earlier work. Furthermore, paradoxically, Keats did more for humanity in creating those poems which were written during the period when he was immersed in meditation and poetry.

In his essay Bridges gives short shrift to the three finished tales. Of *Isabella* he says, "The story is unpleasant, and is the worst executed of the three." The characters remind him of Pre-Raphaelite paintings, of figures in a faded tapestry in whom "the brilliance of the raiment has outlasted the flesh-colour." He thinks *The Eve of St. Agnes* more powerful, but he dislikes the machinery of the story, particularly the bedesman and his chapel that never appear again after the opening scene, and also Porphyro's feast for Madeline that "serves no purpose but to enrich the description." Yet this machinery does provide coloring, and the tale as a whole "is very rich in the kind of beauty characteristic of Keats." *Lamia,* although structurally good, is very uneven in style. The first few lines are "light and sure," but other passages are badly flawed and some lines sink to bathos. *Lamia* is written in heroic couplets, and this fact gives Bridges opportunity to write an incisive paragraph on the proper and improper use of the heroic couplet in English. Chaucer used it with skill. His lines have a buoyancy made possible by terminal vowels and inflections that were common in Middle English but have now disappeared or become mute. In the hands of Dryden and Pope and their disciples the couplet became heavy and polished and not fit for narration. It "passed in a dull generation for a triumph of classic grace." Later poets tried to lighten the couplet, to recover the grace of Chaucer, but "their lightly constructed verse is slovenly." Keats successfully recovered the buoyancy and charm of Chaucer's verse in only a few passages. His use of rhyme and his sense of the integrity of the line are inefficient in *Endymion*. The rhymes either go unnoticed or are too obtrusive. It was this kind of comment that Bridges had in mind when he recommended his essay to Butler. He was dealing with poetry as an art, with matters of form and technique that went beyond the subject of Keats's poems. Bridges showed his scholarly understanding of the development and disintegration of the heroic couplet in English in this critique written in 1894. He demonstrated his own practical mastery of the form in his "Elegy: The Summer-House on the Mound" written a few years later.

Keats's best period, according to Bridges, was that part of the year 1819 when he was most under the influence of Milton and when he wrote his six most important odes. Of these, Bridges ranks the ode "To Autumn" highest for perfection of workmanship, objecting only to the awkward address to the personified Autumn, "Think not of them." But he argues that several other odes, though faulty, have greater passages of poetry. Bridges was particularly moved by "the splendour of the *Nightingale*," which is a perfect expression of sorrow and of an ecstasy that transcends sorrow, yet there are faults. The next to the last stanza is fanciful and superficial, for man is just as immortal as the nightingale although Keats implies otherwise. Also, the introduction of the last stanza is artificial, and the elf, derived from William Brown of Tavistock and supplied to rhyme with "self," is disastrous. The last six lines, however, are great, and the poem as a whole contains more beauty than any other poem of the same length in the language. The "Ode on Melancholy" ranks next but is flawed in the second stanza where Keats exhibits his usual weakness in depicting human passion by equating the beauty of his mistress's anger with roses, peonies, and rainbows. Bridges likes the last fifty lines of "Psyche," but not the beginning. He ranks in fifth place "Ode on a Grecian Urn," a surprisingly low rating. Is it justified? The central theme of the poem as expressed in the first stanza, the supremacy of ideal art over nature, Bridges calls true and beautiful, but he finds its amplification in the rest of the poem "unprogressive, monotonous, and scattered." The concluding lines he considers successful because of "their forcible directness." The famous crux *Beauty is truth, truth beauty*, about which so much has been written in this century, seems to bother him not at all. In his severe handling of this poem one observes Bridges's classical criteria at work. The rational content of a poem is as important as the style. He grants that the details of the ode are beautiful, but beautiful repetitive details in themselves are not enough if they do not advance the thought.

Bridges places "Indolence" at the bottom of his list of six odes, for the details of the poem are arbitrary in meaning and do not contribute to any central theme. He also calls attention to the unfinished "May Ode" for its fine description of the Greek poets and to two odes in *Endymion* of which the ode to Pan is the weaker because of its vague personification and its monotonous rhythms. High praise goes to the ode to Sorrow (in spite of its weak opening and a weak fourth stanza), particularly for the "pictorial description of the Bacchic procession," which is "unmatched for life, wide motion, and romantic dreamy Orientalism."

In his discussion of the odes Bridges's criticism is at its best. He is exacting and fearless in examining faults. Yet he is equally ready to give high praise when it is justified.

Bridges's treatment of the sonnets is also exacting and discerning. He selects the ten best out of sixty for especial attention, but before doing so he gives us his highly interesting analysis of the sonnet form, an analysis that he mentioned to Butler in the correspondence cited above.[34] He distinguishes between a sonnet in its external form—a poem of fourteen lines in iambic pentameter with a certain rhyme scheme usually called Shakespearean or Italianate—and a true sonnet. A true sonnet has the aforementioned external form together with a certain kind of subject matter. "The typical sonnet is a reflective poem on love, or at least in some mood of love or desire, or absorbing passion or emotion." Bridges then supplies by way of illustration a one-paragraph summary of the history of the epigram,[35] in which he points out that it started as an inspiration to mark an event and express an appropriate emotion, but that its terseness and pathos were soon used for other purposes, and finally that in the hands of city wits it became the medium for the "well-bred jeer; a sad fall from Simonides." So, too, the "sonnet form has been as loosely and variously used as the epigram." Bridges then gives a brief account of the Horatian ode and points out that a number of Milton's sonnets in subject matter are closer to the odes of Horace than they are to Petrarch's sonnets. And there are also many sonnets of trivial subject matter that might be more properly classified as occasional verse. Returning then to Keats, he lists his ten best true sonnets, that is, poems written in the external sonnet form that are reflections on some absorbing emotion. They are: "Much have I travelled," "When I have fears," "Come hither all sweet maidens," "Four seasons," "Bright star," "O soft embalmer," "I cry your mercy," "As Hermes once," "The day is gone," and "Time's sea." He considers the first eight to be nearly faultless and among the best in the language, although he finds weaknesses in the eighth line of the first, in the concluding couplet of the second, and in the fourth line of the ninth.

Of the verse epistles, Bridges finds little to interest him except the one to Reynolds dated March 1818, and of the lyrical poems only "La Belle Dame sans Merci" merits attention. Providing the original "knight-at-arms" instead of "wretched wight" is kept in the first line, the poem is "above the reach of criticism." The play *Otho the Great* he dismisses as a failure.

In his general comments on Keats's diction and rhythm, Bridges defends the poet's use of the suffix *y* when added to the substantive to form adjectives such as *spangly* gloom and *pipy* hemlock because the new locutions work in context, and he defends on the same grounds the suffix *y* when added to an adjective to form a new adjective. "I never heard of anyone objecting to Shakespeare's 'I can call spirits from the vasty deep.' Indeed, what is in question is very much the same with the words as with the spirits, whether they will come when you do call for them." Keats's diction may be faulted, however, in its overuse of certain words such as *bees, marble, silver,* and *tiptoe.* Also, he says, "the *melting, fainting, swimming, swooning,* and *panting* words are over-frequent." But this faulty diction is largely overcome in the later style. Some of the flaws in his rhythms may be attributed to mistakes in Keats's pronunciation, such as his pronouncing of *perhaps* as a monosyllable and *fire* as a disyllable. Keats all too frequently introduced an instability into his rhythms by his careless use of the monosyllable-disyllable combination such as *camp-mushroom,* which is normally pronounced cámp-músh-room, but which must be awkwardly pronounced cámp-mushróom in the line "That camp-mushroom, dishonour of our house" if the rhythm is to be preserved. Yet Bridges defends Keats's awkward inversion of the last foot in the line "Bright star would I were steadfast as thóu art" because it suggests "the irony of impossibility," an argument that is difficult to follow.

In his concluding section Bridges summarizes Keats's virtues, laying especial stress on his ability to concentrate "all the far-reaching resources of language on one point, so that a single and apparently effortless expression rejoices the aesthetic imagination at the moment when it is most expectant and exacting, and at the same time astonishes the intellect with a new aspect of truth." The description of this power, which according to Bridges is the "highest gift of all in poetry"—in its emphasis on concentration, surprise, suddenness, and its combined appeal to the imagination, emotions, and intellect—reminds one of the significant "charged moment" of the Pre-Raphaelites. It is also reminiscent of James Joyce's epiphany and of Ezra Pound's definition of the successful image as "an intellectual and emotional complex in an instant of time," both of which apparently derived from the Pre-Raphaelites and were dominant in early twentieth-century aesthetics. And Bridges's selection of passages from Keats to illustrate the power reminds one also of Arnold's touchstones. Bridges's touchstones from Keats are:

> The journey homeward to habitual self.
>
> *(Endymion, 2.276)*

> Solitary thinkings: such as dodge
> Conception to the very bourne of heaven.
>
> *(Endymion 1.294–95)*

> My sleep had been embroider'd with dim dreams.
>
> ("Ode on Indolence," 1. 42)

Another virtue of Keats that Bridges admired and, indeed, succeeded in emulating in his own poetry, is his ability at word painting, often with a few phrases to suggest scenes of vast size, as these lines from *Endymion*:

> The woes of Troy, towers smothering o'er their blaze,
> Stiff-holden shields, far-piercing spears, keen blades,
> Struggling, and blood, and shrieks.
>
> (2.8–10)

Keats, in his reaction against the stereotyped diction of the eighteenth century, drew "his imagery from common things, which are for the first time represented as beautiful." These fresh images derived from common things are sometimes too plentifully supplied in *Endymion* and elsewhere; nevertheless, they account for much of the charm of Keats's poetry; yet the practice becomes a fault when Keats attempts to depict feminine beauty in terms of natural beauty, for it was the beauties of nature that moved him most, and, indeed, he never did succeed in depicting human passion, the love of man for woman, successfully.

Keats's absolute seriousness toward his art also commands Bridges's respect, and yet he feels that Keats was negligent "in the castigation of his poems." This lack of self-restraint is directly attributed to Keats's prolific imagination; he was of all poets one of the most frequently "inspired," and he should have been more selective of the images that crowded his mind. It was fortunate that at one time in his career he fell under the influence of Milton whose chastening example he needed after his immersion in Shakespeare and Spenser.

Bridges ends his essay with a defense of his critical method. Criticism has no "better function than to discriminate between the faults and merits of the best art: for it commonly happens, when any great artist comes to be generally admired, that his faults, being graced by his excellences, are confounded with them in the popular judgment, and being easy of imitation, are the points of his work which are most likely to be copied."

I have dwelt at length on this essay for it seems to me to be not only one of Bridges's best pieces of criticism but also one of the best essays on Keats ever written. Bridges undertook his task (after considerable hesitation) supported by innate good taste, a sufficient historical knowledge of English poetry, and the keen perceptions of a practicing poet. He succeeded in achieving a just appraisal of Keats's entire career and in ascertaining what was the best work of a great but very uneven writer.

Gerard Manley Hopkins

Bridges and Gerard Manley Hopkins met at Oxford in 1863 where Bridges was at Corpus Christi and Hopkins at Balliol.[36] Similar interests in literature and music led to a close friendship interrupted in 1866 by Hopkins's conversion to Roman Catholicism, a step of which Bridges did not approve. But around 1877, when each discovered that the other was writing poetry, the friendship was renewed and maintained, chiefly by correspondence, until Hopkins's death in 1889. Shortly thereafter Bridges approached C. H. Daniel of the Daniel press with plans for a selection of Hopkins's poems, edited by Bridges with notes and a memoir of Hopkins as well as a note on the poems by Hopkins himself.[37] For reasons not known, the project was stopped and Bridges's edition did not appear until 1918. In the meantime,

Bridges published the complete text of seven of his friend's poems in A. H. Miles's *The Poets and the Poetry of the Century* (London, 1893) [38] and six selections in his own anthology *The Spirit of Man* (London, 1916). His correspondence with Miles[39] indicates that Bridges took great care with the format and accuracy in the presentation of his friend's poems. The same care is obvious in his own 1918 edition of the poems, which immediately gained a strong underground backing among a few young poets in the United States such as Yvor Winters and Hart Crane and also among the Imagists and others in England. But Hopkins's poetry did not win wide recognition until the 1930s. Bridges has been criticized for his delay in the publication of the bulk of the poems, but the criticism is unjustified. The poetry-reading public was not ready in the 1890s for a large selection of Hopkins's poems. It was better to introduce them gradually into anthologies. The public was just barely ready for the poems in the 1920s. Bridges has also been criticized for his "Preface to Notes" in the back of his edition. This editorial commentary has been omitted as no longer relevant in the most recent edition of Hopkins's poems, but I think the omission is not justified, although Bridges's critique is understandably resented by those who believe a major poet can do no wrong. Bridges took poetry professionally and seriously (much more so than his friend), and he felt it necessary to comment briefly on some of Hopkins's faults. He warns the reader that he is about to encounter a gifted but idiosyncratic and difficult poet. There is first of all, Bridges points out, the prosody of the poems, which Hopkins called *sprung rhythm,* in which the poet used a system of scansion, involving seven different marks, that was far too complicated. Bridges quotes from a letter from Hopkins agreeing with him that the scansion should be simplified. Then there are various mannerisms such as errors of taste when Hopkins describes the hills "as a stallion stalwart, very-violet-sweet," and perversion of feeling as in the "nostrils' relish of incense along the sanctuary side" or "the Holy Ghost with warm breast and with ah! bright wings." These expressions represent efforts to force emotion into theological channels, according to Bridges.

There are also faults of style about which Bridges is severe: "These blemishes in the poet's style are of such quality and magnitude as to deny him even a hearing for those who love a continuous literary decorum." Hopkins's two "extravagances" are

"*Oddity* and *Obscurity*," and Hopkins himself admitted to the first fault, for in aiming at that which is unique and distinctive, at *inscape,* he discovered that "it is the vice of distinctiveness to become queer." Hopkins said that in rereading his "Eurydice" he was at first appalled by its raw nakedness and violence but that it all came right when read aloud—he wrote for the ears. This is the poem that contains, among other remarkable lines, the following:

> Death teeming in by her portholes
> Raced down decks, round messes of mortals.

As for obscurity, Bridges felt that Hopkins did not realize how obscure he was, particularly in his use of ellipses in which a relative pronoun was missing, as when he wrote "Squander the hell-rook ranks sally to molest him," meaning "Scatter the ranks that sally to molest him." Hopkins liked the packed line in which most of the words were poetic; hence his impatience with colorless relative pronouns. Also he (mistakenly, according to Bridges) sometimes seemed to feel that ambiguity was a positive good, a virtue that enriched the meaning; hence, he frequently leaves a grammatical part of speech ambivalent and consciously employs homophones ambiguously. Finally, his rhymes are sometimes repellent. Bridges cites as a horrible example the rhyme for *communion* in "Eurydice":

> This very very day came down to us after a boon he on
> My late being there begged of me, overflowing
> > Born in my bestowing,
> Came, I say, this day to it—to a First Communion.

The above critique of Hopkins's faults appears to me to be perfectly sound; in fact, the list of blemishes might have been considerably extended. It was Hopkins's idiosyncrasy to push things to extremes so that awkward and harsh locutions exist side by side with passages of great delicacy. In his prosody also he went too far. As Bridges said, "A simple theory seems to be used only as a basis for unexampled liberty." But, as Bridges points out, had Hopkins lived he would probably have developed a more mature and reserved style as evidenced by his powerful dark sonnets written toward the end of his life.

Other Poets

At the turn of the century Richard Watson Dixon (1833–1900), Canon of Warkworth, was known to a few scholars as the author of the *History of the Church of England* in six volumes, two of which were published after his death. But he also wrote poetry,[40] which was never popular, although it was admired by both Bridges and Hopkins. Dixon was an assistant master at Highgate School for a brief period when Hopkins was a student there, and after Hopkins became a priest he wrote to Canon Dixon recalling his school days and expressing admiration for the Canon's poems. A correspondence followed that lasted until the end of Hopkins's life. Bridges heard about Dixon from Hopkins in 1878, and in 1879 he made a trip to the rectory at Hayton near Carlisle to meet him; he eventually commemorated his visit and subsequent friendship with Dixon in "Eclogue I: The Months," which begins:

Man hath with man on earth no holier bond
Than that the Muse weaves with her dreamy thread:
Nor e'er was such transcendent love more fond
Than that which Edward unto Basil led.

Bridges was much taken by Dixon as a person. A firm and lasting friendship developed, maintained by correspondence, by Dixon's visits to London where he used Bridges's residence while engaged in research for his *History* at the British Museum, and by later visits of Bridges to Dixon at the rectory in Warkworth, Northumberland, where Bridges says, he made the worn chair beneath the Severn picture of Keats in Dixon's study his own. The two friends last saw each other in the fall of 1899 in London and in Oxford where Dixon received an honorary degree in divinity and was made honorary fellow of Pembroke College. The first meeting of the two became a pattern for subsequent meetings as poetically idealized in Bridges's *Eclogue*. In his Memoir of Dixon that prefaces the selection of his poems, Bridges said that they rambled in the woods, played lawn tennis, and talked by the fire far into the evening. At his first sight of the Canon, Bridges was immediately struck by his appearance and his introspective, mystic manner. "Under the heavy black brows his eyes did their angelic service to the soul without distraction."

Of his early poetry, Bridges says "It reveals a mind revelling to excess in transcendentalist beauty and mystical meditation." This mysticism is present throughout his later poetry, combined with a Pre-Raphaelite medievalism that came from the Oxford Brotherhood, particularly from the earliest poetry of William Morris. Like Keats, Dixon glorified the weakness of excessive passion—often in a medieval setting. Love, as Dixon depicts it, is usually hapless. Bridges describes it as "a pitiable and pardonable disaster into which man's celestial spirit is ensnared." His poetry abounds with responses to the beauties of nature, which sometimes encourage philosophical reflection in the manner of Wordsworth. When he philosophizes on nature or on other subjects, his style, says Bridges, is likely to be abstract and tedious. When he describes nature, his style ranges from the dreamy and diffuse to the precise image making of the Pre-Raphaelites. Bridges particularly admired "Song" of which he wrote, "I should say that the destiny of this poem is that it will always be found in any collection of the best English lyrics,"[41] and he included it with fourteen other selections from Dixon in *The Spirit of Man*.

The small poem is what Dixon does best.[42] He can capture a brief lyrical moment inspired by a scene in nature. However, in my opinion, the bulk of Dixon's verse is facile, dull, and derivative. There is no attempt to create striking new images and rhythms as in Hopkins. There is none of the hard-won prosodic skill of Bridges. Bridges's admiration and affection for Canon Dixon as a man have obviously influenced his critical estimate of him as a poet.

Another very minor poet who received Bridges's attention was Digby Mackworth Dolben (1848–1867), and here too Bridges's personal interest in the man led him to overrate the poet. In his eloquent Memoir of Dolben published as the introduction to his edition of the poems,[43] Bridges tells of his friendship with the young poet who died at the age of nineteen. Dolben's home was Finedon Hall in Northamptonshire, an impressive structure (judging by the picture in Bridges's edition of the poems) with spacious grounds. Bridges's mother was descended from a Dolben; she frequently visited Finedon Hall in her youth and told her son stories about it when Bridges was a child. It was natural, therefore, that a close friendship should have developed between Dolben and Bridges when they met at Eton in 1862. Bridges was the older by four years, and the new boy came under his care and guidance. Dolben was very different in personality from Bridges. He was tall, pale, delicate, abstracted, and nonathletic; but both liked poetry and both had an overriding concern with religion—a concern that became an obsession with Dolben as he developed extremely high-church views that led him toward Roman Catholicism, and for which he was suspended from Eton in the summer of 1863. He died in 1867 by drowning while swimming near Finedon Hall.

In comparing his own poetry with that of Dolben, Bridges wrote his now famous statement:

> Our instinctive attitudes toward poetry were very dissimilar, he regarded it from the emotional, and I from the artistic side; and he was thus of a much intenser poetic temperament than I, for when he began to write poetry he would never have written on any subject that did not deeply move him, nor would he attend to poetry unless it expressed his own emotions; and I should say that he liked poetry on account of the power that it had of exciting his valued emotions, and he may perhaps have recognized it as the language of faith. What had led me to poetry was the inexhaustible satisfaction of form, the magic of speech, lying as it seemed to me in the masterly control of the material: it was an art which I hoped to learn. . . . Dolben imagined poetic form to be the naïve outcome of peculiar personal emotion.[44]

The chief inspiration of Dolben's poetry was his intense religious experience, often expressed in imagery reminiscent of the Pre-Raphaelites and in diction reminiscent of Tennyson. The other influence was classical. He developed a pagan ideal of beauty from his readings in Greek literature, an ideal that probably ran counter to his Christian faith and that probably caused him considerable remorse. Even his best poetry is today considered stereotyped, sentimental, and derivative.

Bridges also wrote brief essays on Mary Coleridge (1907), George Darley (1906, 1908, 1928), and Lord de Tabley (1903), all very minor poets. Miss Coleridge has never been widely read and Darley and Lord de Tabley are now forgotten. Nevertheless, despite the slightness of their subjects, these essays are of some interest for their incidental observations on English poetry. In the course of evaluating Mary Coleridge's verses, Bridges makes one of the most significant statements of his entire career on the subject of modern poetry:

> It may be difficult to say what the artistic requirements of modern poetry are or should be, but two things stand out, namely, the Greek attainment and the Christian ideal; and art which nowadays neglects either of these is imperfect; that is it will not command our highest love, nor satisfy our best intelligence.[45]

In the beauty and originality of her expression and in her profound spirituality, Miss Coleridge, according to Bridges, has neglected neither the Greek attainment nor the Christian ideal and, for that reason, she is superior to Heinrich Heine, whom she resembles, for Heine, despite his formal excellence, is lacking in spirituality. The delicate and ethereal verse of Miss Coleridge also owes much to her friend Richard Watson Dixon (who, as shown above, was also a friend of Hopkins and Bridges). Her penchant for the supernatural owes something to Blake, of whom Bridges says, ". . . we call him a visionary, and mean by that, he was overmastered by clear, internal presentations in which he had unshaken faith, and took great pleasure."

It is difficult to find faults in Bridges's well-written and perceptive comments on those poems by Mary Coleridge that he particularly likes, but in general he rates her too highly. The essay was written in 1907, a few weeks after her sudden and unexpected death. It is therefore more a tribute than a critical evaluation.

George Darley, the author of a number of lyrics and of *Ethelstan* and *Becket* (historical plays in verse), was born in the same year as Keats and died in 1846. He was once well known as a person and as a poet of the Romantic school. Bridges's essay, as it appears in the *Collected Essays* (no. 5), is a composite of an article published in 1906, of a review of Darley's collected *Poetical Works* published in 1908, and of a note written in 1928 or 1929 after a visit with Colleer Abbott who had just published a *Life* of Darley.

With Darley, Bridges is at a proper distance from his subject, and some of his comments on the poet's more egregious poems are devastating. He finds many faults, and all of his faultfinding appears to be justified:

> . . . there are few of Darley's lyrics which can claim high excellence, and none that we should put into first rank. Besides their weakness of sentiment and fancy, they lack content or definition; and his rhythm is often let loose on the matter, instead of supporting it, with the inevitable result that what meaning there is is waved away.[46]

However, he admires the blank verse of *Ethelstan,* although the play itself is a failure. And he has a high regard for the two completed cantos of *Nepenthe,* particularly for the two-hundred-line introduction to the second canto. His respect for *Nepenthe,* an obscure allegory on, to use Darley's own words, "the folly of discontent," was reiterated in 1916 when he included six selections from it for his anthology *The Spirit of Man.* No reader of today will share Bridges's enthusiasm for this poem.

Lord de Tabley's reputation has dwindled to a footnote in the pages of literary history; yet he had some reputation in Bridges's day, and Bridges wrote the favorable review of an edition of his poems that was reprinted in his *Collected Essays* (No. 7). De Tabley (1835–95), who traced his pedigree to William the Conqueror, held a social position that must have tempted him to pursuits other than literary; yet he persisted in his disappointing efforts to establish himself as a poet. His play *Philoctetes* (1866) achieved some popular success, but after that his work dropped from sight until in 1891 Alfred Miles published (in an anthology) a selection of his poems that drew Bridges's attention. Bridges corresponded with de Tabley, met him, and encouraged him to bring out a volume of poems in 1893 that was fairly successful, but his later books received little attention. It is difficult to understand Bridges's liking for the work of this nonoriginal and prolific poet.

For his articles on Emily Brontë, Wordsworth and Kipling, Dryden on Milton, and Dante in English literature, Bridges had more substance with which to work, although the results are not

comparable with his major essays on Shakespeare and Keats.
With Emily Brontë's poems he is severely judicious. She eschews
ornament, is indifferent to aesthetic beauty, and she never
mastered the techniques of poetry. Many of her rhymes are com-
monplace. She did not perfect a style and it is therefore easy
to find bad examples of her verse. Yet she was a genius. She can
move us deeply when she deals with the bare truth in a plain
style as in "Fall, leaves, fall!," "If grief for grief can touch thee,"
"Strong I stand," and her poem on the death of Branwell. Bridges
sums up her achievement:

> We must not expect either full artistic technique or sustained
> height of diction; she works without them: and this plainness
> may deceive; for it is a genius that is speaking, and in her
> speech the common words have regained their essential and
> primal significance, and, being the simplest, are therefore for
> her the best means of direct verbal touch with felt realities.[47]

Bridges's comments on Wordsworth in a review of Lane
Cooper's concordance to the poems are somewhat surprising. Like
the late Yvor Winters, he seems to have felt that the Lake Poet
took himself too seriously:

> No poet ever took himself more seriously than did William
> Wordsworth; however wide his outlook he lived as a sectary
> in a closed system, and imagined that whatever he happened
> to think was of primary importance. . . . He would probably
> have thought a complete concordance to his works inevitable
> and necessary, so we may congratulate his shade on the sort
> of honorary degree now conferred upon him.[48]

Because he is reviewing a Kipling dictionary in the same
article, Bridges finds an opportunity to comment on something
shared by these two very different poets, a matter that is of particular interest because of the date. The review was published in
1912 when the Imagist movement under the leadership of Ezra
Pound and T. E. Hulme was just getting started. Pound believed
that the language of poetry could be renewed by the employment
of colloquial diction and "free verse" rhythms. Like Emerson,
he wished to return to the language of common men, having
been persuaded to do so by his friend Ford Madox Ford. Pound
did not always practice what he preached; nevertheless, this is

what he was preaching in 1912. Similarly (and perhaps unaware at this time of Pound) Bridges in 1912 said that Wordsworth, Kipling, and J. M. Synge had this in common—they tried to employ the living speech of common men to bring freshness to their poetry. Bridges, however, has reservations about this reform of poetic diction. These poets, wrote Bridges, thought that "a decaying speech is capable of dialectic regeneration." At first, he continued, there is delight at the novelty, but "its strangeness itself becomes a mannerism."[49] Bridges then makes an observation that the Imagists would have welcomed. He said that Wordsworth and Kipling seem to be unaware that the old verse forms themselves are worn out and need renovation: "There are abundant signs that syllabic verse [i.e. conventional accentual-syllabic verse] has long been in the stage of artistic exhaustion of form which follows great artistic achievement."[50] He acknowledges that Wordsworth and his contemporaries "actually wrought miracles of original beauty with the old forms," but in so doing they completed the exhaustion of the old forms so that much of their work and the work of succeeding poets is tedious. It was these considerations that led to Bridges's own experiments in stress prosody, classical prosody, and neo-Miltonic syllabics in which he succeeded in creating new rhythms. But he did not attempt to change his poetic diction to the language of the common man, perhaps because he feared he might develop the mannerisms evident in some of Wordsworth's, Kipling's and Synge's poetry and perhaps, too, because such a change would have been uncongenial to his instinctive poetic taste.

"Dryden on Milton" (first published in 1903), is an excellent example of Bridges on the attack. The essay is devastating. He first shows the insincerity and emptiness of Dryden's famous epigram in praise of Milton—"Three poets in three distant ages born" (in which Dryden states that Milton combines the virtues of Homer and Virgil)—by giving another quotation by Dryden that states the exact opposite—that is, that no one will ever equal or excel Homer and Virgil. He also demonstrates Dryden's lack of enthusiasm for Milton elsewhere in Dryden's critical writings. Dryden was obviously the kind of poet who could turn out urbane verses of praise or blame as expediency rather than conviction required. With examples taken from Dryden's mishandling of Chaucer, Bridges then proves that Dryden "sinks to dullness of metre, dullness of rhythm, dullness of rhyme (of which he was

most proud), dullness of matter; a dullness gross as his ruinous
self-conceit."[51] He refutes Dryden's criticism of Milton's inability
to rhyme by pointing to Milton's masterly use of rhyme in
"Lycidas" and Dryden's misuse of rhyme in the epigram on
Milton and in *Annus Mirabilis*. He concludes his essay with,
". . . if all poetry had been like Dryden's, I should never have felt
any inclination towards it."

"Dante in English Literature,"[52] a review of Paget Toynbee's
book on the subject, briefly calls attention to certain aspects
of the Dantean influence, direct and indirect, on English poetry.
Dante had a strong influence on Chaucer, but was then neglected
(with the exception of Milton and Gray) until Henry Cary's
inferior translation early in the nineteenth century, which unfortunately was admired by Coleridge, Landor, Wordsworth,
and others. Indirectly (and more fortunately) he has had an
influence on many of the best English poets through Milton.
Bridges does not analyze in any detail the major debts Chaucer
and Milton and the others owed to Dante's style and versification.
He points out, however, that Byron and Shelley, when they
adopted the *terza rima* of the *Commedia*, made the mistake of
running on their three-line stanzas continuously instead of closing
them as Dante did, and thus they lost the crispness of the Italian's
verses.

J. W. Mackail's lectures during his first two years as the
Oxford professor of Poetry were published in a volume entitled
The Springs of Helicon. Bridges's review of the book in 1909
for the *Times Literary Supplement*[53] gave him an opportunity
to make a few evaluations of the weaknesses and virtues of the
three poets discussed in the volume—Chaucer, Spenser, and
Milton. Bridges had a high opinion of Mackail, but he felt that
the Oxford professor's response to these major poets was at times
undiscriminatingly enthusiastic. He objected to Mackail's description of Chaucer's *Troilus and Criseyde* as a perfect and consum-
mate masterpiece. Bridges admires the poetic beauty of the last
book, but he dislikes the "extreme Pandarics" of the earlier books.
He finds flaws in Chaucer's characterizations. Troilus, as Chaucer
depicts him, was an ass and therefore does not win our sympathy.
Criseyde is not (as Mackail claims) like a Shakespearean heroine.
Shakespeare's heroines were maids; Criseyde is a widow and perhaps a mother. Chaucer made an artistic blunder when he
introduced a 120-line speech on free will (translated from the

Latin) into a passionate love speech by Troilus. And the love affair, so managed and handled by Pandarus, is impossible to idealize. Chaucer's real success, according to Bridges, lay "in the humanity of his sketches from life." His "higher flights" are mostly translations and less successful than his characterizations in *The Canterbury Tales*. As for Spenser, Bridges cannot agree with Mackail's ranking of the *Epithalamion* as the greatest of the English odes. The poem is prolix and unimaginative. He agrees with Mackail's high praise of Milton, but not with his description of him as an isolated figure like an eagle on top of a cliff before dawn nor with his statement that Milton had no great influence on the poets that followed him. According to Bridges, Milton's methodizing of Chaucer's metrical inventions had considerable influence; furthermore, Keats himself fell under Milton's spell. In fact, Bridges believed, Milton was the strongest of all influences on English poetry during the nineteenth century.

The Defense of Poetry

Of Bridges's general essays on poetry, the most fundamental is "The Necessity of Poetry," which was delivered as a lecture on November 22, 1917, to the Tredegar & District Cooperative Society. In language that, because of the nature of his working-men audience, he carefully kept nontechnical, the laureate enunciated his own Sidneyian *Defence of Poesy*. His purpose was ". . . to give . . . a theoretic view of the fundamental basis of poetry . . . and justify the claim of poetry to that high place which is and always has been granted to it. . . ."[54] He begins his theoretical view with this definition: *Poetry is an Art. Art* is the expression of ideas in some sensuous medium. The ideas, taking material forms of beauty, make a direct appeal to the emotions through the senses. The medium of poetry is words, and this fact makes poetry somewhat different from the other arts, for words are themselves ideas, or the symbols of ideas, which cannot be said of the mediums of sculpture, painting, music, and so on.

In his examination of words as ideas or symbols of ideas, Bridges makes a distinction between the use of words in science, philosophy, and practical affairs on the one hand, and poetry and literary prose on the other. In making this distinction, he investigates the origins of ideas or concepts in the mind. He develops what appears to be a theory of innate ideas—ideas or concepts are present in the mind from the beginning, but they may be refined, reformed, and rearranged spontaneously or by the stream-of-sense impressions brought in by the outer world. Some of these innate ideas arise in the conscious mind. Some (and here Bridges shows his awareness of the new psychology) are in the subconscious mind. Furthermore, the stream of sensation itself that stimulates these subconscious concepts may not be a conscious experience, but may go directly to the brain without one's being aware of it.

Now what has all this to do with poetry? Poetry uses concepts in their natural condition. "Its art is to represent these spontaneous conjunctions of concepts, as they affect the imagination."[55] The scientist is at the extreme opposite from the poet. He is trained to use concepts denotatively with limited, definite meanings; the poet builds his "temple preferably with the untrimmed stone, or—to take Shelley's metaphor—it is in 'thought's wildernesses' that the poet finds the home of imagination."[56] That is, the poet uses words, ideas, connotatively "with all their multiple facets of confused irridescent fringes," but in so doing he expresses truths as important to humanity as those expressed by the scientist.

So much for the poetic medium of words as ideas. Bridges now turns to words as vocal sounds. The poet (as distinct from the scientist) attempts to make his expression beautiful in sound. Beauty of thought should be expressed in beautiful language; the best means of beautifying speech is *rhythm;* hence, poetry is written in meters, that is, in systems of rhythms that repeat themselves, as distinct from prose, which may be written in nonsystematized rhythms. Why metered rhythms should be more beautiful than nonmetered rhythms or no discernible rhythms at all is difficult to explain, but it seems to be a psychological fact that men love patterns. By means of metered sound, poetry achieves artistic beauty, and artistic beauty always "exhibits a mastery, a triumph of grace," of difficulties overcome so completely they seem to disappear. This "triumph of grace" is the mark of great art. Furthermore, the mind takes pleasure in discerning slight variations of a definite form, in recognizing difference in sameness. In successful poetry each line is as different as the individual leaves of a tree, although every line has the same metrical norm. Beautiful poetry must have correct diction as well as meter, that is, the right words in the right order with "an agreeable sound of them in sequence."

Bridges concludes with some philosophical observations on the relationship between poetry, morals, and religion—all three of which "spring from those universal primary emotions of man's spirit, which lead us naturally toward Beauty and Truth." He rejects the popular notion that poetry is nonmoral. "Pure Ethics is man's moral beauty, and can no more be dissociated from Art than any other kind of beauty." He rejects, too, the idea that "art is nothing but competent expression," for that which is being expressed is as important as the method of expression. Great art does not express ugliness, and in saying this Bridges denies the fashionable relativism of the twentieth century: "The championship of ugliness seems to me to be but a part of the general denial of the ordinary distinctions between good and bad of all kinds." As for religion, which Bridges defines as the personal communion between the soul and God, its best expression is in poetry, and, indeed, twentieth century poets may release the English people from slavery to the false conceptions of the God of the Reformation, a slavery made possible initially by the power of Hebrew poetry and by the beauty of the English translation of the Old Testament. Art of all kinds was also employed in enslaving men to the ecclesiastical system of Rome. But now a new Christianity of love, unity, and brotherhood may, through poetry, come into being.

Several of the ideas in "The Necessity of Poetry" were reasserted and further developed twelve years later when Bridges presented a talk entitled "Poetry" as the first of the Broadcast National Lectures delivered for the BBC. on February 28, 1929. At this time Bridges was concluding his composition of *The Testament of Beauty,* and, as Mrs. Bridges explained when she reprinted the talk, the poet laureate took the opportunity to "write a lecture round parts of the work which was wholly absorbing him at the time."[57] The essay is a helpful gloss on several difficult passages in the poem.

In "Poetry," there is the same combination of idealism, materialism, and evolutionism that is found in *The Testament of Beauty.* In describing his development as a poet, Bridges states that he is a Platonist, for he believes in the reality of eternal ideas that exist outside the mind; he is a materialist because, before becoming aware of these ideas, he realizes that they must be received in the human brain by means of the animal senses; he is an evolutionist, for he believes that man's life has its basis in the material world (as does that of animals and the lower forms), but he also believes that man is capable of progressing from the material life to the intellectual life and eventually to the spiritual life. There is a progression, then, from the atom to the vision of God. Paramount in this progression is the idea of beauty, which possesses some men as an obsession. It is the consciousness of an absolute idea that arises in the mind of man as spontaneously and as fully coordinated as a flower, which Bridges calls "the picture of a special grace." In an eloquent passage Bridges describes how he believes these intangible forms, aspects of the eternal idea of beauty, are brought to birth in the "conscient" mind:

> We neither know nor seek to understand by what creative miracle the soul's language is written in perishable forms. Yet we are aware of such existences—crowding, intangible phantasies investing us on all sides, active presences striving to force entrance into our minds like bodiless, homeless souls, pleading in dumb urgency to be brought to birth in our conscient existence, as if our troubled life were the life they longed for: as if eternity should crave for mortal existence, even as we mortals thirst for immortality.[58]

The will of man is powerless to fashion these ideas. They fashion themselves. They have the quality of beauty, a quality that provokes spiritual emotion in the soul. In the poet this spiritual emotion is a kind of transcendental ecstasy similar to the heuristic trance of the mathematician when he discovers new principles of his science. And just as these ideas arise spontaneously in the mind, so the creative act of the artist is also the spontaneous interplay of these ideas, which coordinate themselves and draw their imagery from sensual forms. Nevertheless, in the performance of his art (the carving of a statue, the writing of a poem), the artist must employ great diligence and labor.[59]

Bridges concludes his talk with an exhortation on the value of beauty in the education of children. Love of beauty is innate, but it may be improved by education. If children are surrounded by a good and beautiful environment, they will instinctively imitate beauty in their own artistic expressions, and also they will develop virtue, which is beauty of conduct. Thus at an early age, the child's spiritual life will be born and he will become his own Ideal. Because beauty is the food of the soul, the relatively new invention of radio should be used to nourish the spiritual growth of mankind, particularly in the dissemination of great music.

Appendix to Chapter 2

Poems in Classical Prosody

I. Published poems in classical prosody. First date is of composition when known or probable. Second date is of first publication.

A. Original poems

> The Fourth Dimension   1901; 1912   [Hendecasyllablic]
> Now in Wintry Delights   1902; 1903   [Dactylic Hexameter]
> Pythagoras   1902; 1909   [Scazons]
> Elegiacs/ Ah, what a change!   1902; 1912   [Elegiac]
> Anniversary   1902; 1912   [Elegiac]
> Epitaphs
>> Fight well, my comrades   1902; 1912   [Elegiac]
>> I died in very flow'r   1902; 1912   [Elegiac]
>> When thou, my beloved, diedst   1902; 1912 [Elegiac]
>> Where thou art better I too were   1902; 1912 [Elegiac]
> To Catullus   1902; 1925   [Hendecasyllabic]
> To Sir Thos. Barlow P.R.C.P.   1902; 1925
> See through long summer hours   [The Busy Bee] 1902; *Times Literary Supplement,* August, 28, 1943 [Elegiac]
> Peace Ode   1902; 1903   [Alcaic]
> On Receiving Trivia from the Author   1903; 1930 [Iambic]

To a Socialist in London   1903; 1903   [Dactylic hexameter]

Johannes Milton, Senex   1903; 1912   [Scazons]

Elegiacs/ Amiel   1903; 1912   [Elegiac]

Ode: O that the earth   1904; 1905   In *Demeter* [Iambic]

Chorus of Oceanides: Gay and lovely is earth   1904; 1905   In *Demeter*   [Choriambic]

To—Fair has befal'n   1905; 1905   [Alcaics in Stone's Phonetic Prosody]

Mazing around my mind   1913; 1914   [Elegiac]

Who goes there?   1913; 1914   [Elegiac]

Askest thou of these graves   1914; 1920   [Elegiac]

By our dear son's graves   1916; 1920   [Elegiac]

B. Adaptations, Translations, Paraphrases

Walking Home (from the Chinese)   1902; 1912 [Elegiac]

The Ruin (from the Chinese)   1902; 1912   [Elegiac]

Revenants (from the French)   1902; 1912   [Elegiac]

Communion of Saints (from André Chenier)   1902; 1912   [Elegiac]

Povre Ame Amoureuse (from Louise Labbe, 1555) 1902; 1912   [Sapphic]

Song: Lo where the virgin veiled (from Blake)   1904; 1905   In *Demeter*   [Alcaic]

Ibant Obscuri   1905; 1909   [Dactylic Hexameter]

Mortal though I be (from the Greek)   1905[?]; 1912 [Elegiac]

ΠΟΙΚΙΛΟΘPON'   All-ador'd, all glorious Aphrodita 1910; 1925   [Sapphic]

Evening (from Blake)   1912; 1912   [Alcaic]

Priam and Achilles   1913; 1916   [Dactylic hexameter]

All of the above poems except those listed below may be found in the collected edition of 1953:

On Receiving Trivia from the Author (privately printed, Stanford Dingley, 1930). In Ewelme Collection, Mc-Kisson Library, University of South Carolina, Columbia, S.C.

Peace Ode   In *Collected Poems* (1912)

To—Fair has befal'n   *Academy*, May 1905.

See through long summer hours   *Times Literary Supplement*, August 28, 1943, p. 420.

C. Unpublished poems

The Coming of Spring   In Bodleian MS Eng. Poet. d. 46, fol. 32

Bright hues . . .   In Bodleian MS Eng. Poet. d. 46, fol. 33

II. Stone's Prosody: Bibliography

A basic bibliography for a study of William Johnson Stone's rules of classical prosody for English verse and of Bridges's revisions of these rules: William Johnson Stone, *On the Use of Classical Metres in English* was privately printed in 1898; it was reprinted in London: Henry Frowde, 1899; and reprinted with slight revision in the 1901 edition of Bridges's *Milton's Prosody*, (London: Oxford University Press, 1901); this reprint omits section VI, which gives examples of quantitative verse in English by Stone. See Bridges, a "Summary" of Stone's prosody, listing Bridges's modifications of Stone's rules together with Bridges's "Epistle to a Socialist in London" in *Monthly Review* 12 (July 1903): 150–67; it was reprinted with further modifications and observations as a "Note on Stone's Prosody" by Bridges in *Ibant Obscuri* (London: Oxford University Press, 1916). "Now in Wintry Delights," is the title of both a note on Stone's prosody appended to the first edition of this poem (1903), pp. 19–24, and a review essay in *Times Literary Supplement*, April 10, 1903, pp. 109–10. "Prefatory Remarks on Virgilian Rhythms," an essay on the Virgilian hexameter, introduces the first printing of the adaptation from Virgil, "Ibant Obscuri" in *The New Quarterly* 2 (January 1909): 3–33, followed by a note referring to his differences with Stone; this essay is reprinted as an introduction to the book edition of *Ibant Obscuri*. A prefatory note to the "Poems in Classical Prosody" in the 1953 collected edition summarizes Bridges's critique of Stone. B. A. P. Van Dam, "Robert Bridges, *Milton's Prosody*, and William Johnson Stone, *Classical Metres in English Verse*," in *Englische Studien* (1903) unfavorably comments on both Bridges and Stone. See also Albert Guérard, *Robert Bridges: A Study of Traditionalism in Poetry*, Cambridge, Mass.: Harvard University Press, 1942, pp. 279–81 and passim; Simon Nowell-Smith, "Bridges's Classical Prosody," *Times Literary Supplement*, August 28, 1943, p. 420.

The Letters and Memorials of William Johnson Stone (privately printed, Spottiswoode & Co., Ltd., Eton College, 1904), has letters and poems (some in classical meters) by Stone as well as information about his life.

III. William Johnson Stone

William Johnson Stone, the son of Edward Daniel Stone and Elizabeth Theresa Stone was born December 12, 1872. He went to Eton and then to King's College, Cambridge, where he received his B.A. in 1895. He was an assistant master at Radley College, Abingdon, from 1897 to 1899 and was then assistant master at Marlborough from 1899 until he died of pneumonia February 28, 1901. By 1898 he had completed his treatise on classical meters in English, writing to his brother Ned from Radley College, "The dissertation is making a great stir here. I have antagonists but far more sympathy than I dreamed of. . . ." Bridges's probable first meeting with Stone occurred in December 1898. In an unpublished letter [MS in Worcester College, Oxford] to C. H. Daniel dated December 23, 1898, Bridges referred to a man named W. J. Stone who came to Yattendon to sleep and dine. Stone visited Yattendon again in the spring of 1899 and wrote a poem in quantitative verse to Mrs. Bridges thanking her for his pleasant stay. [Worcester College MS]

IV. Stone's Theory of Classical Meters in English

Stone believed that it was possible to write English verse in classical meters in which quantity would be primary and accent secondary, although up to that time no one had ever succeeded in doing so except in brief passages. He argued that English words if pronounced accurately have a distinct quantity, a fact that enabled the English poet, if he wished, to write verse that could be scanned according to classical systems; it was a verse that should be read naturally, however, so that the accents set up a secondary counterpoint to the quantitative meter. After making a historical survey of the attempts to write English verse in classical meters from the sixteenth through the nineteenth centuries, he came to the conclusion that the Virgilian hexameters were almost impossible in English and that poets "should go straight to the fountain-head and model our metre not on the Latin but on the Greek," as he wrote in his *On the Use of Classical Metres in English*. He proceeded to transplant the Greek (rather than the Roman) metrical system into English prosody: "It is the chief object of this essay to establish a true quantitative English prosody, and render it easy for any one to distinguish our syllables by the same rules of value as the Greeks did," even though "a beginner would find his path as thickly strewn with thorns as that of a boy learning Latin verses." Stone's rules (modified by Bridges) for determining the quantity of syllables in English may be found on pages 156–64 of Bridges's 1901 edition of *Milton's Prosody*.

V. Bridges's Modification and Critique of Stone's Prosody

Although Bridges is reported to have said that writing English quantitative verse was just a game with him, the fact that he spent a number of years writing over 2,000 lines of verse in classical prosody indicates that he was engaged in a serious experiment. In his introduction to the 1901 reprint of Stone's prosody, Bridges says ". . . as to principles and details, I am in every point in agreement with Mr. Stone's teaching," but he goes on to mention that he is doubtful about Stone's exclusion of elisions similar to the Latin, and he says that he is not as hopeful as Stone was concerning the subjugation of the indeterminate vowel to classical rules of quantity.

As Bridges proceeded to test Stone's rules in the writing of his own classical verse, he (while still basically in agreement with Stone's system) discovered other differences between his own practice and Stone's rules. He agreed with Stone that their system was phonetic—"the verse is for the ear, and not for the eye"—and consequently Bridges made a copy of "Now in Wintry Delights" in phonetic script, a page of which appears in facsimile in the 1903 edition. Syllables, then, are long or short according to the way in which they are spelled. Bridges also agrees with Stone that the making of a short vowel long by position when followed by two pronounced consonants "was not due to any alteration in the vowel-sound, but to the time spent in pronouncing the consonants which followed it." Like Stone, Bridges considers the English *h* when at full power to be a consonant. On the other hand, Bridges cites several differences from Stone —Bridges keeps the words *or* and *for* short before vowels, he maintains classical scansion for proper names, and he elaborates Stone's rules for monosyllables.

Stone denied the common opinion that accent takes the place of quantity in English—yet, Bridges points out, in the sixteen rules derived from Stone, eight are concerned with quantity in some way determined by accent. In his "Observations 1916" Bridges either disagreed with or modified about a half dozen of Stone's rules, and in his prefatory statement to the "Poems in Classical Prosody" in the collected editions, Bridges mentions two chief errors of Stone: (1) that Stone relied too much on the quality of the vowel in determining its syllabic length and (2) that Stone regarded the *h* as always consonantal in quality. Bridges is in disagreement with Stone's evaluation of the *er* sound and with Stone's belief that a vowel (when accented) followed by another vowel is long. Stone scans pīety, Bridges piety. Furthermore, Bridges in his quantitative verse practices Miltonic elision between words and Stone does not. Thus, although Bridges was always careful to give credit to Stone, the system Bridges finally practiced was at least half his own. Eventually, Bridges spoke of his gradual emancipation from Stone's rules and concluded with his final evaluation of his experiments in classical prosody: ". . . the experiments that I have made reveal a vast unexplored field of delicate and expressive rhythms hitherto unknown in our poetry: and this amply rewarded my friendly undertaking."

Appendix to Chapter 4

The Testament of Beauty: Collation of Trial Text with Final Text

This appendix quotes all passages in the trial text that differ in wording from the final text as it appears in *Poetical Works of Robert Bridges with The Testament of Beauty but excluding the eight dramas* (London: Oxford University Press, 1953). Frequently, although not always, the line number of the trial text differs from the corresponding line number of the final text. Line numbers of the final text appear first followed by line numbers in brackets of the trial text. Variants in spelling, punctuation, and capitalization have been disregarded.

Book 1

13–19 [13–20]   with like surprise of joy as oft a traveler feels
who resting on a hill has turn'd about to view
the plain he has left; and seeth it now outspredd
a landscape of far beauty, forest field and stream
mapp'd in perspectiv harmony, and he stands agaze
at pains to recognise his long familiar home
by beauty estranged, merging the stiff outlines of space
as the hard throbs of Time are blent in memory's mist.

23–24 [25–26]   of prodigal gay blossom, and man's kindly skill

	had made fair order'd husbandry of that native Pleasaunce
43 [45]	burst into a crowded holiday of scent and bloom
54 [56]	as thirst and wine are to a man that drinketh
67 [69]	the break of day; when the first lark hath warn'd
85–87 [87–89]	than an old stone-deaf labourer lying awake cheerless and lorn of life may perchance be aware of
	when a whole plague of rats run a mock in his thatch?
106 [108]	And birds are of all animals the most like men
146 [148]	which is no less supremely Nature's Oracle
147 [149]	because it is in man so small and tickle a thing:
149 [151]	a greater and less (and speech will reckon some thoughts great,
155 [157]	whereon our loves and fancies are begotten and buried
172 [174]	they hold internal balance on a razor-edge
179 [181]	But because human sorrow is begotten of man's thought,
212–13 [214–15]	were he but granted his blind wish to be as they
	—whether lark or lion or some high-antler'd stag
217 [219]	as well be a toad in his dark hole. Unlike
237 [239]	cumber'd him with their servility, and his memory
319 [321]	is man's generic essence. A wolf that all his life
334 [336]	would more truly have sung the incarnation of God
361 [363]	Man's mind, Nature's gift to him, her own mirror
366 [368]	Logic of science and dialectic discourse,
371 [373]	of Will and Spiritual aim nor his range of knowledge
414 [416]	Thus I saw Conscient Reason as a natural flower-bud

431–36 [433–37]   Though in the schools 'tis held a contradic-
        tion in terms
  to assert that Mind can exist, if incapable
  of their verbal dialectic to argue things out
  on the method whereby Mind itself is reduced
  to a chaos that calleth on the Creator afresh.

461 [462]   and whereas common opinion may assent in
        error

474 [475]   of ethic theologic and metaphysical truth

517 [518]   they were impell'd as blindly and journey'd
        as wildly

537 [538]   off Vistula's flats and their low murky homes

572 [573]   that he should show to Nature this courtesy,
        and kindly

579 [580]   Shakespeare so delicately put his sanity in
        doubt

590–602 [591–603]   of pyramid and pagoda and picturesque attire,
  the outlandish reliquaries of nebulous time,
  as they dug Mammoths out, and Ichthyosau-
        rian bones
  from cliff or frozen scarp; but now will the
        Orientals
  make westward pilgrimage, like the Magi of
        old,
  and flock to gape at our unsightly novelties,
  factories, machines, and scientific tricks—they
        have seen
  the electric light in the West, and come to
        Worship.
  All things in turn have glory: Glory is
        opinion,
  the one doxology wherewith man praiseth
        God.

  Time eateth away at many an old delusion,
  yet with civilization delusions increase;
  the madness of the people taketh furtiv fire

603–4 [605–6]   sudden as a gorse-bush from the smouldering
        end of

	a loiterer's match-splint, which, unless it be trodden out
613 [615]	by spiritual dishonesty in their brief reign
671 [673]	patterning heavenly beauty, in picture of an idea
686 [688]	as if our troubled strife wer the life they long'd for;
[699]	unto all the fowls of the air and all the worms of the earth
	[This line is omitted in final text.]
702 [705]	Ther is now no higher intellect, not in all the world,
724 [727]	and temper, and now above her globe-spredd net
747 [750]	had been unknown—nay and some English names
749 [752]	won spiritual ecstasy, and emotion'd life
754 [757–58]	to discard the severity of its mantled pose and the deliberate ordering of its antique folds.
	[This has become one line in final text.]
758 [762]	the spiritual combat;—as their forefathers were they,
762 [766]	wreck'd their confederacy in the seven score years
767 [771]	under whose alien Kingship they outreach'd
771 [775]	So 'twas when Jesus came in his gentleness
774 [777]	crown'd him with love above all earth-names of renown

Book 2

45 [45]	sucketh in moisture for its germinating cell
59 [59]	into the crevice, pushing ev'n to disrupt the stones
93 [93]	correction awaited not the spiritual charioteer
103–4 [103–4]	herded together; and on their wild prairies are seen when threatn'd by attack, segregating their **young**

106 [106]   in a front line compact to face their dreaded
                           foe
121 [121]   making a ruse of courage, nor will she get up
137–38 [137–38]   Wherewhile in the miraculous significance
                       of a new spiritual personality, the child
196 [196]   well might be in their strange manner of
                           life—So like it is
198 [198]   as the supreme intelligential principle
298 [298]   hath so vex'd thought that explanation is
                           fetch'd
300 [300]   action of unknown forces is described and
                           summed
326 [326]   the everlasting companionship of his lang syne
343 [343]   of mingled pollen (a thing that so concerneth
                           him)
360 [360]   commingle in rich reveries of the dying year
363 [363]   the prime motive they may be, of all bee-
                           energy
368 [368]   to our city hives and the common workshops
                       of men
379 [379]   not one liveth to sing his *nisi Dominus*
385–88 [385–89]   And as they in turn succumb on their lonely
                           journeys
                       o'erladen above their strength, benighted
                           some, astray
                       or lost in marish haze, waylaid by swooping
                           beaks,
                       some by hard hail laid low with broken wings,
                           or drown'd
                       in sudden rains, until a poor remnant at last
414 [415]   while she run well, oil'd stoked and kept in
                           trim
442 [443]   Now in my poem me-seemeth these poor hive-
                       bees fare
456 [457]   through Reason, of her frailty or of her
                           imperfection
464 [465]   'tis delight to look on him in tireless play
470 [471]   the fair uncial comment that long thought
                           hath penned
473 [474]   his spirit is drawn in the stream, and as a drop

484–85 [485–86]   There is nought to compare . . .
                    And now, were Fortune stable in her loving-
                        kindness
                    [Line 485 of trial text is incomplete.]
497 [498]   and to graces transform'd; so, the lover in life
503–6 [504–7]   he liveth in the glow of an oer-ruling Star
                    fed by whose timeless beams our low ter-
                        restrial Sun
                    is but a cast-off satellite, that borroweth life
                    from the great Mover of all, and with im-
                        mortal fire
509 [510]   But high though the chariot be already
                        mounted
521–25 [522–30]   no parch'd Sahara barren as his sour follies
                        are,
                    no sorrow bitter as his vain tears, no abyss
                        deep
                    as his despair, no death like to his ghostly
                        fear.
                    Then will men, fashioning idols, kneel to
                        monstrous gods
                    abstractions of oblivion and terror, devils
                    born in the shadow of negation—and will
                        "look
                    to death's benumbing opium as their only
                        cure",
                    or even seek proudly to ennoble Melancholy
                    by embracement and make a last Wisdom of
                        Woe
545–46 [550–51]   'Tis such a picture as by mere beauty of
                        fitness
                    convinceth natural feeling with added
                        comfort.
559 [564]   the mystical horror of it may rule in him so
                        strong
595 [560]   scour on their prancing pens after their Man
                        of War
609 [614]   now humbled as the seventy kings who with
                        their thumbs
616 [621]   Thus legendary Titans swarming from Chaos

618 [623]	uprooting mountains in gigantic rebellion
629 [634]	who as the flood rose higher swam from peak to peak
632 [637]	till that too was submerged; while in his crowded ark
638 [643]	riding the tempest out, as a weather-bound barque
691–92 [696–97]	whence she hath fetch'd her high authority of Spiritual judgment? WHENCE THEN COMETH WISDOM?
711 [716]	the speechless workings of the inconscient Mind
751–53 [756–58]	slowly as a modeller in clay. How in itself Reason is powerless showeth when philosophers will treat of ART, the which they are apt to do
779–80 [784–85]	knoweth it for the source and very Cause of Life; and then by science unravelling its physical rays
804 [809]	Seeing then that this Reason, our Teacher in all the schools
806 [811]	its richer faculties depend, and that these powers
812 [817]	and thus Man's trouble came of their divergencies
825 [830]	Between Spiritual Emotion and sensuous form
835 [840]	should rename his Ideas Influences, ther is no man
844 [849]	awakeneth Spiritual Emotion in the mind of Man.
857 [862]	such as convention approveth, not Virtue itself
864 [869]	herein—that her discernment of spiritual things
867–68 [872–73]	upgrew from lower to higher) to the conscience of beauty judging herself by her own beauteous judgment.

883 [888]	of our high English summer in August at the country seat
902 [907]	all "virtue is in her shape so lovely," that at sight
909–17 [914–33]	But 'gainst him I have thought divine **WISDOM** to be

909–17 [914–33] But 'gainst him I have thought divine
WISDOM to be
other than human Reason and thus have
    partly escaped
his paradox that all VIRTUE soever in man
is made by a faculty that cannot produce it—
For tho', virtue being human and man
    reasonable
there is no Virtue apart from Reason; yet
    reason
is no diviner a gift than the virtuous impulse,
and neither is liker than the other to Goddes
    mind
whence both flow and grow together indis-
    sociables
So that what the great Master as I read him
    w^d make
Virtue's efficient cause, this Reason I hold to
    be
nothing but that same Virtue's conscience of
    itself
finding response in minds by disposition
    attuned.
    Virtue hath her degrees: yet even as Beauty
        is One
so Virtue will be of one Essence in all degrees
from formal shapes unto the unbounded
    Vision of God
whereafter man's Desire soareth, hoping to
    attain.
    And whether or no such far fruition is
        won by men
I have shrunk from the Arctic cold of
    Aristotle's heav'n
& the snow-image of his pensive Deity.

940–41 [956–57] welcoming rather the hardships, that, by

                     affraying cowards

                     purge their heroic ranks: and Battle rallieth all

943 [959]   adventurers whose joy balanceth on peril's edge

948 [964]   And 'tis because they feel their Spiritual ecstasy

954–55 [970–73]   But we who hav seen, constrain'd to teach our peaceful folk

                     to fashion, and wield, new instruments of death, to stem

                     the mass'd onrush of scientific savagery

                     wherewith the Prussian warload would have swept the world,

958 [976]   sorrows for which no glory of heroism can atone,

961–62 [979–81]   yet might forget, since in the glad passing of pain

                     Mind is so quick and fain to cast her skin again

                     and Memory is so burdonsome that we well may fear

964 [983]   regardless how her fractious babe hath scratcht her cheek

991 [1010]   that punish'd them so; alas then in what plight are we

995 [1014]   and taken himself infection of the brute's madness

[1017–19]   in place of self-contrition and forgiveness of wrongs

                     was self-glorification and revelry of folly

                     in savage dance around the old idols of our shame.

                         [These three lines, which would have appeared after line 997 of the final text, were omitted from the final text.]

998–99 [1020–21]   amid the flim-flam of the uproarious city

                     my spirit on those first days of jubilant disgrace

[1024–43]   And round the council-table of that high conference,

sat to confirm the peace of Europe at
   Versailles

Peace had no seat; the voice that drown'd
   wisdom was his

who spoke unbending enmity and utmost
   revenge

who with the title of Tyger won his folk's
   applause

when with his hellish motto he sear'd his
   tongue, LA PAIX

C'EST LA GUERRE POURSUIVIE PAR
   D'AUTRES MOYENS.

Means as ignoble as were his passions, Fear
   and Hate—

all the vices of War, without its Heroism

that saving virtue of War, that Heroism
   whereby

full many a humble soul, rousd from its sloth
   had found

spiritual ecstasy in the sacrifice of self.

   While such peacemakers flourish, will the
      Warrior stand

more honor'd than the Statesman, War
   nobler than Peace:

woe to the world! if that be, and woe to man's
   best hope!

for he may see that air-sped chariot crash to
   Earth

consumed in its own flames . . . that chariot
   which afore

Socrates saw mounting the skies, and told
   of it

to Phaedrus as they sat together by the banks
of the Ilissus, talking of the passions of men.

   [This passage, which occurs at the end of
      the trial text, was deleted from the final
      text.]

Book 3

76–77 [76–78]   refineth every means, as those Painters of old who in their sunless chambers taxed all human skill

by underpainting glaze and varnish to perfect

86 [87]   but by fortune of genius to possess such bottles

118 [119]   he indulgeth his time until the day cometh

122 [123]   any cricketer or fisherman, for he too hath follow'd

131–32 [132–33]   for good or ill success to his limit of strength his joy in the doing and his soul in his hand

136–37 [137–38]   that governs thought inhabiteth, where man wandereth into God's Presence—But what heavenly Muse

[After line 151 of the trial text (150 of the final text), there are two ruled lines indicating that Bridges intended to compose two lines here. In the trial text these lines are counted as 152 and 153. These lines were evidently never composed, and they do not appear in the final text.]

157–58 [160–61]   in plants as in animals, yet its apparatus as found in animals is of more special kind—

203–4 [206–7]   to a constant conscient passion, by Reason raised to altruistic emotion and spiritual love.

206 [209]   for as Self from its animal rage grew through Reason

232 [235]   at thatt fair hour of dawn which is holier than day:

235–39 [238–42]   that the sunlight may enter to flush the casket of her virgin promise that excelleth the pride of all the passionate glories that shall squander in death— Twas of that silent meeting that a vision came rapturous as any vision that poet saw

257 [260]   of spiritual emotion (as 'twas said) 'tis plain

260 [263]   and first, as in animals, of his physical form

275 [278]   spiritual effect, and that the Poet included this

278 [281]   *Holy fair and wise is she,* giving to Soul

294 [297]   outlasteth not its brief prime, but must fade

315 [318]   *so Nature pricketh them in hir corages.*

318 [321]   torn from her throne, who is herself Mother

332 [335]	virginity may seem an activ power of soul
335 [338]	So here we are driven to enquire of Reason how it came
338 [341]	at such a judgment. But not lightly to trench
361 [364]	a nest of shares, that glideth to and fro
427–28 [430–31]	to the fulfilment of unattainable desire. Yet in divinest abandon and fullest devotion
451 [454]	because of her higher function and duty therein,
509 [512]	and, pressing Westward in desperate retreat, became
516–17 [519–20]	and wrinkling along the edges of its faltering shell the mountains lean and tumble and pour their ruddy bowels
526 [529]	where tracing up to its source some Heliconian rill
530 [533]	whence-after to the poet all his joy will seem
534–35 [537–38]	Now when Rome's mitred prelates in time cross'd o'er the Alps to hold the Gallic provinces whose overlords and chiefs
560 [563]	and grudging to the pagan what might serve the church,
594 [597]	now again of their buoyancy up-struggling here and there.
602 [605]	with Universitie of learning, Sanctuaries
641 [644]	had striven into outline: which, tho' Passion heeded nor
646 [649]	would seem frivolity if we knew not that we watch
650 [653]	Skysoarers should be hatch'd of such young flutterers
672–73 [675–76]	i' the sunshine with my history, and the names that won and held my fancy and now shall hav place in my line
678 [681]	who had found joy in thatt charity and brotherly will
683 [686]	and (wonder above wonders) here was harbour'd safe

689 [692] Restless and impatient our Reason is ever in
        quest

693 [696] she espouseth delusion & sweareth fealty
        thereto:

699 [702] were trifling with no symbols; their wild
        creed had grown

704 [707] all this visible world to the work of a devil

715 [718] a visible Church to be the devil's device,

719 [722] and troubled now that he could neither
        cleanse nor cure,

722 [725] preached a Crusade within the fold,—thatt
        desperate wrath

726–27 [729–30] outbid the barbarous Huns in cruelty, and in
        the end

        was Raymond's country sack'd and destroyed
        and his folk

752 [755] cast off the first night-terrors of his infant
        mind.

754 [757] led him in joy of spirit to full fruition of life.

780–808 [783–806] —a pleasant thought his Deity with so good
        regard

        to save appearances and ignorant 'twould seem

        that all might be resolved in pure physical
        terms

        by fancied commotions in fancied dimensions
        at the intersection of curvilinear planes—

        But 'twere well ask'd how Beauty came to
        be the lure

        of Love in Man: whereto the answer will be
        on this wise—

        That there is Beauty in Nature and that Man
        loveth it

        are one thing and the same; and neither can
        be set

        apart as Cause of the other: Again twill be
        confessed

        that Nature is not all beautiful nor do all men

        love beauty alike: but since human specialty
        is found

in Reason and Spirit and as Wonder to
  intellect
so for his soul desire of Beauty is mover and
  spring,
'twould come that in whate'er spirit is most
  moved, a man
will most be engaged with Beauty and with
  growth of the soul
will win to truer knowledge of it more and
  more
till Beauty itself be wholly spiritualized,
as in its primal Essence it must be conceived.
But when Reason apprehendeth how 'tis in
  mankind
Nature is thus transform'd, a lover is apt
  to find
the pure spiritual ideal in his transform'd self
and oftimes in his mate the ideal beauty,
  whence
the main delinquencies of his high passion
  ensue.

812 [810]	with every breath, and floodeth all the sluices of life
837–38 [835–36]	or even ugly, with whatever other sympathies they can indulge; And, tho' they know it not, this is
840 [838]	And of the mass since there is little good to look for
862 [860]	now personate in Eve, who should reveal to him
865 [863]	This myth was law to th' Jew and 'twas men of that ilk
882 [880]	as comrades indispensable and of spiritual aid.
885 [883]	can find but small credit with this generation
895 [893–95]	in all deserted lands disseminate whereso'er he hath dwelt—monks, hermits, mystics, catharists

                              nor need we now,
                  [This line is incomplete in the trial text.]

901–2 [901–3]	whence thatt nobility of race and all the honour

which all the world accordeth to our country
hath come,

whether in respect of good or envy of evil
men,

905 [906]   of Saxon temperament, the which being slow
or dead

907–8 [908–9]   And so the character of our common folk,
being built

in the commanding presence of this feminine
grace,

937–40 [938–41]   weaving some age-old figure in their Morris
dancers

the chemist booketh all of them as C+H

and my art is as his to figure diversly

the two persistent semitones of my Grand
Chant.

951 [952]   to the subconscious thwarting of universal lust

953 [954]   of spirit stored in flesh which, affined to her
sex,

973–74 [974–75]   pronounced the one thing needful; and as it
was to her

so is it today to us for our happiness.

977–78 [978–79]   out of slumber into Vision, his Reason ever
the more

findeth the main of Natur at war with his
desire

994 [995]   the claim of Faith. To such despairers Christ
spake

999 [1000]   which thought were the authentic vanity of
vanities,

1005 [1006]   As with the germ-cell which in normal growth
passeth

1035 [1036]   nor delusive perspectives to spiritual sense,

1037 [1038]   in the Wisdom of God: hence men, who
mostly live

1043 [1044]   and were he heaven-inspired he should not
look for thatt

1065 [1066]   that Pheidias wrought, can ever wholly escape

1078 [1079]   its own intention, and in portrayal of Spirit

1090 [1091]   and as pictorial Beauty suffereth defeat:

1094 [1095]   with thoughtful face impassive and averting her head

1122 [1123]   and mimicry of beauty that is the attire of vice.

Book 4

6 [6]   when the sap mounteth secretly and its wintry stalk

11 [11]   with pleasurable ichor of heaven: and where she hath formd

55 [55]   even by the common folk who none the less pursue

82 [82]   the accumulated observation of physical flux

100 [100]   of horror, omnipresent, inescapable,

106 [106]   which is no other indeed that the prime ordinance

126 [126]   is thatt creativ faculty of animal mind

164–65 [164–65]   insured to exult in torture and cruelty

will yet to kind feelings respond at gentle appeal:

168 [168]   take pleasure in self devotion, and punctiliously observe

183 [183]   Denial of Use hath done our Virtue wrong, and some

220 [220]   is at every time the index of his growth in grace;

246 [246–47]   with Beauty hath won to enfranchisement of soul

and made already escape, Soaring away to where

252 [253]   Virtue's pure nativ stock that hath no need of graft

255–57 [256–58]   that in collusion float its credit; and awhile

their ship of state runneth with full bellying sail

for lack of seamanship, like the yacht in the race

273 [274]   but should they look to find solid scientific **ground**

288–94 [289–94]   ere he was born, and sinking deeper his shafts
came on no virgin soil but older walls again
the relics of a city of prior date, whose life
and luxury had succumb'd forgotten of time;
and there
happening on the King's tomb he dug out
from the dust
the treasures of that monarch's lost magnificence

314–15 [314–15]   which the king never thought would love to
eclipse the fame
of all his other memories when he set it up,

325–28 [325–28]   of the oxen that had drawn it, there beside
their bones
lay the bones of the grooms slain together at
their post
with the kings body-guard, each liegeman
spear in hand,
his head crush'd in his helmet; and where
lay the harp

[338–346]   Standing now in the very arena of that
terror,
Envisaging the scene of human sacrifice,
the explorer was dismay'd and greiv'd more-
over at heart
because by script and cypher he had unriddled
this folk
to be the teachers of thatt great Sumerian
Race
whence Aryan culture sprang, himself their
British heir
(in lineage so remote it might be twentyfold
thousandth generation) and he piously had
held
his proud Sumerian kin free of thatt Scythian
crime.
       [This passage, which would have oc-
         curred after line 337 of the final text,
         has been deleted from the final text.]

338–40 [347–49]   Leave Tigris now and Ur. Follow that
Aryan race

to Gunga and Hydaspes in the teaming realm
when Sakya Mune preach'd of gentleness and
    love

342 [351]   at every Rajah's tomb, in Punjab or Cashmire,

347 [356]   deem any outlawry of their ritual Suttee

349 [358]   whose social code withheld not of our Island
    king's

353 [362]   by pagan ethic or Christian, and found by
    insight

359 [368]   than the outraged alien, and neath Liberty's
    name

[371]   and tho' the social optimist be too stiffneck'd
    to see

    [This line (omitted from final text) is
    followed by asterisks indicating Bridges's
    original intention of adding two more
    lines at this point, an intention that he
    abandoned.]

363 [376]   PLEASURE may follow after, taking like
    second place

377 [390]   struggle for Self persistently against all
    hindrances:

388–89 [401–2]   and true logic of Ethic. So, flaunting their
    motto
    'Pleasure for pleasure's sake,' these Hedonists

394 [407]   Becoz 'tis common knowledge that some
    pleasures are bad

397 [410]   Pure Hedonism then is confuted off hand

436 [449]   he being then a housecarl in Loyola's menie,

452 [465]   to make them foolish. Nature neertheless

457 [470]   and their diviner poets—and this the novice
    knew—

459 [472]   The repudiation of Pleasure is a reason'd folly

487 [500]   prayers and reveries that steal forth from
    earth

498 [511]   and beanfields of June would wear a mantle
    thick

512 [525]   so mystics use asceticism, and no man

525–26 [538–39]   deemeth it dutiful and a noble honesty
    coldly to criticize rather than blindly to
    love—

531 [544]   of common speech, since all tongues in the
                       world

563 [576]   and the actual complexities of men's conduct

572 [585]   accommodate   these   principles   when   they
                       compete

598–99 [611–12]   First then of Disposition: . . . unless there be
                       in truth

                     more good than bad in the whole mass-make
                       of mankind

601 [614]   except the inherent harmony and the unity of
                       Good

621 [634]   by the inborn love of Beauty inconsciently

625 [638]   co-ordinating Potencies to Spontaneity,

653–55 [666–68]   Man's perfect happiness to be the realm of
                       heaven

                           within his heart, spake thus 'Take heed'
                             (he said)

                     'Take heed lest ye offend one of these little
                       ones'

685 [698]   virtuous or musical an example as such

726 [739]   tho' he by such complacency should forfeit
                       the prize:

767 [780]   entering as is my wont where all now enter
                       free

830 [843]   of purposive co-ordination,—whence 'twould
                       seem

872 [885]   to'ard self-realisation which continueth on

878 [891]   Now seeing the aim of Socrates it followeth
                       here to inquire

903–4 [916–17]   of the arch-creative potency of Life where-
                       from

                     the senses took existence—thus 'twould seem

920 [933]   be exactly alike and therefore (as 'twas said
                       afore)

938 [951]   Again 'twill follow this same cause no less

954 [967]   is sweetest of all sounds, whose inviting
                       embrace

977 [990]   among the flowers of her setting; and tho'
                       true it be

992–93 [1005–6]   and how horizon'd: Thus the secret of a poem
                     lieth on its face, albeit the effect is inscrutable

1015 [1028]	nor for that the leech when he is call'd in to heal
1027 [1040]	Reason will diagnose the main disorder of Mind
1036 [1049]	like the steel spring in a French clock box'd up
1060 [1073]	and since I see all human activities soe'er
1067 [1080]	towards spiritual conscience hath been duly told.
1092 [1105]	physically and metaphysically in quality
1096 [1109]	the first supersensuous implications of Life
1101 [1114]	driveth) with fierce exultation (albeit we may deplore
1104 [1117]	all Reason and Faith—so old a trouble and great
1113–15 [1126–28]	with the inventiv levity of their enlightenment
	till as an animal that hath fasted too long
	acheth within and for his emptiness will eat [This, the first section of Book 4 of the trial text, ends at line 1135, which corresponds to line 1122 of the final text.]

Book 4, the "Tail Section"

1144 [1157]	in favour of the folk and need of good disciplin.
1258 [1271]	except it be that, like as with unconscient things
1310 [1323]	Wherefor as when a runner who hath run his shift
1319 [1332]	and this direct contact is it with eternities
1321–22 [1334–35]	that oft hath set philosophers adrift in dreams the which Christ taught, when he set up a little child
1364 [1377]	thatt first enthusiasm, then the unbounded promise
1412 [1425]	and ultimate good: which howsoe'er 'ts found
1434 [1447]	which he spake of his great pity and trust in man's love,

The Typescript of Book 4.

This is the "tail section," lines 1136 to 1459, which correspond to lines 1123 to 1446 of final text. The quotations below give the original reading of the typescript before Bridges's emendations.

1130 [1143]	thatt old arrant exile, who, for all her witchcraft
1134 [1147]	Faith being the humaniser of his brutal part
1144 [1157]	in favour of the folk and need of good disciplin
1148 [1161]	which they that use that habit may be seen to hav found
1179–82 [1192–95]	and ever had been, and would be, unless the heavenly Muse
	had known to engage man's art to redeem for his soul
	the beauty of holiness, marrying creativly
	his best earthly delight with his heav'nliest desire,
1189–90 [1202–3]	For any idea so e'er new-born to consciousness,
	if it infect the herd, taketh repetend life
1217 [1230]	breathless and irresisting on the roaring beach.
1258 [1271]	except it be that, like as with inconscient things
1305–6 [1318–19]	For tho' by Beauty it is that we come at WISDOM
	yet not by Reason at Beauty: and now with my words
1315 [1328]	which groweth in the child from the Mother's embrace
1319 [1332]	and this direct is it with eternities
1349 [1362]	as thought in a closed book, where some poet long since
1414 [1427]	and pulleth us instinctively as to a final cause:
1428 [1441]	the wandering Visionary in his dóctrinal ode

Notes

Preface

1. *The Poems of Digby Mackworth Dolben,* ed. with a Memoir by Robert Bridges (London, 1911), pp. xviii–xix.
2. *The Poems of Gerard Manley Hopkins,* ed. W. H. Gardner and N. H. Mackenzie (London, New York, Toronto, 1967). p. 99.

Chapter 1: The Traditionalist Poet

1. Bridges's shorter poems previous to the 1890 collection appeared in a number of small volumes: *Poems* (1873); *Poems* (1879); *Poems,* Third Series, (1880); *Poems* (1884). *The Shorter Poems* of 1890 were selected from these earlier volumes augmented with previously unpublished poems and are grouped into Books I, II, and III. Book IV of this collection consisted of previously unprinted poems. *Shorter Poems Book V* appeared in 1893. Volume II (1899) of *Poetical Works* in six volumes reprinted all five books of the shorter poems and added a section entitled *New Poems.* The one-volume *Poetical Works* (1912) reprinted the five books of shorter poems, the *New Poems,* and added a section entitled *Later Poems. Poems Written in the Year MCMXIII* appeared in 1914 and was reprinted together with a group of new poems on World War I and some miscellaneous verses in *October and Other Poems* (1920). *New Verse* (1925) reprinted the poems in neo-Miltonic syllabics from *The Tapestry* (1925) together with new poems in conventional meter. For complete details see George L. McKay, *A Bibliography of Robert Bridges* (London, 1933). For this discussion of the shorter poems I have considered all of the poems written in conventional meters that have appeared in the above volumes.
2. Percy Withers, *A Buried Life: Personal Recollections of A. E. Housman* (London, 1940), p. 58.
3. The following may be considered landscape poems: "Who has not walked," "Clear and gentle stream," "There is a hill," "The Downs" [in accentual verse], "Indolence," "The upper skies," "The clouds have left the sky," "Last Week of February," "April, 1885," "Spring goeth all in white," "The storm

is over" [in accentual verse], "North Wind in October," "November," and "Dunstone Hill."

4. See particularly "The Downs," "Who has not walked," "Dunstone Hill," and "The upper skies."

5. "Last Week in February," "April, 1885," "Spring goeth all in white," "North Wind in October," "November," "The storm is over." Seasonal description also, of course, appears elsewhere, particularly in some of the poems listed in n6.

6. See "London Snow" [in accentual verse], "Gay Robin," "The summer trees," "The garden in September," "The Palm Willow," "A Robin," "Winter Nightfall," and "Idle Flowers."

7. The following poems appear to fall in this category: "Late Spring Evening," "A Water Party," "Spring Odes I and II," "Morning Hymn," "I praise the tender flower," "I love all beauteous things," "When June is come," "The pinks along my garden walks," "The birds that sing on autumn eves," "Larks," "Asian Birds," "January," "A song of my heart," "First Spring Morning," "Eclogue I," "Now all the windows," "Riding adown," "In still midsummer night," "October," "The Flowering Tree" [in neo-Miltonic syllabics], and "Cheddar Pinks" [in neo-Miltonic syllabics]. "Eclogue I" is an idealized depiction of Bridges's friendship with Canon Dixon. See chapter 5.

8. The following love poems appear to be addressed to an individual lady: "Elegy," "Dear lady," "I will not let thee go," "Cliff-Top," "I found today," "Sometimes when," "Long are the hours," "I made another song," "Wooing," "The Philosopher to His Mistress," "My bed and pillow are cold," "O thou unfaithful," "Thou didst delight my eyes," "The full moon," "Awake my heart," "Songs," "Since thou, O fondest and truest," "My spirit sang all day," "O Love, my muse," "Anniversary," "When my love was away," "My spirit kisseth thine," "Ariel," "So sweet love seemed," "I climb the mossy bank," "To my love," "My delight," "Since we loved," "When Death to either shall come,—" "Wishes," "A love Lyric," "An Anniversary," "Vivamus," "One grief of thine," and "The Philosopher and His Mistress." "Elegy on a Lady Whom Grief for the Death of Her Betrothed Killed" is addressed to the memory of an individual person, but not one loved by the poet. Poems treating the subject of love in general are: "My eyes for beauty pine," "Love on my heart," "Fire of heaven," "Since to be loved," "O Love, I Complain," "Eros," "The Duteous Heart," "In der Fremde" [in neo-Miltonic syllabics], and "The evening darkens over."

9. See the discussion of this poem in Albert Guérard, *Robert Bridges: A Study of Traditionalism in Poetry* (Cambridge, Mass., 1942), pp. 74–75; Robert Beum, "Profundity Revisited: Bridges and His Critics," *The Dalhousie Review* 44 (1964): 172–79; M. L. Rosenthal and A. J. M. Smith, *Exploring Poetry* (New York, 1955), pp. 183–85; Yvor Winters, *Forms of Discovery* (Chicago, 1967), pp. 198–99.

10. Beum, "Bridges and His Critics," 175–76.

11. Ibid., p. 177.

12. See particularly: "Ye thrilled me," "Eclogue II," "Emily Brontë," "To Joseph Joachim," "Buch der Lieder," and "To Thos. Floyd."

13. Giovanni Duprè (1817–82), an Italian woodcarver and sculptor born in Siena, made his home in Florence where he completed his successful recumbent figure of Abel and a bas-relief, "The Triumph of the Cross," over the main door of the church of Santa Croce. Other famous works include his "Pieta" in the campo santo of Siena, "Giotto" in the Uffizi gallery, Florence, and "St. Francis" in Assisi. His last important undertaking, a monument to Cavour in Turin, is considered a failure.

14. See the *London Times,* May 17, 1904, p. 11, for an account of the program.

15. The following poems have been placed in this category: "Dejection," "I have loved flowers that fade," "O my vague desires," "Haste on, my joys!," "Joy sweetest life-born joy," "O youth whose hope is high," "Angel spirits of sleep," "Laus Deo," "The Affliction of Richard," "The north wind came up yester-night," "Weep not to-day," "Eclogue III," "Elegy: The Summer-House on the Mound," "The south wind rose at dusk," "The sea keeps not the Sabbath day," "Pater Filio," "Recollections of Solitude," "La Gloire de Voltaire," "To Robert Burns," "Narcissus," "Our Lady," "The Curfew Tower," "Hell and Hate," "The Excellent Way," "Poor Child," "To Percy Buck," "To Harry Ellis Wooldridge," "The Great Elm," "The Sleeping Mansion," "Vision," "Low Barometer," "The idle life I lead," "Crown winter," "The snow lies sprinkled on the beach," "A Vignette," "Melancholia," "Fortunatus Nimium," "The Tramps," and "Sorrow and joy." Only the principal poems are discussed.

16. See the discussion of this poem by Yvor Winters in "Robert Bridges and Elizabeth Daryush," *The American Review* 8 (January 1937): 355–57.

17. See especially Yvor Winters, "Gerard Manley Hopkins," *The Hudson Review* 1 (Winter 1949): 458–66; reprinted in Yvor Winters, *The Function of Criticism* (Denver, Col., 1957).

18. "The Windmill," "The Winnowers," "A Villager," "Millicent," "The Portrait of a Grandfather," "Hodge," "Simpkin," and "The Widow." "Kate's Mother" is in neo-Miltonic verse and is discussed in the neo-Miltonic section.

19. Among those he kept are "The Fair Brass," "The Chivalry of the Sea," "Trafalgar Square," "Christmas Eve, 1917," "Britannia Victrix," and "To His Excellency"; also "For Pages Inedites" and "Gheluvelt," which are in classical prosody, and "The West Front," which is in neo-Miltonic syllabics.

20. See particularly "Founder's Day," "Regina Cara," "To the President of Magdalen College," "An Invitation to the Oxford Pageant," "Ode to Music," "A Hymn of Nature," "Ode on the Tercentenary Commemoration of Shakespeare," "England to India, Christmas 1918," "England will keep her dearest jewel," and "Verses Written for Mrs. Daniel"; also "Noel: Christmas Eve," which is in neo-Miltonic syllabics and is discussed in that section.

21. The titles are listed in the table of contents only; in the text the sonnets are numbered.

22. McKay, *A Bibliography of Robert Bridges,* p. 5.

23. Ibid., p. 5.

24. This edition was limited to 22 copies; but a larger reprint in black letter was issued in 1890.

25. Guérard, *Robert Bridges,* p. 18.

26. Bodleian MS Don. d. 131, fol. 17–18.

27. Donald E. Stanford, "Robert Bridges and Samuel Butler on Shakespeare's Sonnets: An Exchange of Letters," *Shakespeare Quarterly* 22 (Autumn 1971): 328–35.

28. Note to 1895 edition, p. 168. Bridges has commented on the poem in notes to the first edition (1885), to the revised edition (1894/95), and to the 1898 reprint in *Collected Poems*. See also Bridges's letter to Coventry Patmore in *Fortnightly Review*, March 1948, p. 200. The most learned discussion of *Eros and Psyche* is by Douglas Bush in *Mythology and the Romantic Tradition in English Poetry* (Cambridge, Mass., 1937, reissued 1969), pp. 433–36. See also Guérard, *Robert Bridges*, pp. 20–23, 37–41; Coventry Patmore, *Courage in Politics and Other Essays* (London, 1921), pp. 147–51; C. C. Abbott, ed., *The Letters of Gerard Manley Hopkins to Robert Bridges* (London, 1935), pp. 194, 198, 202–3, 206–8, 212, 223, 245; C. C. Abbott, ed., *The Correspondence of Gerard Manley Hopkins and Richard Watson Dixon* (London, 1935), pp. 126–28; C. C. Abbott, ed., *Further Letters of Gerard Manley Hopkins*, rev. ed. (London, 1956), pp. 357, 359, 430; F. E. Brett Young, *Robert Bridges: A Critical Study* (London, 1914), pp. 192–97; Edward Thompson, *Robert Bridges* (London, 1944), pp. 34–36.

29. Note to 1885 edition, pp. 156–57.

30. Note, 1898 edition, p. 290.

31. See Richard D. Altick, "Four Victorian Poets and an Exploding Island," *Victorian Studies* 3 (March 1960): 249–60.

32. Note, 1898 edition, p. 290.

33. May, sta. 15.

34. August, sta. 27.

35. Louis C. Purser, *The Story of Cupid and Psyche as Related by Apuleius* (London, 1910), p. xliv.

36. These allegorical interpretations are summarized in ibid., pp. 128–33.

37. The letter is in Derek Patmore, "Coventry Patmore and Robert Bridges: Some Letters," *The Fortnightly*, n.s. 169 (March 1948): 196–204.

38. Guérard, *Robert Bridges*, p. 20.

39. Note, 1898 edition, p. 290.

40. Erich Neumann, *Amor and Psyche* (New York, 1956), p. 5.

41. Altick, "Four Victorian Poets and an Exploding Island."

42. Abbott, ed., *Letters of Hopkins to Bridges*, p. 202.

43. Altick, "Four Victorian Poets and an Exploding Island," p. 256.

44. A. M. in *Bookman* (London) 7 (January 1895): 116.

45. Abbott, ed., *Letters of Hopkins to Bridges*, p. 207.

46. Purser, *The Story of Cupid and Psyche*, pp. lxxvii–lxxviii.

47. Robert Graves, *The Golden Ass of Apuleius* (New York, 1951), p. x.

48. See n. 28 for references to letters.

49. *St. James's Gazette*, December 31, 1885, reprinted in Patmore, *Courage in Politics*, pp. 147–51.

50. Erich Neumann, *The Great Mother* (New York, 1955).

51. Erich Neumann, *The History of Consciousness* (New York, 1954).

52. In Neumann, *Amor and Psyche*.

53. Ibid., pp. 77–78.

54. Ibid., pp. 122–23.

55. Ibid., p. 122.
56. Ibid., p. 124.

Chapter 2: The Experimentalist Poet

1. Bridges to Sir Henry Newbolt in Newbolt's *My World as in My Time* (London, 1932), p. 194.

2. Robert Bridges, *Milton's Prosody*, rev. ed. (Oxford, 1921), p. 29 n.

3. Yvor Winters, *The Function of Criticism* (Denver, Col., 1957) p. 82.

4. Bridges, *Milton's Prosody* (1921), p. 2.

5. Bridges published nine poems that he himself identified as being in accentual meters: "And so hot the noon," "I would be a bird," "The Passer-by," "The Downs," "London Snow," "The Voice of Nature," "On a Dead Child," "To Francis Jammes," and "Melancholy." Albert Guérard considers the following to be also in accentual verse: "The hill pines were sighing," "The storm is over," "The Nightingales," and "Ode on the Tercentenary Commemoration of Shakespeare." In addition, the following poems appear to me to be in accentual meter: "A winter's night with the snow about," "A Robin," "A Song of my Heart," "North Wind in October," "The Portrait of a Grandfather," "Fly-catchers," and "The Chivalry of the Sea." The play *The Feast of Bacchus* is described by Bridges as being accentual, and some of the choruses in *Prometheus the Firegiver* appear to be accentual. Also, a case may be made for scanning these poems in accentual verse: "October," "Narcissus," "Our Lady," "The Curfew Tower," "Hell and Hate," "Trafalgar Square," "Christmas Eve, 1917," and "Fortunatus Nimium." The problem of how Bridges intended some of these poems to be scanned is pointed up by a curious note by Bridges that is found in a rare pamphlet, a second edition of the 1873 poems published in 1880 [not listed in McKay], which states that "Poor withered rose and dry" is in the new prosody (accentual verse). Yet the poem scans as accentual syllabic verse. Furthermore, it was written in 1872, before Bridges in conjunction with Hopkins was experimenting with stress prosody. And Bridges never reprinted the note. See Simon Nowell-Smith's letter to the *Times Literary Supplement*, May 12, 1961, for a full account.

6. Robert Bridges, "On the Rules of the Common Lighter Stress-Rhythms, and the English Accentual Hexameter," in *Milton's Prosody* (1901).

7. These rules briefly summarized are: (1) the stress governs the rhythm; (2) the stress must be true speech stresses; (3) stress normally has more power over the syllable next to it than over a syllable removed by an intervening syllable; (4) however, stress has attraction for verbal unity and its own proclitics and enclitics, sometimes overriding rule (3); (5) a heavy (long) unstressed syllable must be contiguous with the stressed syllable that carries it; (6) a stress will not carry more than one heavy syllable or two light syllables on the same side of it; (7) in some cases four or more unaccented syllables may take the place of a stress.

8. In applying the preceding rules to his scansion of stress verse, Bridges recognized the existence of seven kinds of feet: one stressed syllable, falling disyllabic, rising disyllabic, britannic, dactyl and anapest, quadrisyllabic, and five-syllable.

Each of these except the first and last have variant combinations of heavy and light unstressed syllables so that Bridges identifies actually sixteen feet in all!

9. See chapter 5.

10. First published in 1857 in *North British Review* as "English Metrical Critics." Revised as "Prefatory Study on English Metrical Law" in 1878 edition of *Amelia.* This version reprinted in four-volume edition of collected *Poems;* reprinted with slight revisions as "Essay on English Metrical Law," in volume 2 of collected *Poems* (1886). Reprinted several times thereafter. A critical edition of the essay is edited by Sister Mary Augustine Roth, *Coventry Patmore's "Essay on English Metrical Law"* (Washington, D. C., 1961). Both Bridges and Hopkins knew this essay. According to Roth (pp. xi–xii), Hopkins in several letters to Patmore urged revisions of the essay in 1883. Patmore said that he would consider them, but he did not incorporate Hopkins's suggestions into his 1886 revision. How much was Bridges influenced by this essay? An answer to this question must take into account the statement Bridges made in 1909 in his "A Letter to a Musician on English Prosody" (no. 15), *Collected Essays etc. of Robert Bridges* (London, 1927–36), p. 55: "I have never myself read any of the treatises on English Prosody, though I have looked into many of them." On the other hand, Bridges in a letter to Patmore, August 29, 1883, expressed admiration for Patmore's *Essay.* There are a number of affinities between Bridges's essay on stress prosody and Patmore's essay: (1) Intervals between accents are isochronous. This is a matter of major emphasis in Patmore's essay. Bridges does not emphasize it, but the doctrine is implicit in Bridges's concept of equivalence. According to Elizabeth Cox Wright, *Metaphor Sound and Meaning in Bridges' The Testament of Beauty* (Philadelphia, 1951), Bridges extended the concept from the foot to the entire line in *The Testament of Beauty.* That is, every twelve-syllable line in the *Testament* is isochronous with every other twelve-syllable line. (2) Relationship between meter and the speaking voice. This is fundamental in Bridges's "New Prosody." The stresses are all speech stresses. (3) Close relationship between the rhythms of poetry and music. Hopkins's concept of sprung rhythm has affinities with these three doctrines. Also, Patmore's praise of Anglo-Saxon alliterative meters and his insistence that English rhythm tends to be dipodic may have been taken over by Hopkins. Some of Patmore's influence on Bridges may therefore have come through Hopkins. Of the affinities of Patmore's and Hopkins's theories, Harold Whitehall in "Sprung Rhythm," *Gerard Manley Hopkins by the Kenyon Critics* (Norfolk, Conn., 1945), p. 37, says "Hopkins' sprung rhythm . . . follows Patmore's theories almost to the letter." According to Whitehall, Hopkins instinctively agreed with Patmore that English rhythms are essentially dipodic without calling them such. Sprung rhythm, according to Whitehall, is dipodic rhythm. Patmore also points out that Milton in his blank verse frequently substituted the trochaic foot for the iambic foot in any of the five positions in the line. Bridges in his explanation of his own neo-Miltonic syllabics calls this practice the "freeing of the foot," but argues that Milton did it in any of the first four positions but not in the fifth. It might be added that Patmore in his essay strongly advises against the attempts to write English in quantitative or Classical meters, citing Daniel's arguments against Campion. Bridges did not follow this advice.

11. C. C. Abbott, ed., *Further Letters of Gerard Manley Hopkins including his Correspondence with Coventry Patmore* (Vol. 3 of the letters of Hopkins) (London, 1938), p. 208.

12. See Derek Patmore, "Coventry Patmore and Robert Bridges: Some Letters," *The Fortnightly*, n.s. 169 (March 1948): 196–204; Derek Patmore, "Three Poets Discuss New Verse Forms," *The Month*, n.s. 6 (August 1951): 69–78; Abbott, ed., *Further Letters of Gerard Manley Hopkins*, rev. ed. (London, 1956); Basil Champneys, *Memoirs and Correspondence of Coventry Patmore*, 2 vols. (London, 1900); Derek Patmore, *The Life and Times of Coventry Patmore* (New York, 1949).

13. Bridges probably began his experiments in accentual meters soon after he read Hopkins's "The Wreck of the *Deutschland*," completed in 1875. He did not (as far as present evidence indicates) put his rules for accentual prosody into a formal essay until over twenty years later when he published the first version of his essay on stress prosody in *Milton's Prosody* (1901, revised 1921). Albert Guérard points out that Bridges in his early accentual poems broke some of his own rules; however, it is probable that some of these rules were formulated after the composition of the poems. The main rules that Bridges probably had in mind from the beginning can be inferred from his letter to Patmore in 1883: "You will more easily see what it is by what I have written in it than I could explain in a few words—the foundation of it is natural stress . . . with attention to quantity, i.e. not to use unaccented long syllables as if they were short syllables,—and not to admit any conventional accents" (See D. Patmore, "Coventry Patmore and Robert Bridges: Some Letters," pp. 196–97). A few years earlier Hopkins was writing to Canon Dixon, "This then is the essence of sprung rhythm: *one stress* makes one foot no matter how many or how few the syllables" (C. C. Abbott, ed., *The Correspondence of Gerard Manley Hopkins and Richard Watson Dixon* [London, 1935], p. 23). Hopkins also stated that sprung rhythm should express natural speech rhythms, but in practice Bridges follows the principle more closely than Hopkins. It is often difficult in Hopkins to tell *where* he intended the accent to fall. Both Bridges and Hopkins agreed that in accentual verse one stress makes one foot so that a foot could consist of from one to usually not more than four syllables.

14. See Hopkins's letter to Bridges, no. 30, April 3, 1877, in C. C. Abbott, ed., *The Letters of Gerard Manley Hopkins to Robert Bridges* (London, 1935), pp. 32–40. Hopkins wrote a series of notes on Milton's prosody that he may have shown to Bridges.

15. Bridges's "On the Elements of Milton's Blank Verse" appeared in H. C. Beeching's 1887 edition of Book I of *Paradise Lost* and in the same year as a separate pamphlet. In 1889 Bridges published his pamphlet *On the Prosody of Paradise Regained and Samson Agonistes* and in 1893 a limited edition of *Milton's Prosody* (regular edition 1894). A revised edition of *Milton's Prosody* was published in 1901, which included William Johnson Stone's essay on quantitative verse in English as well as the first version of Bridges's essay on stress prosody. The final edition of *Milton's Prosody* (1921) omitted Stone's essay but retained a revised version of Bridges's essay on stress prosody.

16. As quoted in Jean-Georges Ritz, *Robert Bridges and Gerard Hopkins 1863–1889. A Literary Friendship* (London, 1960), pp. 117–18. Bridges's italics.

17. Bridges, *Milton's Prosody* (1921), p. 99.

18. Abbott, ed., *Letters of Hopkins to Bridges,* p. 71, in a letter dated February 22, 1879.

19. Ibid., p. 77.

20. Ibid., pp. 81–82.

21. Ibid., p. 82.

22. Ibid., p. 112.

23. Ibid., pp. 111–12.

24. Ibid., p. 111.

25. Ibid., p. 122.

26. Ibid., p. 260.

27. Bridges, "A Letter to a Musician on English Prosody" (no. 15), *Collected Essays,* p. 71.

28. Bridges, *Milton's Prosody* (1921), p. 91. And see Lindon Stall, "Robert Bridges and the Laws of English Stressed Verse," *Agenda* 2, nos. 2–3: 96–108.

29. In a note on the meter of her poem "Air & Variations," *The Southern Review,* n.s. 9 (July 1973): 645.

30. *The Letters of Sir Walter Raleigh,* ed. Lady Raleigh, 2 vols. (New York, 1926), 1: 390–91.

31. There is an interesting comment on this poem in Bridges's unpublished letter to Henry Newbolt (Bodleian MS Eng. lett. c. 303) dated July 6, 1911. "You ask about my old early attempt in stress prosody 'O bold majestic downs,' whether I was on the Sussex downs. The answer is yes. I used to be a good deal on the Sussex downs when my headquarters were London."

32. Albert Guérard, *Robert Bridges: A Study of Traditionalism in Poetry* (Cambridge, Mass., 1942), p. 27 cites the authority of Mrs. Bridges for stating that the poet began his poems in classical prosody in 1898 (on p. 115 he gives the date as 1896). Simon Nowell-Smith, in a highly informed and cogent letter to the *Times Literary Supplement,* August 28, 1943, p. 420, argues that both these dates are too early and demonstrates that according to evidence in extant manuscripts, the earliest date is 1901. He also demonstrates that most of the quantitative verse was written between 1901 and 1905. Nowell-Smith had access to his own collection of Bridges material (one of the best in private hands), as well as to the manuscripts in the Bodleian library. From the evidence at present available, the last poem in quantitative verse was "By our dear son's grave . . ." dated by Bridges April 1916. A number of the dates of composition cited in the appendix of this chapter were taken from Nowell-Smith's article and verified by manuscripts now in the Bodleian library.

33. Robert Bridges, *Ibant Obscuri* (London, 1916), p. 154.

34. Bridges, *Milton's Prosody* (1901), p. 30.

35. William Johnson Stone, *On the Use of Classical Metres in English* (1899), p. 50.

36. Bridges, *Ibant Obscuri,* pp. 142–43.

37. Ibid., p. 6.

38. Ibid., p. 140. Bridges's italics.

39. Ibid., p. 141.

40. Ibid.

41. Ibid., p. 139.

42. Ibid., p. 141.

43. Ibid., p. 143.

44. Ibid., p. 144.

45. Ibid., p. 145.
46. Bodleian MS Don. d. 131, May 8, [1903].
47. Ibid., Sept. 14, [1903].
48. *Times Literary Supplement,* April 10, 1903, p. 109.
49. Ibid.
50. Ibid.
51. "The West Front" is undated but was obviously written during World War I. It was first printed in *October and Other Poems,* 1920. The other eleven poems in neo-Miltonic syllabics, all of which appeared in *The Tapestry,* privately printed in London in 1925, with dates of composition are: "The Flowering Tree" (1913), "Noel: Christmas Eve" (1913), "In der Fremde" (1913), "Epitaph: Hubert Hastings Parry" (1920), "Cheddar Pinks" (1921), "Poor Poll" (1921), "The Tapestry" (1921), "Kate's Mother" (1921), "The College Garden" (1921, "The Psalm" (1921), and "Como se Quando" (1921).
52. See Nicolas Barker, *The Printer and the Poet* (Cambridge, 1970); Nicolas Barker, *Stanley Morison* (Cambridge, Mass., 1972). Information in this chapter about the relationship between Bridges and Morison is taken from these volumes and from letters in the Bodleian library.
53. Barker, *Printer and Poet,* p. 1.
54. As quoted in Barker, *Stanley Morison,* p. 146.
55. Barker, *Printer and Poet,* pp. 37–38.
56. Robert Bridges, *The Tapestry* (London, 1925), p. [3].
57. Robert Bridges, *New Verse* (Oxford, 1925), p. [v].
58. *XXI Letters: a correspondence between Robert Bridges and R. C. Trevelyan on "New Verse" and "The Testament of Beauty"* (Stanford Dingley, 1955), p. 3.
59. Ibid., p. 8.
60. See the note by Mrs. Bridges in Bridges, *Collected Essays* (no. 15), p. 86.
61. Bridges, *Collected Essays* (no. 15), pp. 87–91.
62. Ibid., p. 90.
63. Robert Bridges, *Poor Poll* (privately printed at the Oxford University Press, 1923).
64. "Cheddar Pinks," however, is printed in lines of 6+5 because the poem "came to him that way" (Bridges, *Collected Essays* [no. 15], p. 90).
65. Bridges, *Milton's Prosody* (1921), p. 60.
66. See John Sparrow, *Robert Bridges* (London, 1955), p. 165; Edward Thompson, *Robert Bridges* (London, 1944), pp. 100–101; R. C. Trevelyan, "Prosody and the Poet Laureate," *The New Statesman* 24 (December 13, 1924): 296–98; *XXI Letters,* passim.
67. Thompson, *Robert Bridges,* p. 100.
68. Ibid.
69. *XXI Letters,* p. 4.
70. Yvor Winters, *Forms of Discovery* (Chicago, 1967), p. 203.
71. Sparrow, *Robert Bridges,* p. 165.
72. *XXI Letters,* p. 4. A remarkable statement from the author of *Milton's Prosody!*
73. Ibid., p. 7.
74. Robert Beum, "Syllabic Verse in English," *Prairie Schooner* 31 (Fall 1957): 265.
75. Sister Mary Gretchen Berg, *The Prosodic Structure of Robert Bridges' "Neo-Miltonic Syllabics"* (Washington, D. C., 1962), p. xliv.
76. Ibid., p. 79.

Chapter 3: The Dramatist

1. See C. C. Abbott, ed., *The Letters of Gerard Manley Hopkins to Robert Bridges* (London, 1935), pp. 126, 138, 141, 146–49, 152–53, 159–62 165–68, 172–73, 176, 185, 192, 200–201, 217, 229–30, 243–44.

2. Abbott, ed., *Letters of Hopkins to Bridges*, p. 126.

3. Ibid., p. 243.

4. Ibid., p. 159.

5. Ibid., p. 160.

6. Ibid.

7. Carl Grabo, *Prometheus Unbound: An Interpretation* (New York, 1968), p. 167.

8. Ibid., p. 113.

9. Albert Guérard, *Robert Bridges: A Study of Traditionalism in Poetry* (Cambridge, Mass., 1943), pp. 153–54.

10. William Riley Parker, *Milton's Debt to Greek Tragedy in Samson Agonistes* (Baltimore, Md., 1937), p. 177.

11. Paulette Hooper, "Robert Bridges and the Masque Form: A Critical Study of Demeter: A Mask and Prometheus the Firegiver" (M.A. thesis, Louisiana State University, 1973), pp. 41ff.

12. Ibid., pp. 48ff.

13. *Demeter* was first published in 1905 by the Clarendon Press, Oxford.

14. From title page of reprint of *Demeter* in 1912 *Collected Poems.*

15. See Hooper, "Robert Bridges and the Masque Form," pp. 64–65, 106–7.

16. Guérard, *Robert Bridges*, p. 306.

17. See Hooper, "Robert Bridges and the Masque Form," pp. 64–65, 80–81, 104–5.

18. *Correspondence of Robert Bridges and Henry Bradley 1900–1923* (Oxford, 1940), p. 51.

19. F. E. Brett Young in his *Robert Bridges: A Critical Study* (London, 1914), p. 190, says that it was written in one month. Bridges in a letter to Henry Bradley dated March 17, 1904, says, "I have been these last 3 or 4 weeks at it, and it's nearly finished" (*Correspondence*, p. 43). From Bradley's letter to Bridges May 13, 1904, it is known that the masque was in rehearsal at Somerville College by early May (*Correspondence*, p. 47). Bridges sent Bradley the completed MS on May 26 (*Correspondence*, p. 50).

20. *Correspondence*, p. 43.

21. Erich Neumann, *Amor and Psyche* (New York, 1956), pp. 62–63.

22. Bridges, *Demeter*, p. 59.

23. Ibid., p. 66n.

24. Bodleian MS Eng. lett. e. 30.

25. A. Momigliano, *The Cambridge Ancient History* (New York, 1934), 10: 702.

26. So called by Agrippina in Bridges's play, a reference to Seneca's satire on the dead Claudius and his deification entitled *Apocolocyntosis Divi Claudii,* the Pumpkinification of Claudius, literally "transformation into a gourd." The term was probably similar to our "cabbage-head" meaning stupid fellow, hence "The Deification of a Cabbage-Head" would be a fair translation. Bridges's use of the epithet indicates his probable familiarity with Seneca's satire.

27. Guérard, *Robert Bridges*, p. 306. There were, however, as Guérard notes, a great sufficiency of unimportant plays on Nero in various languages.

28. Donald E. Stanford, "Robert Bridges on His Poems and Plays: Unpublished Letters by Robert Bridges to Samuel Butler," *Philological Quarterly* 50 (April 1971) : 287–88.
29. See Abbott, ed., *Letters of Hopkins to Bridges*, pp. 160, 179.
30. Guérard, *Robert Bridges*, p. 132.
31. A. Momigliano, *Cambridge Ancient History*, 10: 710.
32. Ibid., p. 728.
33. Allan Perley Ball, *The Satire of Seneca on the Apotheosis of Claudius* (New York, 1902) , p. 23.
34. See Abbott, ed., *Letters of Hopkins to Bridges*, pp. 208–10.
35. Guérard, *Robert Bridges*, pp. 135–38.
36. Ibid., p. 138.
37. Bodleian MS Eng. lett. c. 302.
38. Item 17 of the Ewelme catalogue, McKisson Library, University of South Carolina, Columbia, S.C.
39. Stanford, "Letters by Bridges to Samuel Butler," p. 288.
40. In Henry Newbolt, "On the Line," *The Monthly Review* 6 (March 1902) : 12–16.
41. Bodleian MS Eng. lett. c. 302.
42. Ibid.
43. As quoted in W. B. Yeats, *Ideas of Good and Evil* (New York, 1961) , p. 200.
44. Ibid.
45. Bodleian MS Don. d. 135.
46. Stanford, "Letters by Bridges to Samuel Butler," p. 286.
47. Gilbert Norwood, *The Art of Terence* (Oxford, 1923) , p. 44.
48. See Leo Spitzer's essay in Bruce W. Wardropper, ed., *Critical Essays on the Theatre of Calderon* (New York, 1965) .
49. See A. E. Sloman, *The Dramatic Craftsmanship of Calderon: His Use of Earlier Plays* (Oxford, 1958) .
50. Guérard, *Robert Bridges*, p. 306.
51. The program for the production is in the McKisson Library, University of South Carolina, Columbia, S.C. These two performances have been overlooked by Bridges specialists. George L. McKay, *A Bibliography of Robert Bridges* (New York, 1933) , p. 5, and Guérard, *Robert Bridges*, p. 123, state that the play was never acted. The existence of the Cheltenham program was brought to my attention by Paulette Hooper.
52. *Correspondence*, pp. 113–14.
53. The letter to an unknown correspondent is inserted in a copy of *Achilles in Scyros* in the McKisson Library.
54. Among the most probable sources of Bridges's play are Statius, *Achilleid*; Hyginus, *Fabulae*; Ovid, *Metamorphoses*; Philostratus Junior, *Imagines*; Apollodorus, *The Library*, and John Lampriere, *A Classical Dictionary* (various editions) . See Douglas Bush, *Mythology and the Romantic Tradition in English Poetry* (Cambridge, Mass., 1937, reissued 1969) , p. 441 n. 26, and Guérard, *Robert Bridges*, pp. 162–63.
55. See Statius, Apollodorus, and Philostratus.
56. The trumpet blast occurs in Apollodorus, Philostratus, and Statius.
57. Statius *Achilleid* 1. 853ff., translated by J. H. Mozeley in the Loeb Library edition.
58. Statius *Achilleid* 1. 888ff.

59. *Correspondence*, pp. 33–34.
60. See "The Laureate's Play," a notice in the *London Times*, January 8, 1930, p. 10.
61. Bodleian MS Don. d. 131.
62. The MS LRA. 6. 10. of Bridges letters to C. H. Daniel and to Mrs. Daniel is in the Worcester College Library, Oxford.
63. First published in Book IV of *Shorter Poems* (1890).
64. John Garrett Underhill, *Four Plays by Lope de Vega* (New York, 1936), p. xvi.
65. Stanford, "Letters by Bridges to Samuel Butler," p. 290.

Chapter 4: The Philosophical Poet: *The Testament of Beauty*

1. See the note of M. M. B. (Mrs. Bridges) in Robert Bridges, *Collected Essays etc. of Robert Bridges* (no. 15) (London, 1927–36), p. 86.
2. See Simon Nowell-Smith, "A Poet in Walton Street," *Essays Mainly on the Nineteenth Century Presented to Sir Humphrey Milford* (London, 1948), p. 68.
3. Bodleian MS Don. d. 113, fol. 102–3.
4. Nowell-Smith, *Essays*, p. 66.
5. Ibid.
6. Ibid., p. 69.
7. Edward Thompson, *Robert Bridges* (Oxford, 1944), chap. 12.
8. Published in part in *XXI Letters: a correspondence between Robert Bridges and R. C. Trevelyan on "New Verse" and "The Testament of Beauty"* (Stanford Dingley, 1955). Edition limited to 68 copies. Page numbers at the end of quotations from the Bridges-Trevelyan correspondence refer to this volume.
9. Nicolas Barker, *Stanley Morison* (Cambridge, Mass., 1972), p. 145.
10. Ibid., p. 212. The page numbers in parentheses at the end of the longer quotations indicate pages of this volume.
11. Ibid., p. 265.
12. Ibid., p. 254.
13. Nowell-Smith, *Essays*, p. 69.
14. Thompson, *Robert Bridges*, chap. 12.
15. Nowell Charles Smith, *Notes on The Testament of Beauty* (London, 1931), p. 85.
16. See chap. 2, above.
17. Elizabeth Cox Wright, *Metaphor, Sound, Meaning in Bridges' The Testament of Beauty* (Philadelphia, 1951).
18. Ibid., p. 53.
19. Bodleian MS Don. d. 131, fol. 73. The letters to Logan Pearsall Smith quoted in this chapter are unpublished. They are in the Bodleian Library, Oxford.
20. George Santayana, *Persons and Places*, vol. 3, *My Host the World* (New York, 1953), pp. 80–81.
21. George W. Howgate, *George Santayana* (Philadelphia, 1938), p. 289.
22. Bod. MS Don. d. 131, fol. 93, dated October 6, [1918].
23. Ibid., fol. 105, dated New Year's Eve [1920].
24. Ibid., fol. 182, dated September 12, 1924.
25. Ibid., fol. 216, dated January 24, 1926.

26. See Harold A. Larrabbee, "Robert Bridges and George Santayana," *American Scholar* 1 (1932) : 167–82.

27. George Santayana, *Soliloquies in England and Later Soliloquies,* vol. 9 of the Triton Edition (New York, 1937) , p. 4.

28. George Santayana, *Persons and Places,* vol. 1, *The Background of My Life* (New York, 1944) , p. 190.

29. Santayana, *My Host the World,* pp. 97ff.

30. Howgate, *George Santayana,* p. 201.

31. Bridges, "George Santayana" (no. 19) , *Collected Essays,* p. 143. This review first appeared in the *London Mercury,* August 1920.

32. Ibid., p. 144.

33. Ibid., p. 147.

34. Ibid., p. 151.

35. Ibid., p. 153. Santayana discusses this point in his letter to Bridges dated August 29, 1920, in Daniel Cory, ed., *The Letters of George Santayana* (New York, 1955) , pp. 182–84. He states that Bridges's view of Christianity seems to be "whatever is best or truest in the belief and sentiment of people calling themselves Christians." His own view of Christianity includes "such eschatology and such supernaturalistic hygiene for saving the soul as the Christian churches have developed." He argues that Bridges's Christianity was certainly prevalent in London in the nineteenth century, but not his own views.

36. Cory, ed., *Letters of Santayana,* p. 156.

37. Ibid., p. 157.

38. Ibid., p. 162.

39. Albert Guérard, *Robert Bridges: A Study of Traditionalism in Poetry* (Cambridge, Mass., 1942) . See especially chap. 13.

40. Willard E. Arnett, *George Santayana* (New York, 1968) , p. 48.

41. Ibid., p. 60.

42. Ibid., p. 140. Arnett's italics.

43. Howgate, *George Santayana,* p. 219.

44. Santayana, "Aversion from Platonism," *Soliloquies in England,* p. 23.

45. Santayana, *Soliloquies in England,* p. 112.

46. See Santayana's letter to Bridges dated May 10, 1928, in Cory, ed. *Letters of Santayana,* pp. 233–34.

47. Ibid., p. 243. The letter (pp. 243–45) is dated November 4, 1929.

48. Ibid., p. 244.

49. Ibid.

50. Ibid.

51. Ibid., pp. 244–45.

52. Santayana, *My Host the World,* p. 84. Santayana's italics.

Chapter 5: The Critic

1. Robert Bridges, *Collected Essays etc. of Robert Bridges* (London, 1927–36). There are thirty numbered essays.

2. Bodleian MS Don. c. 65.

3. According to a penciled note on his correspondence with Smith in Bodleian MS Don. d. 131.

4. Donald E. Stanford, "Robert Bridges and Samuel Butler on Shakespeare's Sonnets: An Exchange of Letters," *Shakespeare Quarterly* 22 (Autumn 1971): 328–35.

5. They are in Bodleian MS Don. d. 131.

6. Stanford, "Bridges and Butler on Shakespeare's Sonnets," pp. 332–35.

7. Ibid., p. 334.

8. Ibid., p. 332.

9. Bodleian MS Eng. lett. e. 30.

10. Bridges, *Collected Essays* (no. 1), p. 25. "The Influence of the Audience" was first printed in 1907 in volume 10 of the Stratford edition of Shakespeare's works. It was subsequently reprinted as a separate volume in 1926 in America by Stanley Morison and reprinted as the first essay in *Collected Essays* in 1927.

11. Bridges, *Collected Essays* (no. 1), p. 21.

12. See his letter to A. H. Bullen, November 21, 1906, in Bodleian MS Eng. lett. e. 30.

13. Bodleian MS Eng. lett. e. 30.

14. Augustus Ralli, *A History of Shakespearian Criticism*, 2 vols. (London, 1932), 1: 237.

15. Irving Ribner, "Shakespeare Criticism 1900–1964," in *Shakespeare 1564–1964, a Collection of Modern Essays by Various Hands*, ed. Edward A. Bloom (Providence, R.I., 1964), pp. 194–208.

16. Ibid., p. 198.

17. Alfred Harbage, *Shakespeare's Audience* (New York, 1941), pp. 151–52.

18. In *Shakespeare Association, A Series of Papers on Shakespeare and the Theatre* (London, 1927), p. 200.

19. Harbage, *Shakespeare's Audience*, p. 153.

20. See a series of letters from Bridges to Bullen beginning April 16, 1894, in Bodleian MS Eng. lett. e. 30.

21. In Bodleian MS Don. c. 79, fol. 85–88.

22. Donald E. Stanford, "Robert Bridges on His Poems and Plays: Unpublished Letters by Robert Bridges to Samuel Butler," *Philological Quarterly* 50 (April 1971): 284.

23. Ibid., p. 286.

24. Bodleian MS Don. d. 131, fol. 237.

25. Bodleian MS Eng. lett. e. 30, fol. 54.

26. Ibid., fol. 56.

27. As reprinted in 1929 in Bridges, *Collected Essays* (no. 4).

28. Ibid., p. 77.

29. Ibid., p. 79.

30. Ibid., p. 80.

31. Ibid., p. 91.

32. Ibid., pp. 107–8.

33. Ibid., p. 109.

34. Stanford, "Letters by Bridges to Samuel Butler," p. 284.

35. Years later, in 1926, Bridges wrote to L. P. Smith, "I am pleased with my account of the epigram" (Bodleian MS Don. d. 131, fol. 237).

36. For the Bridges-Hopkins relationship see Jean Georges Ritz, *Robert Bridges and Gerard Hopkins 1863–1889. A Literary Friendship* (London, 1960). His account is so full and detailed that it would be useless to attempt to repeat it here.

37. Letters from Bridges to Daniel concerning this abortive edition are in the Worcester College Library, Oxford. See Simon Nowell-Smith, "Bridges, Hopkins, and Dr. Daniel," *Times Literary Supplement,* December 13, 1957, p. 764, and Ritz, *Bridges and Hopkins,* pp. 157–58. Ritz points out that Bridges also discussed with Daniel in 1880 plans (which never materialized) for an anthology that would include poems by himself, Hopkins, Dolben, and Dixon.

38. The poems are in vol. 8 of Miles's anthology and are preceded by a four-page foreword by Bridges. The poems are: "A Vision of Mermaids" (1862) —a selection of 35 lines; "The Habit of Perfection" (1866); "The Starlight Night" (1877), "Spring" (1877); "The Candle Indoors" (1879); "Spring and Fall" (1880); "Inversnaid" (1881); and "To—" (1889), beginning "The fine delight that fathers thought. . . ." In addition, Bridges quoted thirty-six and one-half lines from Hopkins's other poems in his foreword. Bridges must also be given some credit for the inclusion of poems by Hopkins in H. C. Beeching's anthologies *Lyra Sacra* (London, 1895) and *A Book of Christmas Verse* (London, 1895). Beeching was the rector of Yattendon church and a friend of Bridges. In his notes to the poems in both volumes Beeching refers to Bridges's memoir of Hopkins and the selections of his poems in Miles's anthology. The poems in *Lyra Sacra* are "Barnfloor and Winepress," "God's Grandeur," "Heaven Haven," and "Morning, Midday, and Evening Sacrifice." "Thee, God, I come from" is quoted in Beeching's note. The one poem in *A Book of Christmas Verse* is "Mary Mother of Divine Grace, Compared to the Air We Breathe."

39. Owned by Gordon Ray of the Guggenheim Foundation.

40. His poems include *Christ's Company* (1861), *St. John in Patmos* (1863), *Historical Odes and Other Poems* (1864), *Mano* (1883), two volumes of odes, eclogues, and lyrics, and finally *The Story of Eudocia and her Brothers* (1888). Bridges edited a selection of his poems prefixed by a Memoir: *Poems by the Late Rev. Dr. Richard Watson Dixon* (London, 1909).

41. Bridges, ed., *Poems by Dixon,* p. 196.

42. But for another opinion see C. C. Abbott's interesting evaluation of Dixon's poetry in the Introduction of *The Correspondence of Gerard Manley Hopkins and Richard Watson Dixon* (London, 1935). Abbott thinks well of the long narrative poem *Mano.*

43. Robert Bridges, ed., *The Poems of Digby Mackworth Dolben* (London, 1911). The Memoir was reprinted in Robert Bridges, *Three Friends* (London, 1932).

44. Bridges, ed., *The Poems of Dolben,* pp. xviii–xix.

45. Bridges, "Mary Elizabeth Coleridge" (no. 6), *Collected Essays,* p. 212.

46. Bridges, "George Darley" (no. 5), *Collected Essays,* pp. 187–88.

47. Bridges, "The Poems of Emily Brontë" (no. 9), *Collected Essays,* p. 264. First published in 1911 as a review of Clement Shorter's edition of Brontë's poems.

48. Bridges, "Wordsworth and Kipling" (no. 13), *Collected Essays,* p. 27.

49. Ibid., p. 30.

50. Ibid., pp. 30–31.

51. Bridges, "Dryden on Milton" (no. 10), *Collected Essays*, p. 274.
52. First published in 1909; reprinted in Bridges, *Collected Essays* (no. 8).
53. Reprinted in Bridges, *Collected Essays* (no. 12).
54. Bridges, "The Necessity of Poetry" (no. 28), *Collected Essays*, p. 194.
55. Ibid., p. 209.
56. Ibid., p. 213.
57. Bridges, "Preface," *Collected Essays*, 10: ix. The lecture was reprinted in *Collected Essays* (no. 29).
58. Bridges, *Collected Essays* (no. 29), pp. 248–49.
59. Bridges has not changed the position he took over twenty years earlier in his ironical review (first published in the *Times Literary Supplement*, November 21, 1907) of Stopford Brooke's *Studies in Poetry*. The review was reprinted in Bridges's *Collected Essays* (no. 11). There Bridges raised objections to Brooke's statement that "unconscious logic" was responsible for the structure of such poems as Shelley's "Ode to the West Wind." Brooke had written that as Shelley composed his poem, the first lines came "leaping from his lips in a moment—thought, emotion, metre, movement—all rushing together into a self creation," to which Bridges replied that in the actual process of composing the poem, Shelley was probably aware of what he was doing and quite consciously planned its structure.

Selected Bibliography

A. M. "Eros and Psyche," *Bookman* 7 (January 1895) : 116.

Abbott, C. C., ed. *The Correspondence of Gerard Manley Hopkins and Richard Watson Dixon.* London: Oxford University Press, 1935.

_____, ed. *Further Letters of Gerard Manley Hopkins including his Correspondence with Coventry Patmore.* London: Oxford University Press, 1938. Revised edition, 1956.

_____, ed. *The Letters of Gerard Manley Hopkins to Robert Bridges.* London: Oxford University Press, 1935.

Altick, Richard D. "Four Victorian Poets and an Exploding Island." *Victorian Studies* 3 (March 1960) : 249–60.

Arnett, Willard E. *George Santayana.* New York: Washington Square Press, 1968.

Bailey, John. "Poems of Robert Bridges." *Living Age* 199 (December 3, 1893) : 556–63.

_____. "Poetry of Robert Bridges." *Living Age* 278 (August 30, 1913) : 515–29.

Baker, Howard. *Ode to the Sea and Other Poems.* Denver, Col.: Alan Swallow, 1966.

Ball, Allan Perley. *The Satire of Seneca on the Apotheosis of Claudius.* New York: The Columbia University Press, 1902.

Barker, Nicolas. *The Printer and the Poet.* Cambridge: University Printing House [privately printed], 1970.

_____. *Stanley Morison.* Cambridge, Mass.: Harvard University Press, 1972.

Beeching, H. C., ed. *A Book of Christmas Verse.* London: Methuen & Co., 1895.

_____, ed. *Lyra Sacra.* London: Methuen & Co., 1895.

Berg, Sister Mary Gretchen. *The Prosodic Structure of Robert Bridges' "Neo-Miltonic Syllabics."* Washington, D.C.: Catholic University of America Press, 1962.

Beum, Robert. "Profundity Revisited: Bridges and His Critics." *The Dalhousie Review* 44 (1964) : 172–79.

_____. "Syllabic Verse in English." *Prairie Schooner* 31 (Fall 1957): 259–75.

Bradley, Henry. *Correspondence of Robert Bridges and Henry Bradley 1900–1923*. Oxford: Clarendon Press, 1940.

Bridges, Robert. *Achilles in Scyros*. London: Edward Bumpus, 1890.

_____. [A review of] *Achilles in Scyros*. "Poetical Works of Robert Bridges. Vol. III." *The Athenaeum* 3872 (January 11, 1902): 40.

_____. "[A review of] *Achilles in Scyros*." *Bookman* 2 (September 1892) : 183.

_____. "[A review of] *Achilles in Scyros*." *The Spectator* 66 (March 14, 1891) : 382–83.

_____. *The Christian Captives*. London: Edward Bumpus, 1890.

_____. *Collected Essays etc. of Robert Bridges*. London: Oxford University Press, 1927–36. [30 numbered essays]

_____. *Correspondence of Robert Bridges and Henry Bradley 1900–1923*. Oxford: Clarendon Press, 1940.

_____. *Demeter. A Mask*. Oxford: Clarendon Press, 1905.

_____. *Eros and Psyche. A Poem in Twelve Measures. The Story Done into English from the Latin of Apuleius*. London: George Bell and Sons, 1885.

_____. *Eros and Psyche*. Rev. ed. London: George Bell and Sons, 1894.

_____. *The Feast of Bacchus*. Oxford: H. Daniel, 1889.

[_____]. *The Growth of Love. A Poem in Twenty-Four Sonnets*. London: Edward Bumpus, 1876.

_____. *The Growth of Love*. 2d ed. Oxford: H. Daniel, 1889. [79 sonnets]

_____. *The Growth of Love*. Vol. 1, *Poetical Works*. London: Smith and Elder, 1898. [69 sonnets]

_____. *The Humours of the Court*. London: George Bell & Sons and J. & E. Bumpus, 1893.

_____. "[A review of production of] *The Humours of the Court*." "The Laureate's Play." *London Times*, January 8, 1930, p. 10.

_____. *Ibant Obscuri*. London: Oxford University Press, 1916.

_____. *Milton's Prosody* [Bound with William Johnson Stone, *Classical Metres in English Verse*]. Oxford: Clarendon Press, 1901.

_____. *Milton's Prosody with a chapter on Accentual Verse and Notes*. Rev., final ed. Oxford: Clarendon Press, 1921.

_____. "[A review of] Mr. Robert Bridges's 'Demeter'." *Living Age* 246 (August 19, 1905) : 506–8.

_____. *Nero. Part 1.* London: George Bell & Sons and J. & E. Bumpus, 1885.

_____. *Nero. Part 2.* London: George Bell & Sons and J. & E. Bumpus, 1894.

_____. *New Verse.* Oxford: Clarendon Press, 1925.

_____. *Now in Wintry Delights.* Oxford: Daniel Press, 1903.

_____. "[A review essay of] *Now in Wintry Delights.*" "Quantity and Accent. Mr. Robert Bridges's New Poem." *Times Literary Supplement*, April 10, 1903, pp. 109–10.

_____. *October and Other Poems.* London: Heinemann, 1920.

_____. *Palicio.* London: Edward Bumpus, 1890.

_____, ed. and intro. by. *Poems by the Late Rev. Dr. Richard Watson Dixon.* London: Smith, Elder & Co., 1909.

_____, ed. with a Memoir by. *The Poems of Digby Mackworth Dolben.* London: Oxford University Press, 1911.

_____, ed. *Poems of Gerard Manley Hopkins.* London: Humphrey Milford, 1918.

_____. *Poetical Works of Robert Bridges.* 6 vols. London: Smith, Elder & Co., 1898–[1905].

_____. *Poetical Works of Robert Bridges Excluding the Eight Dramas.* London: Oxford University Press, 1912.

_____. *Poetical Works of Robert Bridges with the The Testament of Beauty but excluding the eight dramas.* London: Oxford University Press, 1953.

_____. *Poor Poll.* London: Oxford University Press, 1923. [Privately printed]

_____. *Prometheus the Firegiver.* Oxford: H. Daniel, 1883.

_____. *The Return of Ulysses.* London: Edward Bumpus, 1890.

_____. *The Shorter Poems.* London: George Bell & Sons, 1890.

_____. *Shorter Poems Book 5.* Oxford: H. Daniel, 1893.

_____. *The Spirit of Man.* London: Longmans, 1916.

_____. *The Tapestry.* London: privately printed, 1925.

_____. *The Testament of Beauty.* Oxford: Clarendon Press, 1929.

_____. *Three Friends.* London: Oxford University Press, 1932.

Bush, Douglas. *Mythology and the Romantic Tradition in English Poetry.* Cambridge, Mass.: Harvard University Press, 1937. Reissued 1969.

Byrne, Muriel St. Clare. "Shakespeare's Audience." In *Shakespeare Association, A Series of Papers on Shakespeare and the Theatre.* London: Oxford University Press, 1927.

Calderón, D. Pedro de la Barca. *Las Comedias.* 4 vols. Leipzig: Ernesto Fleischer, 1827–1830.

Champneys, Basil. *Memoirs and Correspondence of Coventry Patmore.* 2 vols. London: G. Bell and Sons, 1900.

Cory. Daniel, ed. *The Letters of George Santayana.* New York: Scribner's, 1955.

Daryush, Elizabeth. "Air & Variations," note on meter of poem. *The Southern Review,* n.s. 9 (July 1973) : 645.

de Vega, Lope. *Obras.* 15 vols. Madrid: Establecimiento Tipográfico, 1890–1913.

Freeman, Edward Augustus. *The History of Sicily from the Earliest Times.* 4 vols. Oxford: Clarendon Press, 1891–94.

Grabo, Carl Henry. *Prometheus Unbound: An Interpretation.* New York: Gordian Press, 1968.

Graves, Robert, ed. and trans. *The Comedies of Terence.* Chicago: Aldine Publishing Co., 1962.

————, ed. and trans. *The Golden Ass of Apuleius.* New York: Farrar, Straus & Young, 1951.

Green, David Bonnell. "A New Letter of Robert Bridges to Coventry Patmore." *Modern Philology* 55 (February 1958) : 198–99.

Guérard, Albert. *Robert Bridges: A Study of Traditionalism in Poetry.* Cambridge, Mass.: Harvard University Press, 1942.

Harbage, Alfred. *Shakespeare's Audience.* New York: Columbia University Press, 1941.

Hooper, Paulette. "Robert Bridges and the Masque Form: A Critical Study of Demeter: A Mask and Prometheus the Firegiver." Master's thesis, Louisiana State University, 1973.

Howgate, George W. *George Santayana.* Philadelphia: University of Pennsylvania Press, 1938.

Inveges, Agostino. *Annals,* in *Nobilario viceregio capitaniale e pretoriano in Palermo nobile.* Part 3. Palermo, 1651, p. 104.

Kellog, G. A. "Bridges's *Milton's Prosody* and Renaissance Metrical Theory." *PMLA* 68 (March 1953) : 268–85.

Kerényi, C. *Eleusis: Archetypal Image of Mother and Daughter.* New York: Pantheon Books, 1967.

Larrabbee, Harold A. "Robert Bridges and George Santayana." *American Scholar* 1 (1932) : 167–82.

McCarthy, Denis Florence. *Dramas of Calderon . . . Translated from the Spanish.* London: Charles Dolman, 1853.

Mackail, J. W. "*Prometheus the Firegiver.* By Robert Bridges." *The Academy* 655 (November 22, 1884) : 834–35.

McKay, George L. *A Bibliography of Robert Bridges.* New York: Columbia University Press, 1933.

Miles, A. H. *The Poets and the Poetry of the Century.* London: Hutchinson & Co., 1893.

Momigliano, A[rnoldo]. *The Cambridge Ancient History.* Vol. 10, chapter 21. New York: Macmillan, 1934.

Neumann, Erich. *Amor and Psyche.* New York: Pantheon Books, 1956.

————. *The Great Mother.* New York: Pantheon Books, 1955.

————. *The Origins and History of Consciousness.* New York: Pantheon Books, 1954.

Newbolt, Sir Henry. *My World as in My Time.* London: Faber & Faber, 1932.

————. "On the Line." *The Monthly Review* 6 (March 1902) : 12–16.

Norwood, Gilbert. *The Art of Terence.* Oxford: B. Blackwell, 1923.

Nowell-Smith, Simon. "A Poet in Walton Street." *Essays Mainly on the Nineteenth Century Presented to Sir Humphrey Milford.* London: Oxford University Press, 1948.

————. "Bridges's Classical Prosody New Verses and Variants." Letter to *Times Literary Supplement,* August 28, 1943, p. 420.

————. "Bridges's Debt to Hopkins." Letter to *Times Literary Supplement,* May 12, 1961, p. 243.

————. "Bridges, Hopkins, and Dr. Daniel." *Times Literary Supplement,* December 13, 1957, p. 764.

Parker, William Riley. *Milton's Debt to Greek Tragedy in Samson Agonistes.* Baltimore, Md.: The Johns Hopkins Press, 1937.

Patmore, Coventry. *Courage in Politics and Other Essays.* London: Oxford University Press, 1921.

————. "Robert Bridges' *Eros and Psyche.*" *St. James's Gazette,* December 31, 1885. [Reprinted in *Courage in Politics,* pp. 147–51]

————. "Robert Bridges' *Prometheus the Firegiver.*" *St. James's Gazette,* March 9, 1885. [Reprinted in *Courage in Politics,* pp. 143–47]

————. See Roth, Sister Mary Augustine.

Patmore, Derek. "Coventry Patmore and Robert Bridges: Some Letters." *The Fortnightly,* n.s. 169 (March 1948) : 196–204.

————. *The Life and Times of Coventry Patmore.* New York: Oxford University Press, 1949.

————. "Three Poets Discuss New Verse Forms." *The Month,* n.s. 6 (August 1951) : 69–78.

Purser, Louis C. *The Story of Cupid and Psyche as Related by Apuleius.* London: G. Bell & Sons, 1910.

Raleigh, Lady, ed. *The Letters of Sir Walter Raleigh.* 2 vols. New York: Macmillan, 1926.

Ralli, Augustus. *A History of Shakespearian Criticism.* 2 vols. London: Oxford University Press, 1932.

Ribner, Irving. "Shakespeare Criticism 1900–1964." In *Shakespeare 1564–1964, a Collection of Modern Essays by Various Hands,* edited by Edward A. Bloom. Providence, R.I.: Brown University Press, 1964.

Ritz, Jean-Georges. *Robert Bridges and Gerard Hopkins 1863–1889. A Literary Friendship.* London: Oxford University Press, 1960.

Roberts, J. Slingsby. "Nero in Modern Drama." *Fortnightly Review,* n.s. 79 (January 1906) : 83–95.

Rosenthal, M. L. and Smith, A. J. M. *Exploring Poetry.* New York: Macmillan, 1955.

Roth, Sister Mary Augustine, ed. *Coventry Patmore's "Essay on English Metrical Law."* Washington, D.C.: The Catholic University of America Press, 1961.

Santayana, George. *Persons and Places; the Background of My Life.* 4 vols. New York: C. Scribner's Sons, 1944–1953.

————. *The Works of George Sanatyana.* 15 vols. New York: C. Scribner's Sons, 1936–1937.

Sloman, A. E. *The Dramatic Craftsmanship of Calderon: His Use of Earlier Plays.* Oxford: Dolphin Book Co., 1958.

Smith, Logan Pearsall. *Little Essays Drawn from the Writings of George Santayana.* London: Constable and Co., 1920.

Smith, Nowell Charles. *Notes on the Testament of Beauty.* London: Oxford University Press, 1931.

Sparrow, John. *Robert Bridges.* London: Oxford University Press, 1955.

Spitzer, Leo. "The Figure of Fenix in Calderon's El principe constante." In *Critical Essays on the Theatre of Calderon,* edited by Bruce W. Wardropper. New York: New York University Press, 1965.

Stall, Lindon. "Robert Bridges and the Laws of English Stressed Verse." *Agenda* 2, nos. 2–3: 96–108.

Stanford, Donald E. "Robert Bridges and the Free Verse Rebellion." *Journal of Modern Literature* 1 (September 1971) : 19–31.

————. "Robert Bridges and Samuel Butler on Shakespeare's Sonnets: An Exchange of Letters." *Shakespeare Quarterly* 22 (Autumn 1971) : 328–35.

————. "Robert Bridges on His Poems and Plays: Unpublished Letters by Robert Bridges to Samuel Butler." *Philological Quarterly* 50 (April 1971) : 281–91.

Stone, William Johnson. *Classical Metres in English Verse.* Oxford: Clarendon Press, 1901. [Bound with Bridges's *Milton's Prosody.* See Bridges, Robert]

————. *On the Use of Classical Metres in English.* London: Henry Frowde, 1899.

Thompson, Edward. *Robert Bridges.* London: Oxford University Press, 1944.

Trevelyan, R. C. "Prosody and the Poet Laureate." *The New States-man* 24 (December 13, 1924) : 296–98.

_____. *XXI Letters: a correspondence between Robert Bridges and R. C. Trevelyan on "New Verse" and "The Testament of Beauty."* Stanford Dingley: The Mill House Press, 1955.

Twitchett, E. C. "The Poetry of Robert Bridges." *London Mercury* 21 (December 1929) : 140.

Underhill, John Garrett. *Four Plays by Lope de Vega.* New York: Scribner's Sons, 1936.

Whitehall, Harold. "Sprung Rhythm." *Gerard Manley Hopkins by the Kenyon Critics.* Norfolk, Conn.: New Directions, 1945.

Winters, Yvor. *Forms of Discovery.* Chicago: Alan Swallow, 1967.

_____. *The Function of Criticism.* Denver, Col.: Alan Swallow, 1957.

_____. "Gerard Manley Hopkins." *The Hudson Review* 1 (Winter 1949) : 458–66. [Reprinted in *The Function of Criticism*]

_____. *In Defense of Reason.* New York: The Swallow Press and W. Morrow and Company, 1947.

_____. "Robert Bridges and Elizabeth Daryush." *The American Review* 8 (January 1937) : 355–57.

_____. "The Shorter Poems of Robert Bridges." *Hound & Horn* 5 (January–March 1932) : 321–27.

Withers, Percy. *A Buried Life: Personal Recollections of A. E. Housman.* London: J. Cape, 1940.

Wright, Elizabeth Cox. *Metaphor Sound and Meaning in Bridges' The Testament of Beauty.* Philadelphia: University of Pennsylvania Press, 1951.

Yeats, W. B. *Ideas of Good and Evil.* New York, Macmillan, 1961.

Young, F. E. Brett. *Robert Bridges: A Critical Study.* London: Martin Secker, 1914.

Index

Page numbers for illustrations are in italics